918/6

Capitol Hill Library
AUG 17 2016

NO LONGER PROPERTY OF
SEATTLE PUBLIC LIBRARY

The Emancipation of Cecily McMillan

The Emancipation of Cecily McMillan

an american memoir

CECILY McMILLAN

NATION
BOOKS
New York

Copyright © 2016 by Cecily McMillan

Published by Nation Books, an imprint of Perseus Books, a division of
PBG Publishing, LLC, a subsidiary of Hachette Book Group, Inc.
116 East 16th Street, 8th Floor
New York, NY 10003

Nation Books is a co-publishing venture of the Nation Institute and the Perseus Books
Group

All rights reserved. Printed in the United States of America. No part of this book may be
reproduced in any manner whatsoever without written permission except in the case of brief
quotations embodied in critical articles and reviews. For information, address the Perseus
Books Group, 250 West 57th Street, 15th Floor, New York, NY 10107.

Books published by Nation Books are available at special discounts for bulk purchases in the
United States by corporations, institutions, and other organizations. For more information,
please contact the Special Markets Department at Perseus Books, 2300 Chestnut Street,
Suite 200, Philadelphia, PA 19103, or call (800) 810-4145, ext. 5000, or e-mail special.
markets@perseusbooks.com.

Library of Congress Cataloging-in-Publication Data
Names: McMillan, Cecily, 1988- author.
Title: The emancipation of Cecily McMillan : an American memoir / Cecily
    McMillan.
Description: New York : Nation Books, 2016.
Identifiers: LCCN 2016000493 (print) | LCCN 2016001136 (ebook) | ISBN
    9781568585383 (hardback) | ISBN 9781568585390 (e-book)
Subjects: LCSH: McMillan, Cecily, 1988- | Radicals—United States—Biography.
    | Generation Y—United States—Attitudes. | Occupy movement—United
    States. | BISAC: BIOGRAPHY & AUTOBIOGRAPHY / Personal Memoirs.
Classification: LCC HN90.R3 M38 2016 (print) | LCC HN90.R3 (ebook) | DDC
    303.48/4092--dc23
LC record available at http://lccn.loc.gov/2016000493

10 9 8 7 6 5 4 3 2 1

Contents

Photographs follow page 142

Introduction

by Pussy Riot's
Nadya Tolokonnikova
and Masha Alyokhina

On May 9, 2014, we met with the brilliant American activist Cecily McMillan in the Rose M. Singer Center on Rikers Island. She has amazing political charisma, a trait not every social or political activist can successfully cultivate. Cecily's efforts are aimed at challenging social indifference, a hurdle she personally fell victim to on May 5 of that year in a district court in Manhattan. Cecily idealizes volunteering, solidarity, and mutual consideration of other people's struggles, but her ideals were nowhere to be found in that court. When Cecily was condemned, she was taken hostage by the court, a court that represents the city she called home, the city where Occupy Wall Street was born.

The day after Cecily was found guilty, nine of the twelve jurors wrote a letter to the judge expressing their horror at Cecily's sentence and requesting an alternative punishment. The jurors had not understood the article used to accuse Cecily, nor were they aware that the article stipulated imprisonment. The jury's change of heart calls to mind a quote from Luke 23:34: "They know not what they do."

Cecily's conviction is the perfect example of why her efforts as an activist are needed—the inability of the jury to accept Cecily's problems as their own, to take the time and consideration during her trial to seek justice, resulted in her imprisonment.

Cecily told us with great pride that her ability to talk to people of different backgrounds and groups is one of her most valued traits. Her ultimate goal is to find ways to bring together disparate social groups and create a platform for shared, collective action. At various points in her life, Cecily has found herself in completely different strata of American society, switching from one layer of language and experience to another. This is the heart of Cecily's aim—to master these "other tongues," to understand the social circles outside of the ones into which she was born, raised, and made her career, and to understand other people's experiences. We saw her do this with her fellow prisoners in Rikers, and we see her do this as a prison reform activist now. Cecily wants to gradually recover the lost dialogue between the 1 percent who own everything and the 99 percent who have to live in the shadows. While those in power want to silence undesirable voices, it is Cecily's goal to return those voices to the people who have been deprived of them.

Cecily McMillan's case and her work today reflect a global struggle. The court's verdict and imprisonment of this young woman marks a dangerous new direction in the United States, one that has repercussions in those countries that are indirectly impacted by US domestic policies. These countries include Russia, where the government is introducing conservative laws and suppressing the political activity of its citizens. More and more often, Vladimir Putin and his team are citing the practices of other countries, including the more recent and unsavory efforts to suppress dissent in the United States, to justify their actions.

But Cecily, like activists all over the world, has not given up. More than ever, she is doing the work of a true patriot.

CHAPTER 1

Child

*M*y mother always said we were perfect for each other; she never wanted to be a parent and I never wanted to be a child. Her water broke on a Friday, but she didn't notice because "it didn't gush like in the movies." The following Tuesday, she was hospitalized for an infection and found out she was in labor; I was overcooked and her body was trying to get rid of me. And so it was that I was rejected into this world at 12:42 p.m. on September 20, 1988—very late and very sick. Before I was removed to intensive care, the nurse let my mother hold me for a minute. I was hairy all over and covered with rashes; she turned to my father and said, "Oof! She's kind of homely, isn't she?" She was only twenty-one, and he was a young twenty-seven—neither knew anything about babies or ever intended to be parents. When the hospital handed me over a week later, my mother said, "I can't believe they're letting her go home with *us*."

"Us" was James Emerson McMillan and Maria Celina Mutrux-Barrera. Dad, a "man's man," is six-foot-four with a sturdy structure and supersized features undermined by bright blue eyes that give away his sensitive interior. Mom, in turn, stands four-eleven, short with delicate features—fair skin, dainty nose, high cheekbones—and watchful brown eyes that hint at the turbulence beneath her calm, cool surface. He's a red-blooded, red-headed (you guessed it!) Irish Amurican from southeast Texas. She's a blue-blooded, dark-featured (*yes*, documented) immigrant from across that ever-so-messy southern border of the United States. The two are opposites in almost every way and, so, it took a pretty odd set of events to throw them together. More than anything, though—like everything then and, really, since—their fates were intertwined with oil.

Mom was born in 1967, to an affluent family of doctors and businessmen, learned ladies and prima ballerinas. She and her two brothers grew up in Mexico City attended to by a household staff and educated by nuns at a private Catholic school. This lifestyle was afforded by a combination of her mother's inherited wealth and her father's lucrative oil investments—that is, until the 1982 Mexican Crisis changed everything. It was the biggest recession since the 1930s: oil prices tanked and dragged the value of peso down with them. Her father's business went bankrupt, and her mother's savings weren't worth anything anymore. Trying to salvage a future for their children, her mother traded in the remains of the family estate for a small house in Brownsville, Texas, while her father traveled for months on end, chasing an endless stream of get-rich schemes. He never did reclaim his fortune, though, and, one day, he just never came home. A proud, devout woman, scorned and ashamed, Abuela was left alone to raise three kids, forced to sell her jewelry to feed them—and, later, Mary Kay makeup. Along the way, she became riddled with depression and hardened by resentment, but the kids, as they always do, paid the highest price: Samuel, the oldest, got married and had a kid at the age of eighteen; William, the youngest, got into drugs and committed suicide at the age of seventeen; while Mom, in the middle, got out—ran away, couch-surfed to Austin at the age of sixteen. By eighteen, though, she'd gotten herself into college and was taking classes at Lamar University in Beaumont, Texas.

A portside city on the Gulf of Mexico—eighty miles east of Houston and sixty west of Lake Charles—Beaumont was founded in 1838, following the Texas Revolution against Mexico. Initially a small center for cattle raisers and farmers, by the end of the century, it would become a major lumber and rice-milling town with an active shipping center, stimulated by the Civil War Reconstruction effort. The promise of work and available lands attracted both new immigrants and southern migrants alike. Among the thousands came Dad's ancestors from "the Carolinas"—a hearty group of artisans and day laborers who settled all over southeast Texas. And though milling had put Beaumont on the map, it was drilling that made it world famous: in 1901, a well struck oil at Spindletop field and rained for nine days straight; it was the largest gusher the world had ever witnessed, the first ever found on the US Gulf Coast, and the beginning of the Texas oil boom. Sixty years later, the oil continued to flow and my grandfather began his lifetime career as a pipefitter for Mobile Chemical Oil. That same year my grandmother gave birth to my father in Beaumont, Texas, and, there, he met my mother—twenty-five years to the day later.

It was the summer after her freshman year. He was out celebrating his birthday at *Mason's*, a New Wave club. Mom and Dad ran into each other haphazardly on the dance floor and fell prey to the sultry, trance-inducing beat of Soft Cell's "Tainted Love"—talk about foreshadowing! By the time I was born, though, they had moved to Atlanta, Georgia, where she worked as an office assistant for a legal firm and he managed a Domino's Pizza. Home was the dingy basement apartment of a large Victorian house in the Inman Park Historic District—a neighborhood on the east side of the city, established in 1890 as Atlanta's first suburb. Lucky for them (and me too, I suppose), we lived right next door to my father's mother, Grandmommy Kay, his half brothers Erik and Kevin, and Granddaddy Harlon, stepfather to all three. "Team Cecily" was also joined by Abuela, who flew in for my birth and stuck around the first few weeks to help out. And after her my Great-Grandmommy Grace, who came in from Beaumont just as soon as she'd managed the recent death of her husband, and my would-be great-granddaddy, Emerson Heartfield. The way Grandmommy Kay told it, her father was dying from cirrhosis when it was announced that I'd be a girl; he vowed "to live long enough to see the first one born into the family since Kay," but, unfortunately, he missed me by a week.

According to Mom, the parade of family kept coming for months, and I was "just a ham" for all of the attention, but even then "difficult to keep up with." You might say—as Daddy often did—that I was "born stubborn, determined to do things *my way*." At seven months, my first word was "no," and I refused to crawl—I scooted, stood up, and staggered from one steadying handhold on a chair or coffee table to the next until I could manage without them. As soon as I could walk, I ran. Of course, though, I don't remember any of that. Much to my parents' chagrin, my first memory is of eating a cockroach. I must have been about three years old. There was a tin of raisins in the middle of the coffee table. I leaned across and slid it toward me, but the lid was loose—it toppled off the edge and all the raisins fell out. "Uh-oh!" I looked around for my parents. And when no one came running, I raked most of them back into the tin. Then, on hands and knees, I snatched up the stragglers and stuffed them into my mouth. Flat on my belly, I found another handful under the couch and *crunch!* Wait, I thought, that's not right, and I sat straight up and spit the mouthful out. Sifting through the chewed up bits, I found either end of a half-chewed cockroach. Till this day, I *still* don't eat raisins.

By that time my parents had returned to Beaumont to run their own Domino's Pizza franchise, and the three of us were living at 1569 Main Lane. If you drive a couple of miles past the city limit headed west toward China, Texas, you'll pass Beaumont Municipal Airport on the right. Main Lain is on your left, past Doug's Auto Salvage. If you get to the Exxon-Mobile Chemical Plant, turn around—you've gone too far. A couple hundred feet down, our home was the little yellow trailer on the right (beside two houses on the same lot.) The property belonged to Pop, my father's father, and his second wife, Momma Jean—my father's "mother," never "*step*mother"—having raised him more than anyone else. Pop, like I said, was a pipefitter for Mobil, and Momma Jean was a clerk for Southwestern Bell Telephone Company; they worked hard, saved up, and bought the land outright in 1969, but it was several years before they could afford to put a house on it. In fact, Pop's parents, Pawpaw and Caca (the unfortunate shortening of Clyda) were the first to make the move. While still working full time unloading oil tankers and rail cars for Pure Oil Company, Pawpaw single-handedly built a home for himself and his wife in the center of the lot. Then a year later, he helped Pop build his dream house next door: a large, red brick, four bedroom complete with an inground pool. Carpentry was the family trade, and Pawpaw had been at it since he could walk—in fact, he had a four-inch dent in his skull from a misplaced ax while pulling firewood at age three.

In 1990, my parents purchased the mobile home secondhand from family friends and backed it right into the last remaining plot of that four-acre-long cornerstone of the American Dream. By then Pop and Momma Jean's youngest son, Jarrod, had gone off to college so everyone was excited to have children around again—I say child*ren* because, unbeknownst to me, Mom was pregnant with a second child. I was twenty-two months old when I became a sister. James William, or Baby James, was born July 14, 1990. He was my first and only sibling—after that second happy accident, Mom went ahead and got her tubes tied. My parents weren't ready for another child, and I wasn't ready for a brother. Photographs and videos depict me as a charismatic, curly-haired tot-star always at the center of attention. I can be seen dancing in a black leotard and ballet slippers atop the living room table to a theater in the round of friends and family, posing in a tiara and a sash that reads "Tiny Miss Valentine's" beside a towering pageant trophy as Mom calls "cheese!" and shaking blue-and-white pom-poms as Dad tosses me into the air and cheers, "Touchdown!" at the TV. It must have been hard for me to go from starring in my own one-woman show to being but one of two in a sibling duet, because sharing the spotlight did not come easy. From the moment his crib appeared in *my room,* I saw it as an invasion, and when Baby James arrived with blonde curls and blue eyes as bright as mine were green, it was a declaration of all-out war. Dad came in one day to find me whacking the infant invader over the head with a toy broom; apparently, I was "just trying to look and he pulled my hair!" That was a capital offense that I would not let go unpunished—not then or any time since. Mom remembers my being very territorial. When she would go to the bathroom, I would run after her and Baby James would run after me then I would slam the door in his face and lock him out—sometimes, I would be extra sneaky about it, and she wouldn't notice until he was banging and screaming on the other side.

You'll have to take their word for it, but it sounds right to me; certainly my earliest memory of James is of us fighting. I think it was the summer before I turned five, so he would have been about three years old. I remember sprinting out of the trailer into the pounding rain, wearing nothing but Barbie underwear and rain boots. I neared the middle of the yard and glanced over my shoulder before stopping. I can still see him tearing toward me, lagging only a few yards behind. He was wearing Pull-Ups and my old red cowboy boots; they were far too big for him, and he nearly tumbled with each stride. I took advantage of the lead, bent down, and scooped up a fistful of mud. He slid to a stop and I made my move: mud-ball right to the face! I turned and retreated in anticipation of his counterattack, but when I looked back, he wasn't running after me. He was plunked down in a puddle, with his face in his hands. I returned and cautiously reached down to comfort him when two small hands seized my ankles and slammed me backward to the ground. Never to be outdone, James jumped on me with *two* fistfuls of mud. Hours later we trudged home hand in hand, boots and underpants black and soaking, singing, "It's raining, it's pouring, the old man is snoring!"

As far as childhood memories go, it's pretty nondescript. But for that reason, it's precious to me: it's reminiscent of the short period of happiness and normalcy we shared together on those four acres. After James was born, my parents sold their Domino's franchise to go to college. Dad went full time for accounting while Mom studied nursing part time and worked part time at a Dillard's department store. They were often gone all day, but every morning we shared a big family breakfast with my grandparents and great-grandparents; after everyone else left for school or work, James and I stayed behind with Caca and Pawpaw. Each week we took a day trip to some Native American reservation, historical battleground, or national preserve, and on Sundays we went to church, but most of the time we just played outside. Once out the door, I was captain and James, deputy, of a fearless band of explorers: Snowy, a wily white mutt that rarely stayed in line, Lady, a wise old golden retriever always at our heels, and Perkins, a chunky but spunky pug that often fell behind. Barefoot with backpacks stocked with supplies—peanut butter, pocket knives, toilet paper, and so on—we set out for all-day archeological digs in the cow pasture next door, snake hunts through the overgrown lot behind us, or fishing expeditions in the creek up the street. As instructed, when the sun began to set we almost always returned home—tired and thirsty and ready—for dinner. Sometimes, though, we got so caught up in a mission (or stuck so high up in a tree) that the family would divvy up into search parties to come retrieve us. For that next week we'd be "grounded"—sentenced to bake cookies with Caca or help her make patchwork quilts, to watch *Wheel of Fortune* with Pawpaw or help him make home repairs—then it was back to the adventures of James and Cecily.

More than normal or happy, even, our childhood was damn near storybook—until, as fairytales usually go, a dark spell fell over our kingdom and poisoned my parent's marriage. For Mom and Dad, fighting was normal, and James and I knew how to handle it: we would run and get Caca and she would sort them out *real quick.* Then, *poof!* Right after James's fourth birthday, Caca disappeared. "She's on a trip," is all anyone would say. "Don't worry, though, she'll be back soon!" With nowhere to run, James and I just hid in the closet and covered our ears. Still, we could hear the shouts echoing off the walls, the dishes smashing to the ground, Dad running after Mom, Mom slamming the door behind her as she left. Tears streaming down our faces, we'd race outside just in time to watch her taillights fade away.

When Caca came home a few weeks later, she wasn't strong enough to hold my parents' marriage together anymore—she was falling apart herself. She returned to us a skeleton in a wheelchair, a plastic tube wrapped around her face attached to a metal tank. The night before her return, Momma Jean and Pop had told us that she'd gotten sick and that we needed to be gentle with her; I thought they meant she had a cold or something, but Caca was the strongest person I knew, the matriarch of our family. I couldn't imagine her being weak until I saw it for myself. As it turned out, she'd gotten asbestosis from washing Pawpaw's clothes, and, rather than traveling, she'd been staying at a cancer treatment center in Houston. It was her last hope. Our family hadn't told us because they'd hoped they wouldn't have to—that she would get better. But she didn't.

Christmas was bittersweet that year. It was the last we shared together as a family, and our last with Caca. We tore through a bunch of little presents—craft kits, fishing poles, stocking stuffers—then James and I, a little dejected, followed Momma Jean and Pop outside to find our real present: a go-cart topped with an oversized bow. The big finale, though, was a black pug so tiny it fit in the palm of Daddy's hand. Uncle Jarrod brought it out in a gift bag and carefully placed it on Caca's lap—by then she was confined to a wheelchair and had tubes coming out from everywhere. Before she could open it, though, the bag toppled over and the puppy popped out. It took one look at Caca with those big, bulgy eyes then jumped up and licked her right in the face. She laughed so hard that Pop had to turn up her oxygen, but it was well worth it to see her come alive again. Caca passed away just after the New Year. Pawpaw named the puppy Angel in her memory.

Nineteen ninety-five started out bad, and only got worse from there. Mom and Dad kept fighting, and James and I spent more and more time in my closet. Then that summer, after I'd graduated from kindergarten and James from pre-K, Mom and Dad sent us on our first trip to Atlanta alone; they made a big to-do about us being "big kids now" flying all by ourselves, but I knew something was off. So when we returned from Grandmommy Kay's and they told us they were getting a divorce, I wasn't exactly shocked. James cried right away and Mommy did too. But I cried only once Daddy did. I'd never seen him cry before, and I felt sad for him. More than anything, though, I felt relief. Even then, I knew it was the right thing for Mommy. She was always crying and leaving, and every time she drove off I was scared that she wasn't coming back.

This time, Dad explained, Mom was moving out for good, and we could either go with her or stay with him. It wasn't *just* a choice between them, though: if I went with Mom, I'd have to leave Momma Jean, Pop, and Pawpaw behind. But if I stayed with Dad, Mom wouldn't have anyone. Dad had the house and all that family, but Mom only had James and me—without us, who would make her smile? When she was sad, I would cover my eyes with both hands then jump out and shout, "Magic happy!" James, meanwhile, would take her face into his hands and give her "pretty eyes," blinking one eye after another "like they do in old-timey movies." Between the two of us, we could usually cheer her up. I worried about what might happen if we weren't there. So I chose Mom, and James, of course, chose me. Then the three of us packed our bags and left our suburban home for a two-bedroom apartment on the wrong side of town.

Adjusting to life in that cramped apartment in a new neighborhood was a difficult transition for James and me, but my parents decided it was the only way they could afford to live apart and still provide us a good education. When James and I had begun pre-K and kindergarten the year prior, they'd sent us to a private Christian school because Beaumont public schools had a notoriously bad reputation—they insisted that James and I have every opportunity available to us. After the divorce, Mom paid rent while Dad paid tuition; though they'd both graduated Lamar University that summer—Dad with an accounting degree and Mom with a nursing license—$4,000 tuition for two kids was still a stretch for their starting salaries.

I hadn't thought about it until we moved out with Mom, but all our neighbors before had always been white—now there were only a few families that looked like us. It was the first time James and I had ever lived with blacks and Mexicans—unless you count Mom, but we didn't because in our minds she was white, not brown like the others. It was also the first time we'd ever lived with other kids—and there were *so* many of them! We didn't care what color they were, we were just excited to have new playmates. Every day we played hide-and-go-seek, tag, or red rover until Mom called us home for dinner. We'd groan and (eventually) give in, complaining, "Everyone else gets to stay out after dark!" The reality, of course, was that no one else's parents were around to make them go inside.

One day we were all playing in the courtyard when I noticed a black girl in braided pigtails about my age watching from the side-lines. I invited her to join us, but she just stood there and looked at me like she didn't understand. I grabbed her hand to bring her over, but she jerked back and brandished a kitchen-knife at me. (Maybe she'd never had a *white* neighbor before.) One night, a teenage boy with untreated schizophrenia stabbed both his sister and grandmother then ran door to door attacking anyone who answered—his attempted killing spree left one dead and many wounded before one resident opened the door and shot him. That was "home" during the week, but we really went home on the weekends—to Dad and the rest of our family. Our grandparents, especially, tried to cushion the disruption by affording us their undivided attention: Momma Jean would take me antiquing and let me pick out little trinkets, Pop would take James hunting and teach him how to shoot.

Everyone tried so hard to make us feel loved, but James and I still felt angry and confused. One day, I just stopped eating—a week later, I was hospitalized for malnutrition. The idea must've come from something my ballet teacher said—like, "tuck in those tummies, bal-lerinas can't be fat"—because Mom pulled me out of ballet after that and put me in gymnastics instead. And though my appetite soon re-turned, I didn't feel any better. Instead of taking my frustrations out on myself, I began taking them out on school. I told all my friends about sex and had them keep diaries detailing what they would do with their future husbands. During the parent-teacher conference, my Christian teachers approved of the marriage prerequisite but were otherwise horrified with my seven-year-old fascination with sex.

"What exactly do you think *it* is?" "Mommy and Daddy used to do it," I explained. "I saw them once—it's when two people kiss naked." "We're going through a divorce," my parents explained. "She's having a hard time with it."

James acted out at school, too, but—again, never to be outdone—took it to a whole other level. He'd always had a flair for disruption, but after the divorce, his games took a darker turn. On his first day of kindergarten, he rose before every student, parent, and teacher of the incoming class and introduced himself: "My name is James William McMillan, and when I grow up I want to be the devil reincarnated as a vacuum cleaner!" We *still* don't know where he got that from—TV, maybe? But he was always picking up on things no one else thought twice about. For his first show-and-tell, Mom suggested he bring in his baseball glove; James had a different idea: he smuggled in a buck knife and proceeded to pantomime the proper way to gut a deer before it was confiscated and he was suspended. His favorite game was hide-and-go-seek, and, on more than one occasion, his recess period ended with an Amber Alert. Teachers shut their classroom doors, students stayed in their desks while administrators searched the school (sometimes for hours) until someone finally found James fast asleep in a gym mat or curled up in a supply closet.

And after school, at home, when it was just the two of us, we took our frustrations out on each other. During one fight, though, James picked up a shoe and whacked me in the face with it, just above my left eye. There was a cool sensation of something rushing down my cheek then I felt woozy and began wailing. Through the mix of blood and tears, I could see the horrified look on my brother's face just before both my mother *and father* came running. "Daaadddddyyyy!" I reached out for him, relieved he hadn't left yet after dropping us off after school. (Why had I ever thought it the best thing for them to get a divorce?) Dad took me into his arms and shouted at James,

"What did you do *this time!?*" "Let's go," Mom snatched him up, and the four of us got into the car to go to the hospital. While Dad waited with me in the emergency room, Mom took him to the psychiatric ward. I got six stitches, James got one week. He returned home diagnosed with ADHD and zombied out on Ritalin, the '90s "miracle drug."

IT WAS A BREAKING POINT for my parents, both emotionally and financially. They'd tried their best but couldn't make it work apart—they gave it one more go "for the kids." Though still divorced, together they mortgaged a house in one of the nicest neighborhoods in Lumberton, a neighboring town with a good public school system. When they brought us to see it, we squealed in delight: three times bigger than our trailer, it had a playroom just for us, a large backyard for our dogs, and *even* a pool *with* a diving board—best of all, though, we were all together again. We moved in just before Christmas of 1996, but Dad was gone by the end of spring. He went back to Beaumont, and James and I stayed behind, again, with Mom.

By the end of the summer, things had gotten bad again. Mom was struggling to make mortgage payments, to keep us from fighting, and to break off another unwanted relationship. Lance was the father of a kid we went to after-school care with; Mom had only gone out with him a few times before he became really possessive. He'd show up unannounced and bang on the door until she answered; if she didn't, he'd keep calling until she had to take the phone off the hook. One day we came home and she was gone, too. Instead, Abuela was there. She told us that Mommy was sick in the hospital, but she'd be back and better in a week. "Sick like Caca, or sick like James?" I asked. "Like James," she said. That meant that something bad had happened, something she needed to talk about and take pills for. That's what

James said, anyway, referencing his own experience just after the shoe incident.

Whatever happened to her happened right before Diana, Princess of Wales, died in a car crash on August 31, 1997. I remember that because Abuela made us stay home from school to watch the funeral procession on television—Abuela said Princess Diana was a saint. I knew that saints had something to do with Jesus, but I didn't know what exactly. When I asked her, she shouted "Dios mio!" then asked, "Doesn't your mother take you to mass?" "Like church?" I asked and shrugged. "Sometimes we go to Sunday school." She moved her hand to her head then down to her stomach, back up to her left shoulder then across to the right. "What does that mean?" I asked again. "You were born Mexican and baptized Catholic," she was shouting again. "But you don't know Spanish or how to cross yourself!?" After that she stopped speaking English to us and turned the channel to Tele-mundo instead—I think she hoped we'd learn by osmosis.

When Mom came home, she seemed a lot calmer, but she also said "there are going to have to be some changes." First, she quit working at the hospital and got a job with fewer hours, less pay, and, most importantly, less stress at a home health agency. Next, she stuck a "For Sale by Owner" sign in the yard, and just after my ninth birthday pool party, we packed up the house and left. Then James went to live with Dad, and I stayed with Mom. For as much as she wanted to keep us together, she just didn't have the time, money, and energy to take care of us both. From there, Mom and I moved into a trailer park off US 69, the main thoroughfare between Beaumont and Lumberton—the best she could afford on her new salary.

It may have been the only way, but it had a devastating effect on my relationship with James—we still saw each other on weekends, switching back and forth between our parents. But ultimately we lived separate lives, growing more distant each year, each of us, I think, resenting the other for lives that looked greener from the other side only to find out, years later, that neither of us ever had it easier than the other.

The way Mom and Dad had come undone so absolutely, how James and I had been separated entirely, how our family had been torn apart completely—it left a strong impression on me. I began to believe that calm was not the absence of chaos; it was the sign of a storm ahead. To weather it, I learned to expect the worst—after all, high hopes only got you a longer fall down. The trailer Mom and I rented was the first test. It was a portal to another era: it had shaggy green carpeting, a rotary phone, and Elvis Presley wall paneling. Mom thought it was funny; I thought it was beneath us. We'd gone from a big brick home in a quiet neighborhood to a tiny tin box on a busy highway. There weren't backyards or front yards, only parking spots and the spaces around them (often storage for long-forgotten toys or long-dead appliances). There weren't sidewalks to walk or ride bikes on, only the shoulder of the road—every now and then, some kid got hit. There weren't play sets or pools, only the railroad behind the park and the polluted creek beneath it. Every day, I woke up to cars honking, trains whistling, couples fighting, and kids getting beaten—every night, I fell asleep to the same thing.

By the end of the following year, we'd moved two more times. But I came to prefer living that way. When you're always moving, you don't risk falling into a false sense of security. We arrived at the Elvis trailer to find it already occupied by a colony of cockroaches. From the beginning, it was a battle of all-out chemical warfare: our daily offensive was shoot 'em as you see 'em with Raid, but twice they overtook us and forced us to evacuate—we fought back with bombing campaigns to regain control of the territory. Victory seemed inevitable—it was a matter of fact that we *were* more powerful; alas, our resources were no match for their intimate knowledge of the terrain. In the end, the war was won by a guerrilla strategy I call the "Toast Offensive." One night, Mom put a piece of bread in the toaster and when she pushed the lever down, dozens of roaches launched a sneak attack: they swarmed the kitchen and took to her arms as she struggled to unplug their hub and throw it out the backdoor. We pulled out the *very* next day—we didn't lose though; we just stopped fighting. We always told ourselves that we could've won if we'd wanted to.

From the trailer park, we moved to yet another apartment complex; it was nicer than the last we'd lived in—Mom liked the security gate, I liked the pool—but, like the one before, it was a bastion for single mothers. Many left for work before the school bus came and returned long after their kids did. Mom worked a lot too, but she was home more than most mothers and tried to help the others out: she'd send me around to get my friends ready in the morning, and she'd always have extra McDonald's for those who stuck around for dinner. Money was tight, but Mom was stable and I liked the feeling of us facing our problems together. She couldn't give me everything I wanted, but she gave me everything I needed and she always found creative ways to fill the gap between the two. Sometimes she would wake me up at 4 a.m.—the only time she could spare before work—and take me on a Walmart run; we'd circle Skip-Its around our ankles, curl our eyelashes, or color our nails and catwalk outfits up and down the aisles. On the rare occasions that she got off early, she'd check me out of school for a "mental health day"; we'd dress up in our Sunday best then do dessert at a fancy restaurant or test drives at a luxury dealership and sip complimentary lattes as salesmen pitched Mom on "the deal of a lifetime!" "Love the car," she'd say. "Hate the color." One time, she picked me up from school and we drove straight to Lake Charles to see the Glenn Miller Orchestra; it was a twenty-one and over concert and she didn't have tickets, but we snuck in anyway—listening to "In the Mood," watching Mom dance, I felt light and free, happier than I'd felt in a long time, maybe ever. For a short time it was just Mom and me against the world, and we seemed to be winning.

Then, in November 1998, Mom married Jesse and we moved in with him. It wasn't that I didn't like Jesse. And it wasn't that I didn't like his house. I liked it a lot: it was a real home, it was big *and* it was on a lake. I just didn't like that it was *his house,* that living there would mean living by his rules, and that we'd be the ones leaving when it didn't work out. As it turned out, though, I really liked living with Jesse at first, and this time Mom was happier than she'd ever been.

Certainly, they were an odd couple: at the time, Mom was thirty-one, and Jesse was forty-four years her senior. In fact, he had been her patient; she met him while working home health care. But Jesse didn't need help because he was old—if Jesse was anything, it was seventy-five years *young*—but because he was paralyzed. Fiercely American, Jesse was seventeen years old when he enlisted in the Army to serve in World War II. He fought in Germany and was shot by a sniper while disarming a bomb; still, he completed his mission, and, because of him, his platoon advanced. When he'd finish telling the story, he'd point to the Purple Heart hanging framed on the wall and say, "I got that for gettin' my ass shot off." For his bravery (and his legs) the government also gave him a pension. It was enough to live on, but smart investments made him a financially comfortable man. As such, Mom could afford not to work, and anyway Jesse much preferred that she spend her time with him. So when they got married, she quit nursing—and this is the point where I usually say (with an eye roll), "*No,* she *didn't* marry him for his money."

Living with them day in and day out, I can say with certainty that the only thing more spectacular than their age difference was the love they shared. But anyone with an open mind could see that he was a handsome man with a hearty sense of humor, and Mom married him because *no one* made her laugh like he did. And laugh we did . . . at dinner each night and when we played cards or watched movies after; on road trips to vintage car shows and Civil War re-enactments; during barbecues in the summer when I was always in the lake and fall fashion shows when I modeled my back-to-school wardrobe; after gymnastics practices ("How 'bout that wedgie!") and choir rehearsals ("About that high-note?"); through *The Nutcracker* that Christmas, flower deliveries (for both Mom *and* me) on Valentine's, fireworks viewed from a private boat on Fourth of July, and right up to my eleventh birthday when all of a sudden the laughing stopped— or was just overwhelmed by the roar of Jesse's little green monster.

Maybe it had always been there, but at some point love wasn't enough to keep it at bay any longer and it took over. Jesse had never quite gotten over being in a wheelchair, and when he got it in his mind that Mom was going to leave him for a man who could walk, it crippled their marriage. It didn't matter what she said or did—or that all she wanted was to be with him—he got jealous, possessive, and, sometimes, downright mean.

When she wasn't there, he took it out on me: sometimes he'd backhand me for "getting mouthy" or grab my arm hard enough to bruise me, but more than anything he'd cut me down, call me names, and make me feel worthless. His go-to word was "pissant" and one too many times sent me reaching for a bottle of Tylenol PM. I don't think I wanted to die—I'm not even sure I understood what death was. I just wanted to go to sleep so I wouldn't have to deal with his insults anymore. When I woke up a day and a half later, no one even noticed I'd been gone—maybe they'd been too busy fighting? Mom, however, appropriated my idea and went about it more deliberately. I don't know what she did, exactly, but Jesse told me he'd had her "committed to the hospital for suicidal behavior." It would be a few days before we could visit, he said, because she had tried to kill herself in the psychiatric ward and the doctors had started her on an "intensive treatment."

(Apparently, nobody had searched her bag when she went in, nobody had confiscated all the medications she'd been instructed to bring with her, so she'd swallowed them all on the night she was admitted and was all but dead by the time the nurse found her—they'd pumped her stomach just in time, but the doctors prescribed electroshock therapy to keep her alive, to restore her will to live.)

I didn't know what they did, then, to make her stop crying. I just remember feeling *really* relieved to see that she wasn't anymore—even if it did hurt my feelings, a little, when she didn't recognize me. I took her in my arms and laughed, "*Mom,* it's Cecily!" She blushed and told me she was just surprised by how big I'd gotten; I told her about the fifth-grade talent show. My friends and I were doing a dance that I had choreographed to the theme song of the movie *Space Jam.* I put on a big smile and showed it to her. When I finished, she burst into applause and I beamed (for real, this time)—I wasn't sure I would ever see her smile again. The dance won first place that year. Mom couldn't be there in person, but she found a way to be there in spirit: she asked a nurse to look up *Space Jam* characters then painted them on T-shirts, making costumes for all of us. When Mom was released two weeks later, I told her all about the talent show as we snuck into Jesse's and packed everything we could into her car; "If he knew we were leaving," she explained, "he might try to hurt us."

From there we went to stay with Mom's best friend, Domino, and her fiancé, Grant, her three kids, Taurin (my age and my best friend), Brett (two years older and *not* our friend), and Kay-Kay (two years younger and severely autistic)—and a dozen or so Chihuahuas *and* half-dozen Shar-Peis (as per their dog-breeding business). It was a snug fit for the four-bedroom house; Mom and I bunked together, sharing a queen-sized bed. I liked being close to her, liked knowing she was okay. Before bed each night we would talk about our day and listen to music—our favorite was Tracy Chapman, "You got a fast car.

I want a ticket to anywhere." Then she'd hold me, rub my tummy, and sing to me ("You are my sunshine, my only sunshine . . . ") until I fell asleep.

Just after I finished fifth grade, Mom got us a place of our own. When we drove down US 69 in the direction of our old trailer park, I cringed at the thought of Critter War II, but she took a left turn just before it then pulled into a driveway about a mile and a half up Peck Road. "Are we lost?" I asked. "No, silly," she laughed. "We're home." And it really was a home: three bedrooms (with no wheels) with a huge front *and* backyard. "But," I hesitated, "can we afford it?" "I sure hope so," she said. "I already bought it." "Quit playing," I said. "How much is the rent?" "No seriously," she said, "it's ours—we own it." She'd sold our old house to put up the down payment, she explained, then took out a mortgage to cover the rest. "Can we afford *that?*" I asked again. I wanted to be excited for her and for the house, but I didn't see how we could make it work.

After her incident, Mom wasn't ready to return to nursing, so Domino had gotten her a bookkeeping job at the Cuestick, her father's pool hall; she made only $12,000 a year, but she liked her work and set her own hours so we got more time together. A thousand dollars a month was a tough budget to live on, but it was a worthwhile trade-off, so we made it work: at school, I had free meal status, so I ate breakfast and lunch there; after school, instead of day care, I went back to the Cuestick with Mom to play pool, do homework, then eat dinner (a corndog or pizza pocket); Mom said she'd been cleaning houses part-time and planned to pick up more shifts; I offered to help out on the weekends and get a babysitting gig. "Don't be such a worry-wart" she teased, house keys in hand. "We'll figure it out." Rolling my eyes, I reluctantly chimed in, "We always figure it out."

The moment I stepped through the front door of our new house, though, my excitement got the better of me. I raced around from room to room then declared the master bedroom "mine!" It was a big moment for Mom and me: it was the first house she'd bought herself, our first together, and the first *no one* could take away from us.

It was like a dream come true—then Gary moved in. Gary was a work-hard-to-play-hard kind of guy, a construction worker by day and a socialite by night. He was a little funny looking—five foot, eight inches, stout with a bald head, big ears, and buggy eyes—but made up for it with a big sense of humor. He liked to puff out his belly, prop it up like a baby-bump, waddle around—with that gaping grin of his— and ask people to guess how pregnant he was. Somehow, somewhere along the way, people found him attractive. Certainly, Mom did. She met him that summer at the Cuestick and, before autumn rolled around, he was living with us. To me, Gary was just the new Jesse, and I wasn't ready for the sequel. I didn't have a choice though. It may have been my life, but it wasn't my story—Mom was the star, I was just in it. I *did* choose, however, to play a smaller part than I had with Mom and Jesse. The Gary saga began just like before: I liked him, he liked me, he made us laugh, and we were all happy. But, this time around, I saw it for what it was: a tragedy masquerading as a romantic comedy—it's always fun until it's not and someone *always* gets hurt in the end. This time, I vowed, that person would *not* be me. I got close enough to en- joy myself but left room to bail when things got bad. I started packing up my feelings and finding new homes for them.

When I started sixth grade that fall, I made school my safe house: I signed up for spelling bees and essay competitions and even asked my teachers for extra assignments. I wrote for the newspaper, volun- teered with Special Friends (helping disabled students), and became the class representative for the Thanksgiving food drive—I toured the local food bank and was even interviewed on local news. When Mom saw that I'd cleared out all the cabinets, she laughingly scolded, "But Cecily, we *are* the poor!" When I wasn't in class, I took refuge in sports: I went to track practice at 5 a.m. and gymnastics from 6 p.m. to 9 p.m. That spring, I ran cross-country and did cheerleading. Mom and I shared breakfast together each morning, but otherwise I stayed in my room. The four walls were my sanctuary and art was my therapy: I painted hot-pink stripes on two, tire-sized polka dots on the other two, and cow spots on my fan. I'd stay up late most nights and draw or write in my journal while I listened to music; when a line really spoke to me, I'd write it on the wall.

I'd lock myself in during the week and leave on the weekends; I went to Dad's twice a month, and when school ended, I went to Atlanta for a few weeks then split the rest of it between cheerleading and wilderness camp. When summer ended, I came home to find a shirtless Gary day-drinking on the front porch—"I lost my job," he said, then took a drag from his Newport cigarette and exhaled. "But I'm looking for a new one." "I can see that," I muttered as he finished off his Bud Light. "Mom home?" I asked. "Nope," he crushed the can, tossed it, and pulled another from the cooler beside him. "Work. Always work." "*Someone* has to." I retrieved his can from the yard and put it in the trash. "Beer doesn't grow on trees, ya know."

That fall I went off to seventh grade, but Gary stayed on the porch. I'd get off the bus every day, and he'd be there to greet me— "Can't say I wasn't never there for you." And when Mom and Gary started fighting, I started wearing headphones. And as the cans piled up, I piled on more activities: on top of cheerleading and track, I did theater and debate.

But the more I got involved at school, the more I got in trouble. I started taking my anger from home out at school, and, looking back, I think the catalyst for it all came out of the confusion of 9/11. I was just shy of thirteen years old when it happened. I must have missed the bus that morning, because I was watching the news at home when it happened. "Mom, come here! A plane just flew into one of those towers in New York City!" "You had *better* be ready," she called. "I'm walking out the door in ten minutes." "I *aaaam!*" I shouted back, still in my pajamas. I was still there when she came into the living room, "*Cecily!* What did I *just* say?" "But Mom," I said, unable to look away, "*look.*" Dark smoke billowed from the top of the tower; "It's like a *chimney*," I said, and she sat down beside me. Little dots dropped from the middle; "*Jesus.* They're jumping," she said, and I grabbed her hand. A reporter called in from the ground below: "as fire crews are descending on this area, it does not appear"—a plane flew in from the right—"as if there is any kind of effort up there yet"—then exploded into the second twin tower—"*Oh my God!*" he said. "*Oh my God!*" we said and jumped into each other's arms. For the next few minutes we just held each other and silently watched the two buildings burn—then Mom said, "Shit! It's after 9 a.m., I'm so late for work." On our way out the door, I heard the newscaster say, "I think we have a terrorist attack of proportions that we cannot begin to imagine at this juncture."

That was the first time I'd heard the word "terrorist." I didn't know what it meant, and the adults I asked didn't seem to know either. When they tried to explain, they made terrorism sound sort of Disney-esque: like witches out to destroy our kingdom with black magic. I found it difficult to believe that one person, or a small group of people, could be *that* powerful; "magic" like that came from something deeper, some idea or belief. The terrorists, I learned, had been Muslim, so they believed in Islam; which, I was told, was a religious cult of brown men with towelheads and long beards who worshipped war, enslaved women, and hated Christians. That sounded crazy to me, but it was hard to know what to think any more. I learned a lot of new words trying to figure it out, but they didn't help me understand what had happened—if anything, they made it *more* difficult to untangle, and it started to feel like maybe that was the point. From what I could gather, there was an evil man named Osama bin Laden with a crazed army, al-Qaeda, hiding in the hills of some far-off land referred to as the Middle East, Afghanistan, or Iraq, who wanted to destroy America and the Free World using weapons of mass destruction and replace it with Islam. I still wasn't sure about that story—it still left so much unanswered—but it *did* help me answer my original question about the meaning of terrorism. I decided that terrorism was when you force someone else to do things your way.

Global terrorism was a difficult concept to grasp for someone who had never even been out of the South. But locally, it was something I was already familiar with. Lumberton was an all-white town, and most residents were God-fearing Republicans. Teachers refused to teach evolution ("It's blasphemy!"), parents fought to remove *Harry Potter* from the library ("It's witchcraft!"), and kids bullied those they thought were "faggots" ("It's unnatural!"). "Different," in general, was the nice, southern term when someone or something was "just *not* right." Integration was still considered a very different idea, and though Lumberton largely managed to avoid it, the nearby town of Vidor did not get off so easy. In 1992, a federal judge ordered the desegregation of 170 public housing projects in thirty-six counties across east Texas, and Vidor was one of them. A well-known "sundown" town, it had once boasted a freeway billboard that read, "Nigger, don't let the sun set on you in Vidor," and a sign attached to the city limit marker that proclaimed it "KKK Kountry." Both were removed before I was born, but the sentiment lived on. In 1993, John DecQuir became the first black resident of Vidor since the 1920s, and that year three others followed him. KKK rallies erupted, and, by September, the White Knights had run all four out of town. Afterward, the federal government seized control of the local public housing authority and, for several years after, went head to head with Klan members.

I didn't know all this until a black man was murdered in nearby Jasper, which the news called the latest in a string of crimes since the federal attempt to desegregate Vidor (and seemed to suggest that it was further proof that it wouldn't work). In 1998, James Byrd Jr., forty-nine, was walking home when he accepted a ride from a man he had seen around town and his two friends. Instead of taking him home, they drove him to a back-county road where they beat him and urinated on him, before chaining him to the back of their pickup truck by the ankles. They drove for approximately a mile and a half, before dumping his mutilated remains in front of a black church. The autopsy concluded that he had been alive during much of the dragging—marks suggested that he'd attempted to keep his head up—but died when both his head and right arm were severed as he slammed into a culvert. Pieces of his body were ultimately collected from eighty-one locations. The only thing that made it different from the civil rights era was that the three men were ultimately tried and found guilty of murder; the two who were members of white supremacist groups were given the death penalty, and the other got life in prison.

I was in third grade when they were convicted, but even then all my friends had an opinion. They ranged from indignant—"Them niggers been gittin' outta control. *Bout time* someone showed them who's boss"—to empathetic, like me. I thought what had happened was "just terrible, but a black man oughta know better than to git in a car with whites in *Jasper*, for heaven-sakes!" Right or wrong, there was an order to things, and, like it or not, everyone had their place within it. As far as I could tell, things worked just fine as long as people stayed where they were supposed to.

I didn't think about Byrd's murder again until after 9/11. I was at a pep rally for an upcoming football game. The cheerleaders had just performed a routine to Lee Greenwood's "God Bless the USA" when an athlete grabbed the mic and said, "This one's gonna be for the troops—tonight we're gonna go out there and kick ass like they was sandniggers!" The gym went wild as a teacher snatched the mic from him, but I stayed seated, deep in thought . . . sand—*niggers*. I'd never heard that word used for anyone but blacks. What did it mean that it was so easily transferable? Was it just *another* word for "different," sort of like "faggot"? It was then that I thought about James Byrd Jr. and recognized it for what it was: an act of terrorism. Sure, it was no 9/11, but wasn't it motivated by the same principle? I was told that al-Qaeda had hijacked planes and killed thousands of Americans to threaten our country and what it stood for: democracy and Christianity. Similarly, those three men had kidnapped James Byrd Jr. and dragged him to death to threaten integration and what it stood for: equality and diversity. It was then that I understood why segregation could not be allowed to continue, no matter how difficult it would be to change: no one should have to be scared of being black living in a white town. But it was more than that, too. No one should have to be scared of being different, of having different values or views, while living in a country that calls itself a democracy.

When I went home that night, I typed "sandnigger" into Google. I was surprised to learn that there were Muslims living in America. Islam was such a foreign concept, it hadn't occurred to me that its proponents could be my countrymen—but apparently, since 9/11, many people thought they shouldn't be. I was horrified to learn that Muslim Americans were being targeted in some sort of Salem-esque witch hunt. I saw pictures of men beaten bloody (like James Byrd Jr.) and graffiti that read "Die Arab Sandniggers" (like the pep rally). Ironically, though, the articles also noted that many Muslims had moved to America to escape the extremism of groups like al-Qaeda. When I went to church that Sunday, I brought it up in Bible study. They were nice enough about it but essentially said that Muslims were idol worshippers who got what was coming to them—"if they'd *just* accept the power of Christ, he'd save them in this life and the next." But weren't we supposed to live in his image, love thy neighbors, and turn the other cheek? That was the kind of Jesus I liked; whatever brand they were selling, I wasn't buying it. It wasn't long before I stopped going to church and started getting in trouble at school for asking the same questions.

One day, I stayed seated for the Pledge of Allegiance and stood up when everyone else sat down for the moment of prayer. When the teacher sent me to the office, the principal wanted to know why I'd done it. "Because," I explained, "some people aren't Christian, but we have to say 'under God' in the pledge and worship him in prayer." "Don't you believe in God?" he asked. "I do," I replied. "But that's not the point." "Then what is?" he asked. "That you *make* us do it." I said. "What if I wasn't Christian?" "But you *are* Christian," he replied. "But if I *wasn't*," I argued, "it'd be wrong to *make* me worship a different god." "Yeah, well, you'd also go to hell. Do it again," he challenged, "and you'll get a taste of it."

So the next day, of course, I did it again. When I returned to his office, though, he wasn't there—the women's softball coach was. "Let's get this over with," she said, holding a two-inch-wide paddle with holes in it. "Oh, I don't think so!" I laughed. "Whodoya think you are, my mother?" "Believe me," she said. "If you were mine, you'd be getting more than two." "And if you were mine," I said. "You'd sue the school. And *believe me,* my mom will!" "She didn't sign the form against it," she said, "so, the way I see it, you have two options: bend over and take it, or get suspended and take it up with her. But you run track, right? You'd be suspended from meets too." I crossed my arms and looked away until she made to leave. "Fine," I huffed. With a slight smile, she instructed me to "turn around and put both hands on the desk." Behind it hung a portrait of former president George Bush Senior standing, *of course,* in front of an American flag. I gritted my teeth, stared deep into his beady eyes, and choked back a cry each time the paddle hit my backside.

When I went home that night, I wrote in my journal: *They think they can put me in my place, but they can't. My place is wherever I say it is.* And with that silent declaration of war, school was no longer my safe house—it was my battleground. The only thing the paddle had taught me was that I'd lose if I fought alone. So my first strategic campaign was a petition against the school dress code. It allowed for tank tops with two-inch straps but girls with bigger breasts (like me) got written up for cleavage and had to wear a gym shirt all day. "It's not our fault we have big boobs," I lobbied my classmates, "and it's not fair that we're persecuted for them"—boys and girls alike were happy to sign. What better way to build an army? With my newfound power, I also led boycotts against tests and assignments I thought unfair: I'd convince the class to scribble "A" all the way down Scantron forms or all write the same silly answers on worksheets—"She can't fail us all," I'd say. "She'd lose her job."

While I was busy fighting at school, the fighting between Mom and Gary continued at home. Because I was never there, though, I hadn't noticed how bad things had gotten. Then one day, I got off the bus and Gary was gone—maybe he finally got off his ass and got a job, I thought. Mom was gone too, but I figured she was probably working late as usual. But when neither had come home by ten o'clock, I started to worry. Just then, a friend of my mother's stopped by. She told me that Mom was in the hospital. "Psych ward?" I asked. "No," she said. "Emergency room." Gary had beaten the living hell out of her, she explained. "No broken bones, thank God, but she's badly bruised and has a concussion." Apparently, Mom had managed to call 911 before Gary took off and crashed the car during a high-speed police chase. As it turned out, Gary *did* have a job after all: he was a drug dealer. The cops found a bunch of meth in the trunk and locked him up for a few years. He wrote me once, but I never responded. I had nothing to say to him.

But I had a mouthful for Mom. And when she came home the next day, I let her have it: "You always go for guys like Gary. They put you in the hospital. I put you back together. You bring home a new asshole, and we do it all over again. . . . Either you're stupid, or you like the abuse. Whatever it is, I can't care anymore. It's pathetic, you're pathetic—I can't be a part of it!" I didn't mean to be mean, I was just angry—and not *with* her, but *for her.* Mom was my best friend, my biggest fan; "Ceci," she'd always say, "you're not only beautiful, but smart. You can do anything you put your mind to." I thought the same of her, but I couldn't convince her to see it herself. That night, I gave up trying—and gave up on *us* too. I couldn't take care of her *and* take care of myself, so I chose me and let her go. I packed up my room and called Dad to come get me.

CHAPTER 2

Adolescent

*A*fter Mom, I didn't want to be a grown-up anymore. I just wanted to be a normal kid in a normal family. I wanted freshly baked cookies and help with homework, sit-down dinners and backyard barbecues and, thinking ahead, a car for my sweet sixteen and to graduate valedictorian. *Normal,* you know, like *The Wonder Years* or *Boy Meets World.* Dad, in turn, was looking for a little normalcy too. He'd remarried the year prior, and, like me with Mom's men, James hadn't handled it well. But, unlike me, he didn't retreat into his room or run away to friends' houses. Instead, James launched a full-on offensive. He slammed doors and smashed dishes daily, stole things often, and sometimes took a swing at Dad or our new stepmother, Tammy. By the time I called, they couldn't have been happier to take me in and—as per the child custody agreement—turn James over to Mom. It was a trade-off, it seemed, that met everyone's expectations. Too bad we hadn't shared those with each other in advance. Otherwise, we might have seen the disappointment coming.

Dad and Tammy lived in a big house in Copperfield, a nice suburb of Houston. He was now the chief financial officer of a small
company; she was the manager of an apartment complex. They
weren't rich, by any means, but they had enough to live on and then
some. Dad didn't help with homework (probably because I didn't
need it), but he did take me to cheerleading practice. Tammy wasn't
the baking type, but she did pick up dinner on the way home on
nights we didn't eat out. After dinner, they watched HBO down-
stairs, and I watched TeenNick upstairs. On the weekends, he played
tennis, and she did jazzercise; at night, they'd often go out with
friends, and I'd babysit their friends' kids. Sometimes I went shopping with Tammy or to the movies with Dad, or we'd all go bowling.
I also went to sleepovers and birthday parties and ran around with
kids in the neighborhood.

It was almost everything I'd expected—but then there were the
rules: "You have to keep your room clean," "You have to do your
chores," "You can't go anywhere without permission," "You can't go out
with your friends without supervision," "No friends over when we're
not home," "No dating until you're fifteen," "Don't swear," "Don't argue," and on and on. I'd never had rules before. At Mom's, we had
agreements that were discussed and amended together: my room was
mine to keep as I pleased, as long as it wasn't unsanitary; we would
clean together on Sundays, and if I didn't, she'd take care of it herself.
Her methods were unorthodox; one time she broke all the dirty dishes
except for one set for each of us, so we had to wash our dishes if we
wanted to eat. When I went somewhere, I'd tell her where I was going
and when I'd be back; I dated who I liked and told her about it (but
before I'd have sex—"Ew! Mom!"—I was to talk to her first, then we
would find the right birth control). Swearing, we agreed, was generally
vulgar—a crutch lacking both clarity and creativity—but we appreci-
ated its undeniable comedic and emphatic value. Most importantly, we

didn't argue, we debated—and a good point was a good point, regardless of who had made it.

When I tried to debate Dad, though, he said, "No, means no, Cecily. This isn't a democracy—it's a dictatorship. I'm the parent—you're the child. I make the rules—you follow them. Got it?" I nodded yes, but, no, I didn't "get it"—I didn't get any of it. I'd learned from Mom that "no" wasn't an answer—it was an invitation to find another way. I'd learned from the news that democracy (like America) was good and dictatorships (like Iraq) were bad—was Dad testing me? I learned from TV that parents made rules and kids were *supposed* to follow them, but the best characters usually didn't and always learned something—that was just growing up, right? Wrong. They really *did* just want me to obey them. I really didn't want to—and they really didn't care whether I wanted to or not.

Mom knew me well; she knew that if she made rules, I would break them on principle. Dad, however, hadn't spent more than the occasional weekend with me since I was eight years old. He had only seen what I wanted to show him: perfect attendance awards, honor roll certificates, poetry and essays published in the school newspaper, medals and ribbons from track, gymnastics, and cheerleading, photos of me in the spelling bee, in the class play, in the talent show. . . . He'd put them on the fridge, show them off to his friends, and sometimes point them out to James, "Why can't you be more like your sister?" He didn't know all I'd been through with Mom and that I'd done all those things because I wanted to, not because she told me to; she didn't and she didn't have to. I was thirteen when I moved in with him and Tammy, and to them I was just a little girl—their little girl. I realize now that they were just trying to take care of me with all their "you have to," "you can't," "no," and "don'ts," but for as much as I didn't get that then, they didn't get me either. I had been taking care of myself since Dad left, and I was pretty good at it. When I left Mom's, I was looking for stability and safety from them—but a dictatorship wasn't going to work for me.

My room was always messy: shoes, skirts, shirts everywhere from morning outfit changes, and papers, photos, pens, and markers from nightly art projects. But the mess made sense to me—order didn't. Instead of cleaning, I would just cram everything into the closet before Dad and Tammy came in. (Why did *they* care what *my* room looked like?) The same thing went for chores: I'd do just enough to keep things sanitary, but they called it "cutting corners." (A house was a thing meant to be lived in—why did they want ours to look like it wasn't?) My questions, though, were seen as "backtalk," which was always answered with, "You're grounded." "Grounded from what?" I'd scream, stomping upstairs to my room. "You never let me go anywhere, anyway!"

They still wouldn't let me go to the mall or movies without a parent present—*obvious* social suicide. But I didn't argue the point; I went around it. I'd spend the night with a friend whose parents would let us go without them; once there, we'd meet up with boys from school and make out with them. "But, technically," I'd argue when I eventually got caught, "I didn't do anything wrong: I had permission to stay with a friend—when she went out, I couldn't just stay home. And it wasn't a date—we didn't make plans, I just ran into him." The argument itself broke another rule, so I'd earn myself two weeks instead of one! "Fine, whatever," I'd shout. "You're ruining my fucking life!" "Swearing makes three," Dad would shout back. "Fuck!"—"Four!"—"Fuck!"—"Five!"—"Fuck!"—"Six!"—"You!" For added emphasis, I'd slam my bedroom door each time I said it. Then I'd lock myself in and refuse to come out all weekend. Apart from school and a few successful escapes to friends' houses, I stayed in my room for the rest of the school year.

Instead of talking to Dad and Tammy, I saved all my words for school and a few choice ones ended in fights. The first time was in PE when this pretty, popular girl kept picking on this chubby, quiet girl for "smelling bad." "You mean that shit smell?" I finally snapped. "It's not her, it's you. Your head's so far up your own ass, it's no wonder you can't smell anything else." She called me out "to the basketball courts" after school, and I obliged. I told her to walk away and even let her hit me twice before I laid her out; I argued self-defense, and the principal reluctantly agreed, so I didn't get in trouble. About a week later, though, I kicked a guy in the nuts for bullying a special education student, and that got me a week of in-school suspension in a trailer lined with cubicles where you face the wall and "don't talk!" and "do your work!" I spent a lot of time in detention by the end of the school year, but I came to like it there. I'd finish my work and homework by lunch then write in my journal or read whatever I wanted to. I was sent there because the school didn't want to put up with my shit, but the feeling was mutual: I didn't want to put up with their shit either. Overall, I had more freedom being bad than I'd ever had being good—and not only more free time but also freedom *from* expectation. No one expected much from the bad kids, and for that reason I came to like being one.

When seventh grade ended, I went off to sleep-away camp as usual—but, for the first time, I was almost sent home. It was Wednesday dinner—all the campers had on white, collared shirts for worship—and when dessert was served, it was chocolate cake. It was too good an opportunity to pass up. Afterward, when the camp director demanded to know why I'd started the food fight, I was honest with her: "Oh! Come on," I shrugged. "Someone *had* to do it." "In the first place," she scolded, "you and I obviously differ on our idea of a good time. Second of all," she added, "that's strike three. . . ." (I'd already gotten caught twice for sneaking out at night: once to toilet-paper the older girls' cabin, once to make out in the older boys' cabin.) But before she could finish—"You're out!"—I burst into tears and begged

her to let me stay: "Please don't call my Dad! I'll be good, I promise!"
I put on the show she wanted, told her what she needed to hear to let
me stay. I bent the rules but didn't break them: I was "good" the rest of
the session or, really, careful enough not to get caught. From then on
I learned to play the game, to become the master of it—get good
enough to make up my own rules (though I wasn't quite there yet).

Later that summer, I went to Atlanta to visit Grandmommy Kay
and found some real trouble to get into. I went to parties, did shots,
smoked cigarettes, got high, and hooked up with high school boys.
One night, a friend of mine stole her mother's minivan, two bottles of
wine, and a handle of vodka. We drove around drinking and picking
up friends until we filled up on both, then we broke into a private pool
and went skinny dipping. I went to retrieve her car keys from the bottom of the pool and emerged to the sound of sirens. I tossed them to
her, threw on a pair of nearby boxers and a wife beater, and took to the
fence. When I reached the top, blue-and-red lights bounced off the
buildings around me. I leapt down and made a run for it. The sirens
fast on my heels, I cut a corner and dove behind a set of stairs. "Ma'am,"
I heard an officer say, "you can come out now." I stayed where I was
and tried hard not to breathe. "Ma'am," he repeated, "I can see you."—
No you can't—"You can't hide behind *a single step*." Had it been a foot
chase I probably would've gotten away. Instead I sat handcuffed in the
back of his car and thought about what Mom would say: "So what did
we learn?" *I'm better at running than I am at hiding.*

When summer ended, I went back to Dad's and took that lesson
with me: I stopped hiding in my room and started running away. I
was fourteen when I first tried to leave and was only in eighth grade,
but I remember *feeling* very grown up. My friend Kirsten's parents
said I could move in if my parents consented and agreed to pay child
support. I, in turn, drafted an appeal to Mom and Dad entitled "My
Demands":

I don't want to live with either of you—it's too chaotic; I want to live with Kirsten and her parents—I want stability; I want to be legally emancipated but will agree to frequent weekend visits with Mom and monthly dinners with Dad.

To live with Kirsten, I need:

1) $500/month in child support,
2) continued health insurance for my medications, therapy, and dental care,
3) one paid extracurricular activity per year (tumbling, dance, etc.), and
4) paid travel to Atlanta for spring and summer breaks.

I wasn't trying to be unreasonable; I just asked for what I thought it would take to raise myself and do it well. In earnest, I thought it was a small price to pay to get rid of me. When Dad called he declined to discuss my proposal. "I don't negotiate with terrorists," he said. "You have two options: come home or I'll call the police; live here or go to juvie." I didn't see juvenile detention working out well for me, and I wasn't willing to call his bluff, so I went home—but with new terms: "If you make me stay here, I will make your lives a living hell." They, in turn, *did* call my bluff—but I wasn't bluffing.

I was grounded indefinitely, so I did what I wanted anyway. I wore one outfit to the bus—polo shirt, jeans, and Keds—then changed into another—tank top, skirt, and heels—when I got to school and did my makeup there too. "Let the school call," I told my friends. "I'm already grounded—what more can he do?" Spankings. He'd undo his belt, fold it in half, and smack the leather straps together to let me know it was coming. I was fast, though, and, by then, already halfway up the stairs. Round-and-round the house we'd go until I wore him out or he finally caught up to me—the longer the chase, the worse I got it. And the more I got it, the more I acted out. I'd sneak out—climb down from my second-story window—to meet up with friends and make out with boys, to go parties, or just because I could (and couldn't stand to be home). More spankings, more groundings.

Because I couldn't behave myself, Dad and Tammy said I couldn't go to Mexico with them and the rest of the family for spring break. As punishment, they left me behind with a friend—ironic, I thought, because it was all I wanted to begin with. As retribution, though, I planned a little fiesta of my own: I invited the whole eighth-grade class over to my big, empty house that Friday. Word spread so far, so fast, though, that even the teachers knew about it. As such, the office called my parents, who called my grandparents, who called my uncle, who called the police, who, of course, crashed the party before it even started. After "that little stunt," though, the order changed from groundings and spankings to house arrest and beatings, to which I responded with tantrums of epic proportions (tantrums that made James look like an angel).

It was a dynamic that was doomed from the beginning and ended just three weeks after I started high school—with Dad and me in agreement that one of us would kill the other if Mom didn't come get me. So just before my fifteenth birthday, I moved back to Lumberton to live with Mom and start ninth grade at my second high school— but I was under no impression that I'd be there long. I was done being parented, and she wasn't trying to stand in my way. The summer before, I'd gone to Atlanta as usual, but this time I came home with a long-distance boyfriend and a promise to return to him as soon as possible. By Christmas break, I'd saved up enough money to buy a ticket back, and Mom let me stay with a girlfriend, Michaela—"On two conditions: spend *some* time with your grandparents and come back in time to spend Christmas morning with Momma Jean and Pop." It was tradition; James and I always opened gifts with them. But I was fifteen and wasn't going to let "sentimental bullshit" ruin my plan to run away from my parents and move to Atlanta. So I lied to her and even booked a return flight for Christmas Eve to mask my real intentions. That morning, my plane came and went but I didn't get on it—and I'd never planned to. I hugged Grandmommy and Granddaddy good-bye at the airport, walked in, walked out, then got in a car with Michaela. From there, she drove me to her boyfriend's house. He had a basement and absentee parents, so I intended to hide out there while I negotiated the terms of my permanent relocation with my parents—in other words, I'd planned to hold myself hostage.

When I didn't arrive in Houston, Mom called Grandmommy, who said she'd dropped me off at the airport but hadn't heard from me since. Mom went to the police, but my grandparents were more the wiser—they circled around to every location they'd driven me to the last couple of days. So when Grandmommy flew down the basement steps, I froze in shock—she was the last person I'd expected to see. And when she snatched me by the elbow and dragged me back up with a force and speed that sent me literally tripping over myself, I knew I'd never underestimate old people again. Against her "better judgment," she let me stay for Christmas but (literally) put me on a plane the very next day—she walked me all the way to the gate then watched me board. The tears in my eyes dove for my ears when the plane took off, but I wiped them away with a cocktail napkin and reminded myself: *my place is where I say it is—Atlanta will be my home someday.*

SOMEDAY CAME, BUT IT TOOK much longer than expected—it was a year and a half that felt like a lifetime. It was four more houses, three failed runaways, two different schools, and a new stepfather later. It was my first iPod, my first cell phone, my first car later. It was thousands of cigarettes, hundreds of drinks, and dozens of parties later. It was the year after I left cheerleading to commit to theater but the same year that I began my love affair with politics.

It was the summer of 2005, I was sixteen years old, and I'd gone to Atlanta to do "political theater," as Grandmommy called it. "You don't have to choose one, you can do both," she said, suggesting I audition for Youth Creates, a summer training program for teenagers hosted by 7 Stages—an avant-garde theater in her neighborhood "focused on the social, political, and spiritual values of contemporary culture." At the start of my interview, Heidi—the upbeat, twentysomething director of the program—asked about my theater experience. I bragged about my high school's one-act play and my decorated status in the International Thespian Society. Then she asked about my other interests, and I really lit up. I told her about my obsession with politics, how it began with Howard Dean in the 2004 Democratic presidential primaries and his antiwar/propeople platform: pull our troops from Iraq and provide health care for every American, tax cuts for the middle class (instead of for the rich), better public schools for kids, and more affordable higher education for students. I told her about how even his whooping in- spired me, how I'd never seen anyone so excited about politics before, how I'd started the Young Democrats Club to debate the Young Re- publicans, how we'd publicly discussed the war, welfare policy, the rich, how before that, there was no conversation—just one set of values that nobody questioned, how that was wrong, that we, the kids—someday we, the people—wouldn't learn to think if there wasn't room to ques- tion, how it wouldn't be democracy without disagreement, how I worry what will happen if we're all just . . . silent. When I finished, I was breathless. "You'll fit right in at 7 Stages," Heidi said and even offered me a scholarship to attend Youth Creates that summer.

I was excited for the opportunity, but not for the program specifi- cally—I saw it as my golden ticket to Atlanta. Dad and Tammy had since moved to Decatur, an intown suburb of the Atlanta Metropolitan Area. I was to spend the summer with them while James went to stay with Mom. Not yet fifteen, James was already running a minor drug ring at school, selling weed and prescription pills to kids, and had already been busted once by the police. I thought if I did Youth Creates and didn't get in any trouble (played the game well enough), Dad and Tammy would let me stay with them—it wouldn't be the home I wanted, but it would be the change I needed. It would be my golden ticket out of Texas, for good, and the beginning of the rest of my life in Atlanta. A house was good enough for now, I thought, but I soon found myself taken in by the 7 Stages family.

I arrived bright and early the first morning of the program and, after a quick round of introductions, stood in a circle studying the faces of the other twenty kids before me—half of them shades of black and brown. "The tip of the tongue strikes at two upon the teeth," I followed along as we stretched, but my mind wandered off . . . back to that apartment complex in Beaumont, back to that little black girl with the knife, back to that look of fear (or anger?) in her eyes—like she really would stab me (and, maybe, had good reason to). "The tip of the tongue strikes . . ." —my attention back to the faces before me (*I hope they like me*). Just then I noticed that everyone, not just me, had lost focus. I followed their eyes to find the stunningly beautiful woman standing a few feet behind me: she had dark brown skin, long curly dreads, crystal-covered nails, and curves for days thinly veiled beneath a tight, bright-blue dress, delicately poised atop six-inch heels. "Sorry, I'm late—traffic," she said. "But don't let me stop you." Too late. When she spoke, the room fell silent—it was the most powerful voice I'd ever heard or have ever heard since. "Well, hello then!" she said—her sound, somehow both commanding and kind—"I am Nyrobi. Now finish your warm-ups and we'll talk later." We stood there staring until she shooed us away—*I really hope she likes me*. She did—and the others did too.

But Youth Creates wasn't about liking each other so much as learning how to listen and respect each other regardless. Heidi—short, pale-white with blonde, straight hair and as bubbly now as the day she'd interviewed me—announced our assignment that first day: "In the next five weeks, you will focus your efforts toward understanding how individuals from different cultures and walks of life come together to create a richly diverse and richly unified art." We met ten to five, Monday through Friday, and sometimes on weekends, to write, design, produce, and finally perform *Umuganda*—the title of our original play and the Kinyarwandan (or Rwandan) word for "we work together."

The twenty-five scenes were a theatrical grab bag of, well, you name it: modern dance, hip-hop, and puppetry, film noir, show tunes, and poetry. Although amateur and, at times, decidedly immature, we took ourselves and our work *very* seriously. It was an exercise in learning to use our own voices, to find our own truths, and, of course, being teenagers it came with all the messiness adolescence requires. Each scene depicted our views of the world in light of the most recent genocide; recognized our role as Americans in propagating hate both globally through war, neglect, and industry and nationally through homophobia, sexism, and racism; expressed our fears for a humanity that let things like that happen; and questioned what would be left of the world by the time we grew up?

In one scene, I appeared in the audience wearing the American flag like a cape; I danced vulgarly (like a rap video ho) midway down the stairs as they watched in contempt, then I stopped to look around and watch them in contempt. "Iraq."—I delivered with force but otherwise deadpan—"Hospital. Many patients, few beds. Mother feeds crippled sons FDA-approved animal crackers. Can't chew or swallow. Eyes wide open. Staring at America. What did you do?" I ran to the other side of the audience—the flag streaming behind me—stopped, stared, and began again: "Staff Sergeant Eric Alva. US Soldier. A few years older than me. Missing his right leg from the knee down. Fracture in the other. Stepped on a landmine. Television cameras. His mother weeps. What did I do?" I danced delicately this time (like a ballerina) to the stage and finished a pirouette to face the audience. I removed the American flag and replaced it around my head like a burka. "God Bless America," I belted—"only," I charged. "My home sweet home!" As I sang, Addison (a gangly white teenage boy) entered—goose-stepping behind me, wearing a gas mask and cape, swinging a light saber. I went on without noticing him: "Our leaders drop bombs on people just trying to survive and what did we do?" I paused then answered myself, "Nothing"—Addison stuck me down with his light-saber. For a moment, he silently studied my motionless body then he turned to address the audience: "I am your negation. I am he who misleads. I am he that sends children and women to fight the wars. For your iniquities. Your flat-screen TV. Your Coca-Cola. Your SUV. I fight for your rights. Your right to remain silent. To remain blind. Remain deaf and apathetic. You believe in me." He approached an audience member, formed a gun with his hand, and pulled the trigger (almost) silently. "Umuganda," he continued, "Kinyarwandan for 'we work together.' We Americans know all about that." He laughed as the stage faded to darkness. A few scenes later, our play ended with all twenty of us on stage performing an African harvest dance, shouting "Umuganda!" until the lights went out.

Grandmommy was the first to jump up in applause, but Dad and Tammy were nowhere to be seen. Apparently, they'd stormed out during my Captain America monologue. Nyrobi was enough to make up for the both of them, though—she rushed in to hug me and said, "You were spectacular!" When Youth Creates was over, she recommended me for one of two seasonal internships 7 Stages offered in the fall—Heidi agreed (if, of course, I was still in Atlanta).

I spent the rest of the summer trying to convince Dad and Tammy that I'd changed or at least that I'd be easier to put up with than James. Mostly, though, I just tried to stay out of the house and not ask them for anything. I got a part-time job at a pizzeria a half mile up the street in Decatur Square, the downtown business district. I'd work mornings doing food preparation and cleaning the store then man the cash register and make sandwiches until midafternoon. After my shift, I'd head to the green public space center of "the square" and oc-cupy one of the metal picnic tables where I'd read, write, and smoke cigarettes until well after dark.

That's where I met Joel (pronounced Jo-El), the self-proclaimed "magical negro." He was dark and tall, a little chubby with the hint of an Afro, and sixteen, like me, but he had already graduated high school. His family was from Antigua, where, he said, "the schools were better," but really he was the smartest person I'd ever met—and one of the most charismatic and talented, to boot. Joel knew everyone and I never met anyone who didn't like him; he told the best stories, could play any instrument he picked up, and routinely broke into Broadway-worthy song-and-dance routines. Joel was both my first real black and (not-so-openly) gay friend. It was (platonic) love at first sight—though I did propose to him once, but he turned me down and got booed by onlookers—and, from then on, we were inseparable. Joel also worked in the square, directing a creative writing camp at Little Shop of Stories, an independent bookstore, and assistant man-aging a Cold Stone Creamery franchise. He got me a job as a coun-selor at the former and a server at the latter so we could spend all our afternoons and evenings together. When our shift ended around mid-night, we'd bring ice cream home to my parents, then I'd walk him to the bus stop behind my house—buses came and went, but we'd wave them by, too busy talking, singing, and smoking to say good-bye. On Fridays, we'd usually go to Joel's, and I wouldn't come home until after work Monday; my parents were thrilled to let me spend all my time with a gay guy, especially one "so polite and well-behaved like Joel." "I'll take good care of her, sir," he'd say, shaking Dad's hand before he'd kiss Tammy's cheek, and we'd head out (to buy beer with his fake ID and go to weekend-long house parties). Toward the end of summer, Joel introduced me to Max, who quickly became my first Jewish friend—and my first real boyfriend. Together, we were the Three Musketeers, and Atlanta was our playground—for the first time in years, I felt like a normal kid, and a happy one, at that.

As the school year approached, it was enough of a difference to convince Dad and Tammy to give me another chance—at the very least, they figured, I couldn't be worse than James. And they were right, to some degree: I was different from James, but not necessarily better. I wasn't into drugs, but I was into doing things my way. And I wasn't sneaky, like James; I was upfront about it. I wouldn't do chores because I didn't need their money: I had three jobs. I wouldn't follow their rules because I didn't need parents: I had myself. I wouldn't come home, sometimes, because I didn't need a family: I had Max and Joel. They couldn't take anything away from me, because I didn't need anything from them. They couldn't give me back to Mom, or they'd get James again. They could have grounded me—like they used to—but from what: Work? School? Mock trial? Debate? Theater? That's all I did anyway, and I didn't really get in any trouble—so why did they need a say in it? "Because I said so" was—as it had always been—their response. And I did—as I had always done—the very opposite on principle. It made for—as it always had—a very tense dynamic and a very hostile home.

One night, just after my seventeenth birthday, I got especially mouthy with Dad and he lost it. He pinned me to the wall by my neck—my feet dangling in midair—pressed his nose against mine, and told me "how things are going to be." With each word, droplets of spit flew at my face, and after the last one I snapped too. I kneed him in the groin and ran out the front door—no, *that's how* things are going to be (if I don't leave). It wasn't the first time he or the many men I'd called "father" had gotten physical, but it *had* to be the last time. I couldn't take it anymore—I thought I really might kill the next man that laid a hand on me. This time, there would be no demands, no discussion—no ifs, ands, or buts about it—I left that night and never came back.

I couch-surfed for a few weeks before I faced the possibility of real homelessness. I briefly considered going back to Mom's but quickly decided that I'd sooner sleep on a bench than go back to Texas. The night before I was to check into a shelter, I reached out to the only person I knew who might be able to help. In addition to her theater work, Nyrobi also ran a nonprofit organization that empowered adolescent girls in juvenile detentions, shelters, and halfway houses. So when I ran out of couches to sleep on, I called her to figure out what to do next. "Where are you?" she asked. I told her I'd just finished the night shift at Cold Stone Creamery. "Stay there. I'll come get you."

She arrived a few minutes later but didn't—as I had expected—give me advice. Instead, she drove me to her place and handed me a set of keys. "This is your home now," she said, then yelled, "Isaiah!" A handsome teenage boy—dark and charismatic like Nyrobi—came strutting in. She took him under her arm. "Isaiah, meet Cecily," she said, "your new sister." He paused only briefly then rushed over and hugged me. "My sistuh-from-anutha-mistuh!" he shouted, lifting me off the ground. Nyrobi took up the other side making me into a Cecily sandwich. "Welcome to the family!"

With those keys, I not only opened a door on a new life—I crossed a threshold into an entirely new world. When I walked outside the next morning, I first noticed the metal bars affixed to the windows and doors; at the time, I remember thinking, *What interesting decor!*

but soon learned of their strictly practical value. We lived next door to a crack dealer on the one side and a man, on the other, who drank often and often beat his girlfriend. I once heard a gun go off in his house but hid when the police came so he wouldn't know it was me who had called. On the way to school that first morning, I saw the neighborhood for the first time in broad daylight. Fast-food wrappers and liquor bottles lined the streets, children and broken appliances filled the yards, and elderly folks dotted the porches and kept watch from makeshift chairs; the only unified design I could see was the multicolored graffiti decorating the traffic signs, fences, and businesses. It didn't look too different from the apartments and trailer parks I'd lived in with Mom, except I didn't see anyone white. "Nyrobi," I asked, "what neighborhood is this?" "Glenwood," she replied. During my lunch break, I went to the library to Google it: the map showed it sandwiched between Grant Park and Ormewood Park, two eastside neighborhoods just below the north/south divide, or the barrier between white and black Atlanta—uh oh, I realized, I'm on the wrong side.

On the drive "home," I looked out the window with new eyes and asked Nyrobi whether Glenwood was a dangerous neighborhood. "It can be," she said, "but it looks tougher than it is. You'll be fine as long as you don't fuck with people and don't look out of place." I looked down at my peep-toe pumps and polka-dotted dress then looked at myself in the side-view mirror: I was an exceptionally pale teenage girl, with carefully curled hair and a full face of makeup. I would definitely not be "fucking" with anyone, but how could I not look out of place? I looked out at the preteen boys standing in the highway, weaving in and out of traffic, knocking on people's windows, and trying to sell donuts, and it was far away from the lemonade stands I had in the front yard as a little girl. "But Ny," I blurted, then pointed at the boys, "*they're* not gonna believe I belong here—I'm not even sure I do." She pulled over and said, "Get out." "What?" I said, stunned. "Get out," she repeated. "Find your way home, it's not far." "And Cecily," she added, "it's not about color, it's about attitude"—then she drove off. I stood there alone on the side of the road for about fifteen minutes thinking, "This is a seriously sick joke," before I realized she wasn't coming back—and started walking. What should have taken twenty minutes took me two hours.

When I walked in the door, Nyrobi was waiting, "Learn anything?" "Yeah. Which way *not* to go." "What else?" she asked. I paused to consider the right way to say it. "People here look tough . . . but I think it's mostly a front. Like, I was standing on a corner when this tatted-up kid walked by and said, 'You look lost.' I told him that I'd just moved here, how I'd be homeless without you. Honestly—I was such an easy target—I thought for sure he'd rob me. But, instead, he walked me to the bus, waited there until it came, and even told the driver where to drop me off. Oh, and . . . ," I added with a smile, "he gave me a nickname: white-bread!" Nyrobi was right: I didn't need to be black to belong in Glenwood. I just needed to show respect for its residents and respectfully show them that it was my home too.

"Home" was an easy word to say but a hard concept to settle into. When I first moved in, I negotiated a businesslike living arrangement. Nyrobi was great and all, but I wasn't in the market for a mother and knew better than to get attached. I offered her a little rent for the room, and, in turn, she let me come and go as I pleased—with one caveat: "Let me know where you are and when you're coming back." Boy, did she play me like a fiddle. She left me nothing to rebel against, so I didn't rebel. Within a month, I was housebroken: I'd quit all my jobs besides the internship at 7 Stages, got home nearly every night before dinner, and did all sorts of normal family stuff with Isaiah and Nyrobi: watching TV, grocery shopping, and the whole nine. At the expense of my own grandmother's feelings, I even went home with

Nyrobi to her mother's for Christmas. Maybe it was too much, too soon, but I was finally comfortable—which made me antsy. I think it was that feeling, again, of the calm before the storm; but this time instead of waiting for it to come, I created one myself.

Dad and Tammy had moved out of our old house in Decatur in mid-December, but I assumed the lease was still good through the end of the month. It was an empty house, and I still had the keys— why wouldn't I throw a party? On our drive back from Christmas, I texted everyone I knew: *"Bring yourself, your friends, and $5—we're bringing in 2006 with a kegger!"* Early that day, I bought two kegs and a case of champagne for the party, and a bottle of Goldschläger and a six pack of Smirnoff Ice for myself. Later that night, more than two hundred kids showed up—but we never made it to the countdown. Around 10:30 p.m., I'd almost won my second round of beer pong when a woman showed up screaming, "Get the fuck out of my house!" and whacking kids over the head with a cellphone. She must've just called the police, because about a dozen of them showed up right behind her. Everyone ran for it! Out the front door and backdoor, through windows and off the second-floor balcony—someone, I heard, even hid in the basement. The cops blocked off the street the house was on, the one behind it, and even the main street that connected the two; it was blue and red everywhere with the flickering yellow of cops chasing down kids with flashlights. Despite the overzealous effort, only forty-two were arrested, but I was among them. Most just got drinking tickets and were sent home with angry parents, but because I was seventeen (an "adult" in Georgia), I was charged with criminal trespassing and sent to jail.

I spent the better half of my twenty-hour imprisonment totally terrified, trying to inform the guards of "my rights." In the first cell, I met a girl who'd been stabbed; in another cell, I met the girl who'd stabbed her—one after another, I heard both sides and told each girl,

"You're right." In the background wailed a woman for sixteen straight hours, "I didn't kill him, I swear I didn't do it!" Unfortunately, for her, she was covered from head to toe in presumably "his" blood. Well shaken, by the time of my final hour of incarceration, I turned jointly to God and New Year's resolutions (I thought it couldn't hurt to cover both). *If I get out of here,* I promised, *I won't ever come back. And if Nyrobi still wants me, I promise to be good.* After one night in jail, I didn't want to be a bad kid anymore. When I was released, Nyrobi was there waiting. I had never been happier to see her, but she was *really* angry with me. When she finished yelling, she grounded me for two weeks. I beamed. She demanded, "What the hell are you smiling about?" "I was sure you'd kick me out," I said. "How many times do I have to say it," she started yelling again, "for you to believe it: I am your mother. You're stuck with me—So. Stop. Pissing. Me. Off!" After that, I believed it. To Nyrobi, I wasn't a problem child—I was just a child, *her child.* To convince me, once and for all, she made it official and adopted me. Well, technically, she had Mom transfer over parental guardianship until I turned eighteen. Which, incidentally, was about the time the fairytale ended.

It was good while it lasted, though—the best even. Once I accepted her home and her family as my own, I fit into the role of "child" with relative ease. I loved living with Nyrobi, being "hers." She was safe, no need to fight, no matter how I tried. Once I allowed myself to trust her, I started trusting myself too; I tried to ground myself and face my problems instead of running from them—she taught me how to resolve and, even, prevent conflict instead of escalating it. She was like my fairy godmother; my whole world was more balanced, made more sense with her in it. I stopped getting into trouble at school, stopped skipping classes, and even started to enjoy learning—well, US history, at least. I'd always loved history but hated history teachers. But then, junior year, I had Advanced Placement US History with Mr. Patton.

He was tall and bald with a whimsical step, a sharp mind, and, sometimes, a sharp tongue. He didn't teach, he told stories; he didn't sit at his desk (brimming with papers and pacifist paraphernalia), he zigzagged around us, pulling us in with his variety-show style: every lesson, he would play a popular song or speech from the era or otherwise hand out a contemporary news clipping then ask us to respond and prod us into debate. Mr. Patton never told us how to think, but he did inform us of where we'd come from as Americans and challenged us to seriously consider what our country had become since and what changes should happen next. To bridge our identity to the colonial era, he took us outside to play town ball—"the precursor to baseball," he explained, "founded by colonists in the eighteenth century." For the abolitionist movement, he reorganized all the desks into a round, leaving only a small patch of linoleum in the middle—"everyone lay down, pack in shoulder-to-shoulder" he instructed and turned off the lights before reciting Olaudah Equiano's recollection of riding on a slave ship from Nigeria to the British colony of Virginia in 1754. For World War I, he read the firsthand account of Red, a US soldier stationed in the trenches of France who had suffered a shot clean through the head—"It felt like I got hit by a bat!"—then showed us pictures of the man fifty years later who, Mr. Patton revealed, was his grandfather. For World War II, he assigned students to the President Truman hot seat to debate whether or not to bomb Japan. And for the civil rights movement, we all learned the words to "We Shall Overcome" and sang it together as a class. Mr. Patton was a hippie, but he was a real hard-ass, too—he took history very seriously and the role we, *his* students, would play as citizens in crafting the future of America.

It was an infectious idea, something teachers often said but none had ever really made us believe before: that our voices, our actions mattered—that even as teenagers we had a duty as democratic citizens to take responsibility for how our country treats people at home and abroad. Mr. Patton taught us about the Children's Crusade of Birmingham, Alabama, in 1963; how teenagers, like us, organized school walkouts and marches of thousands of kids (including kindergartners) that only kept growing when faced with fire hoses, attack dogs, and paddy wagons; how the jails were so overcrowded, they starting sending kids to the local fairground; how they slept outside on cots and, even then, kept singing freedom songs as they waited for bail. He showed us pictures of them plastered on the front pages of every major American publication and said, "The bravery of those students—more than anything else at the time—shifted the tide of public opinion in support of the civil rights movement." After that lesson, some of us started thinking seriously about our duty as citizens, too.

The movement against President George W. Bush and his War on Terror was already brewing. We had a sense of the lies and dirty dealing that had landing us in Iraq to begin with, and *especially* of our military's blatant disregard for human rights and lives on both sides of it—but until we learned about the Birmingham Children's Crusade, we didn't think we could do anything about it. Within a week, a handful of us had formed a new student group and approached Mr. Patton with the paperwork to become the teacher advisor. "Student Political Action Club," he read aloud then looked us over carefully (almost painfully) and sighed deeply, "I'm gonna get in trouble for this"—he reluctantly signed—"I just know it."

We hung up signs all over school: **DON'T LIKE BUSH?** (the presidential kind) **JOIN SPAC & DO SOMETHING ABOUT IT!** We met once a week, and Mr. Patton taught us about civil disobedience and nonviolent direct action: like the industrial strikes of the US labor movement in the early twentieth century, the burning of President Wilson in effigy by suffragettes in 1919, the conscientious objectors who went to jail instead of fighting during the World War I pacifist movement, the Montgomery bus boycott of the civil rights movement in the 1950s, the student sit-ins at the University of California, Berkeley, in the 1964–1965 free speech movement, the draft-card burnings of the anti–Vietnam War movement in the 1960s, the die-ins of the ACT UP movement advocating for people living with AIDS in the late '80s / early '90s, and so on. It was inspiring stuff, and soon enough we were trying out some of the tactics ourselves. Our first action was a die-in. More than a dozen of us dressed up in all black, got to school early, and blocked all the entrances with our limp bodies; as the students stepped over us, they couldn't help but read the signs around our necks depicting the shocking death toll (on both sides) of the war in Iraq. Next, we organized a student walkout to the first anti-Bush protest in Atlanta. The administration threatened to suspend anyone who participated, but half the student body walked out anyway. Instead they punished only those of us who'd organized it: we got detention and they called our parents. Most of all, though, Mr. Patton got blamed for the walkout, even though he hadn't helped us at all. We wanted to protest for him (like the Berkeley student sit-ins for free political expression), but he wouldn't let us. "It'll just make things worse," he said.

After that, we backed off from direct action so we wouldn't get him in trouble and all joined his other club, mock trial, instead. Twice a week we met with real lawyers in a real courtroom to learn about the legal system and prepare to compete against other high school teams in Georgia. That year, the statewide assignment was *State v. Robin Banks (2006)*, a criminal case of arson and felony murder. The defendant was an environmental activist charged with setting fire to the anticipated site of a new Glutco dealership, maker of the massive SUV, the Guzzler—and for inadvertently killing a homeless woman trapped inside. After a week of studying the case law and characters, Mr. Patton held tryouts for the six lawyer and five witness positions that would make up our competitive team. I was cast as Robin Banks, the activist defendant (falsely accused, of course, with an alibi and history of strict nonviolence). Mr. Patton said that our team was the best he'd ever had: we blew regionals away, advanced past two dozen others to the final four round at state, and ultimately placed third overall. As for me, I won the Best Witness Award for all of Georgia. Mr. Patton was proud of me but suggested that I try out for lead lawyer the following year instead. "You'd be good at it," he said. "Have you thought about law school?" It was the end of my junior year and I felt pretty silly saying it, but I told him the truth anyway: "I haven't even thought about where I'd like to go to college, yet." "Well, when you figure it out," he said, "let me know and I'll write you a recommendation letter—wherever you go, they'll be lucky to have you."

When I talked to Nyrobi about college (and possibly law school) she urged me to seriously consider going to a liberal arts school. She said I was intelligent and capable, but because I'd been to three middle schools and four high schools in five years I hadn't gotten a strong educational foundation—that the only lesson I'd learned is how to work the system. "You know how to bullshit assignments, take tests, and otherwise cheat or talk your way out of requirements." She said I was "resourceful as hell" and "a damn good hustler" but insisted that that alone wouldn't get me into law school or, generally, very far in academia. She told me I needed to go somewhere with small class sizes and professors who enjoy teaching, professors who would appreciate my raw talent enough to help me learn the skills I should have learned already: how to take notes, read critically, formulate arguments, and write academically. All of that sounded pretty dull to me, but I liked liberals and I liked the arts—how bad could it possibly be? Agnes Scott, a women's liberal arts college, was right across the street from my high school, so I took a tour of it one day and audited some classes. Nyrobi's point was clear immediately: the environment was right for me, but the location was all wrong.

As much as I loved living in Atlanta, I couldn't imagine going to college there: I couldn't see myself putting classes before my existing friends and activities or being able to focus without putting some distance between my family and me. Nyrobi agreed, and we both decided that Texas wouldn't work for me either. But because I had never really been anywhere but Texas or Georgia and because I didn't really know anything about college, junior year came to a close with me feeling further away than ever from figuring it out. And had it not been for Zach's date ditching him the week before prom, I might have given up on college altogether or, more likely, would have gone somewhere I hated and dropped out a year later.

Zach was my first, undeniable true love. We'd known of each other peripherally but really met the first time when I was his fill-in date for his senior prom. I felt like I could watch him, listen to him, be with him forever—and, at the time, I thought I might be. Even then, though, I knew it was a long shot. We spent all summer driving around, talking about the people we wanted to be, singing along to Death Cab for Cutie, knowing all along that he was leaving in months, weeks, days to Lawrence University—a small liberal arts college with a conservatory in Appleton, Wisconsin. I didn't really know where that was or whether we'd make it (whatever that meant), but I was surer of Zach than I was of anything else. He was the smartest, most captivating (and inspiring!) person I'd ever met, and when he said the same to me, I almost believed it myself. Whatever college he was going to was bound to be the best, and wherever he was, I wanted to be near him, regardless of the context. I resolved to apply early decision to Lawrence University and go—no matter what happened—if I got in and figure it out later if I didn't.

I'd finally given myself over, let myself believe in whatever magic had charmed my life since I moved in with Nyrobi—and, right then, it ran out. Just before senior year started, I was summoned to the registrar's office. What I'd expected to be a routine graduation consultation turned out to be my getting the boot. Decatur Public Schools had somehow found out that I was living with Nyrobi, so they transferred me out of their district and into hers to do my final year at Henry W. Grady High School. It wasn't a bad school: its mock trial team had rivaled our own, and its debate team was a force to be reckoned with (both at state *and* nationals); it offered more arts programs than Decatur and was the media magnet school of Atlanta. But I didn't care about any of that, though—I didn't want to go to *another* high school!

During that first week, Ny left early for work and Isaiah for basketball practice, leaving me to ride the school bus alone. As I waited at the corner, the Glenwood kids began to gather. Headphones in, head fixed forward, I examined them out of the corner of my eye and I reminded myself what Nyrobi told me when I first moved in: "It's not about color, it's about attitude." When I boarded the bus, though, and my eyes met the piercing stares of dozens of black teenagers, *I froze.* The voice of the bus driver snapped me out of it. "You sleep, girl? Sit down, can't go nowhere with you stuck like that." Laughter erupted, and I slipped into the first empty seat: rather than riding the bus, I felt like I'd been thrown underneath it. I slouched down and stared intently out the window, wondering how the fuck am I going to get through *another year* of this shit.

When the bus met the curb, I was up; when the door opened, I was out. The closer I got to AP Biology, though, the further Glenwood slipped away. Next I had AP Comparative Politics, then AP Environmental Science, and by the time I got to Advanced Theater, the memory of that morning had all but been erased. I'd ridden an all-black bus to school, but I attended nearly all-white classes.

Two worlds collided at Grady: the one I lived in with Nyrobi and the one made up of kids from Inman Park, Virginia-Highland, Lake Claire, and Morningside/Lenox Park. These upper-middle- to upper-class neighborhoods were decorated with luxury cars, well-groomed parks, outdoor tennis courts, and private swimming clubs. That was the world of my classmates—the one I found at once more enticing and, at the same time, less interesting.

I only ever saw the Glenwood kids in my last class, Speech and Debate with Mr. Herrera, which, for me, was technically an intern credit—a subject I'd long since mastered, I was to be his "assistant." That class, in stark contrast to the rest, was almost entirely black; I blushed as I recognized a couple of them from the bus. (Explaining the overt racial divide, Mr. Herrera later informed me, "This course is a requirement for the minimum graduation track, preparing students for entry-level positions or vocational training.") When the bell rang, I walked wearily to the buses. My classmates gathered in one area, the Glenwood kids in another. The divide was clear, but I was unsure which "side" I was on or whether either "side" would accept me.

I had the strange feeling that I'd gone all the way to Atlanta just to find myself returned to the backwardness of Texas. On top of that, I was "the new girl" (again) so I didn't have any friends to complain to. Worst of all, though, the one person who was supposed to be there for me—Zach, my boyfriend—had gone off to college, and things between us had gotten weird and distant. When we began fighting, I started crying and couldn't stop. Once again, everything in my life seemed to be falling apart—I felt outcast and alone, unsure of myself and my place in the world. I turned to Nyrobi to fix it, to fix *me*—to pick up all the pieces and repair whatever was broken. She listened, she gave advice and hugs but none of it made me feel any less fucked up. Where was her magic wand? Why wasn't she waving it? What good was a fairy godmother if she couldn't make everything better?

I resented her for it. "My life is a nightmare!" I started screaming—"I'm here all alone!"—and stomping—"With no one but you!"—and slamming doors. It went on like that for a couple of months until one day Nyrobi said, "I can't do this anymore." "It's cool," I replied; what else did I expect? She'd been so good to me and I'd treated her like shit. I stuffed a change of clothes into a backpack and waved good-bye. "Ces," she called out, tears in her eyes, "you don't have to leave tonight—" "It's cool," I repeated. "I'll get the rest of my stuff later," I said and walked out the door.

On the way to the bus stop, I grabbed my mail and sifted mindlessly through it, trying to avoid the question, where do I go now? A few letters in, a royal blue insignia caught my eye—"It's big!" I shouted and dropped the rest in a hurry to open it. "Congratulations Cecily! We are pleased to announce your acceptance into the Lawrence University Class of 2011. . . ." I read the whole thing out loud then very literally jumped for joy. I pulled out my phone, flipped through my contacts, then put it away. There was no one left to call. *Finally* the bus arrived, and the driver was the first person I told; when she opened the doors, I screamed, "I GOT INTO COLLEGE!" "Congratulations," she said. "Get on now, or get outta the way—folks ain't got all day!" I tripped quickly up the stairs to obey her but wasn't in a hurry myself. I had no idea where I'd stay that night. I took a seat and watched my former neighborhood tear by as we sped away from it. I might be homeless, I thought, but not for long. I smiled back at my reflection in the window—you're going to college!

FOR A FEW MONTHS, I stayed with family friends. But I fought with them too, and when they asked me to leave, my grandparents took me in. They left me alone, and I mostly kept to myself for the rest of the year. It was sort of like a repeat of the year I'd spent in middle school detention—but now, it wasn't just the school and the teachers I was fighting but my friends and family, too. Soon enough, I found myself in social detention, having fought my way into a corner. Once there,

I was content to stay. The same feeling, as before, returned: They don't want to put up with me—good! I don't want to put up with them either.

I went to school, sometimes, when I wasn't working and when I felt like it. It was my fifth high school and the second semester of my senior year; I'd done everything needed to graduate and had already gotten into college, so I showed up only to take tests and turn in assignments so I wouldn't lose my scholarships. After my thirty-ninth absence though, I was called down to the principal's office. He told me that if I missed another day, I wouldn't be allowed to graduate—"Georgia State Law, nonnegotiable." First, I reminded him that the Atlanta Public School System was under fire for alarmingly low academic standards, then I informed him that I had all As including two AP courses—"a fact the newspapers might find interesting given all my absences. Check my record, nonnegotiable." He left for a minute, presumably to check my facts, then returned with a pass: "Show this to your teachers and give it to security on your way out. It's good for the year."

Most teachers seemed all too happy to have one fewer student in their already overcrowded classrooms. But then there was Mr. Herrara—a thirtysomething, khaki and plaid–clad Mexican American (olive, though, not white like me) with a chipper demeanor—who was my speech and debate teacher. He requested that I meet him after school to "discuss the matter." After the final bell, I stood at his door and demanded, "What?" He paused then carefully asked, "Is everything OK at home?" "Home?" I laughed. Then, unrestrained by punctuation or pause, I introduced him to my world: "Visiting hours with Mom—electroshock therapy—doesn't recognize me . . . weekends with Dad . . . all the 'dads'—the smell of beer—bruises on my back, my neck, my wrists . . . James—on drugs—in jail or rehab . . . trailers, apartments—my stuff in boxes—'staying with friends' again . . .

another school, another teacher, just another new girl . . . free lunch and detention . . . vodka shots and cigarettes . . . my body in the mirror, my face in the toilet . . . running away, calling for help—the social workers saying, 'If you're not dead, dying or bleeding, I can't help you'—been on the run ever since."

"Well, I can see why you're angry," he paused. "But what makes you happy?" What a crazy question, I thought, and shot him a look. He didn't budge, though. He just looked right back at me and waited for an answer. "Can't think of anything off the top of my head," I said. "That's okay," he said. "That'll be your assignment. Draw up a list and bring it by Friday?" "Make it Monday," I said. "I'll be out this week." After school that day, I handed him what I'd written and asked for my next assignment. He pretended not to hear me and, instead, read the list right there, *out loud* before me: "Ben & Jerry's Half Baked ice cream. Listening to Modest Mouse every morning. Finding money in my back pocket. Candles. People watching. Henry David Thoreau. A picture of a time I'd forgotten. Color coordinating. Drawing. When I'm driving in traffic and someone lets me in. Surprises! Laughing so hard I can't breathe! Back massages. Finding the perfect pillow, the perfect jeans, the perfect lipstick. Apple juice. A smile from a stranger. Making funny faces in the mirror. Thinking about the meaning of my dreams. Whiteout. Dancing alone in my underwear or with a friend at a concert—just dancing, really, anytime, anyplace. The sound of rain (but not being in it). Being on stage in the spotlight, the audience hanging onto every word I say. *The Plague,* by Albert Camus. The silence of 4 a.m. Those days when I wake up and feel like I can change the world."

As if I weren't already mortified, he asked me, "What did you mean by that last line: 'change the world'?" I would've said anything to get out of there, but he caught me off guard so I told him the truth. I told him all about the Student Political Action Club at my old high school and especially the student walkout: "I was the first to get up and leave.

I was so scared (and so excited!) when I left the classroom. I was going to join a real protest—my first protest! We all got on the train together, talking and laughing like, 'we *actually* did it!' Then we rode downtown, got off, and started marching. I looked around at all the people, the thousands of people chanting. And when I added my voice to theirs, I couldn't really hear mine anymore—well, not above the rest anyway. It was like we were all one, all equal—there was, at once, no difference between any of us and we were all more powerful together. For the first time, I finally felt like I was part of something that mattered—I finally felt like *I* mattered. Like I could really make a difference, you know?"

"Yeah," he said, sort of looking at me funny, "I *do* know—that's why I became a teacher." It was the first of many conversations I had with Mr. Herrera, after school, mostly, or during weekend debate tournaments (I still refused to go to class). He tried to show me how to "redirect the difficulties of my past into dreams of the future." "Don't let your anger consume you," he'd say. "Let it inspire you. Let 'change the world' be your mantra to cope with a world that needs changing." I didn't understand what he meant exactly, but I got that he was saying that there was power in my struggle. By rising above it, I could somehow reclaim it—change it into something of my own, something that would make it all worth it. It was a difficult lesson, but I made some headway by the end of the school year—at the very least, I opened up to him and began sorting through my feelings. In our final meeting, he challenged me to look beyond my personal experience and reassess it from "a universal standpoint—to ask, 'What's the bigger picture?'" I felt like a young Jedi apprentice to his Yoda; I didn't understand what he meant by that yet, but I knew that I would when I was ready to.

When graduation day finally rolled around, my family came to the ceremony. Of course, Grandmommy Kay and Granddaddy Harlon were there (I'd expected as much—I was living with them). But Momma Jean and Pop drove in from Beaumont, and Mom and James flew in from Houston. Even Dad and Tammy came, and Nyrobi too. Uncle Erik and Uncle Kevin, his wife, Aunt Zahna, and their kids, Savannah and Payton, also came to support me. I'm fairly certain it was the largest group there that year. When my name was called, they all rose at once and cheered. And then they kept going as I walked all the way across the stage. I got my diploma, turned to them, held it up, and waved. They all waved back and cheered louder than ever. Afterward, Grandmommy threw a party for me at her house, and everybody showed up for that too. Despite everything we'd been through, they all kept telling me how proud they were.

After I hugged and kissed everyone else good-bye, it was just Mom and me on the front porch swing and two glasses of champagne. "So," she asked, "what do you wanna be when you grow up?" "Mom!" I laughed, "I am grown up!" Then I burped and we giggled. "I *see* that," she said and asked again. "I meant, what do you think you'll be after college?" I thought back to Mr. Patton's lectures on our duty as democratic citizens and to Mr. Herrera's question about the bigger picture and said, "Maybe I'll go to law school . . . or run for office." That sounded crazy when I said it aloud, and I looked to see if she was thinking the same. There wasn't a shred of doubt in her eyes, though, only pride. Tears begin to surface, but before they fell, she clinked her glass into mine. "Cecily," she said, "you can do anything you put your mind to."

Long after she'd gone to sleep, I stayed there swinging and thinking about my life. It hadn't been easy so far, but it certainly had been interesting. I hadn't always gotten everything I'd wanted, or needed, but I *had* learned what those things were and how to separate the two. My family had been broken, but I learned what a family should be (or, maybe, what it shouldn't be). My heart had been broken, but I learned how to survive the absence of love and knew I would love better for it. My spirit had been broken, but I learned how to get back up and keep fighting. And all that fighting had made me the person I was: passionate and strong, ambitious and determined, a lover and a dreamer. I'd always keep fighting for myself, but I didn't want to fight with my family anymore—and by the looks of it, they didn't want to fight anymore either. So, that night, I made myself a promise: I would turn the page on my childhood and start writing my own story. I would let go of my anger and learn how to be happy. I would become a better person and learn to love myself. And, someday, I *would* change the world—or, at least, leave it better than I found it. I was eighteen then and believed college would fix everything (but I'm twenty-six now and still working it out). Nonetheless, that evening was the fairytale ending I'd needed to start moving past the nightmare of my childhood.

CHAPTER 3

Student

"**N**ow Ceci, don't you go off and marry no damn Yankee, you hear?" Momma Jean half-joked, choking back tears. "We'll never see you again." Already crying, I half lied, "Me? Never! I'll be home before you know it." (I had no intention of either getting married or ever moving back.) "You better," Pop grunted and grabbed me into a bear hug. "Now get good grades and *behave!*" When he put me back down, I kissed my grandmother good-bye, then waved them off and watched them disappear—along with the worries of my childhood.

AFTER GRADUATION, I SPLIT THE summer between Texas and Atlanta visiting family, trying to set things right between us before I went off to college. We still had our differences, but they didn't seem as big as before, and it felt good to "get along," to move past bad history and make new, happy memories. I was more stable than I'd ever been; day-to-day living was easier, enjoyable even. At the same time,

James was spiraling out of control. By that summer he'd already been expelled from school for fighting, kicked out of Mom's for drugs, and had since been doing both (in addition to dealing and a little stealing) while couch-surfing or sometimes camping. Then that July, just days before his eighteenth birthday, James flat-lined (literally). He'd washed ten muscle relaxers down with a bottle of vodka. His girl-friend found him unconscious and called 911. The paramedics man-aged to revive him but said he would have died if she'd called even a couple minutes later. I was on the phone with her when it happened—she called me because she knew that I knew how to handle these sit-uations. When he came to, he called it "an accident," and I gave him my best impression of a tough-love, big-sister speech: "High school sucks. You'll go to college next year—everything will be better. Now stop fucking around or you won't make it that far." He didn't buy it, though—and, to be honest, I didn't either. By that point, I'd dealt with it enough that I was pretty unsympathetic to suicide, accidental or otherwise. If James didn't want to live, that was his prerogative. "Next time, take twenty" is what I really wanted to say. "And book a motel for good measure."

After that, I didn't want to be the person my friends and family members called in a crisis anymore, nor did I want to associate with—or allow myself to be infected by—people living in a day-to-day crisis mode. Crisis seemed to me like some sort of virus that spread through communication (concern and care), and I didn't want to be a walking crisis anymore. So I put 1,244 miles between me and James and the rest of it and set out to be the new, normal Cecily: college freshman, class of 2011 at Lawrence University in Appleton, Wisconsin. Law-rence University, in turn, was anything but normal (and proud of it!)—a trait that had defined it from its very conception, and one that I would appreciate only long after I left. If you haven't heard of it, don't worry: I hadn't really either until I got there. Before that, I was really sure of only two things: it was practically on the other side of the world and there would be snow. I'd never seen snow before.

It never occurred to me to ask my parents to take me to college—that was a Momma Jean and Pop thing to do. The fourteen-hour drive took us two days—of my asking, "Are we there yet?"—and, when we finally reached Appleton Monday evening, both said, "Yes!" before I had the chance to ask again. The following afternoon my grandparents drove me to campus to check out my dormitory. We parked near the address then walked past a couple of smaller houses and up to a wide, off-white stone structure four stories tall and covered with windows. Running ahead, I stopped and read aloud the brass lettering lining an archway supported by two bright-white columns: "Russell Sage Hall—this is it!" Once inside, I addressed the frazzled-looking, fuzzy-haired blonde girl seated behind stacks of files on a plastic fold-out table. "Hi, I'm Cecily McMillan," I announced, holding out my hand. "Class of 2011." She introduced herself as the residence life director of Sage Hall. Which sounded, to me, like a glorified nanny—I didn't need one of those; I was all grown up already. "*Sweet*," I said, in a slightly sour tone. "Can we see my room now?" "*Manners, Ceci!*" Momma Jean reprimanded, then apologized to Miss Fuzzy Bubbles. "She wasn't raised in a barn, I promise—she's just excited, thassall." I rolled my eyes and tried again: "*May we puh-lease* see my room?" "Uh, w-well," she stammered, looking at us like she'd never met southerners before, "welcome week starts tomorrow—but *shhhuuurre* I'll check you in." She searched her files for mine, pulled one, and read, "Room 322," aloud, then handed me a set of keys and an orientation schedule and said, "Welcome to college!"

The ancient elevator took what felt like forever to come and another lifetime to get to the third floor. When it dinged open, we turned left into the rat maze of a hallway then followed the glare of long fluorescents down the length of one wall and made another left (twice over) before we finally found room *322*. I jiggled the industrial key into the industrial doorknob and, at long last, pushed open the solid-wood door into my new home. For a moment, I stood in the doorway and took it all in. The two walls forming the southwest corner of Sage were lined with three sets of windows overlooking the slow-moving Fox River and surrounding treescape while the room itself came furnished with two hardwood twin beds, two armoires, two desks, and two bookshelves. "*Oh my God!*" I gasped. Frozen there, I felt my grandparents push up against me to peek in, then both said, "What!?" I all but wailed, "Where are all my clothes and shoes gonna go?" then plopped down on the nearest bare mattress in pre–anxiety attack mode. "Well, don't get upset just yet!" Momma Jean said, sitting beside me. "How much do you have?" I turned into her chest, burst into tears, and heaved, "Every. Thing. In. The. Truck." She cradled my head and shushed me, "Calm down, I can't understand a word you said." A couple minutes later, I sat up and wiped the snot on my face off on my sleeve. "Boy, Jean, she sho' is *ugly* when she cries," Pop teased, and Momma Jean smacked his behind. "Be nice, James, 'for' I putcha in timeout!" I half cried (again) and half laughed along with them, then took a deep breath and repeated, "Everything in the truck is clothes and shoes." "What!?" they said in unison again. And then, for the first time in my life, they were speechless.

"What?!" I demanded. "Ceci-poo," Momma Jean said in a sensitive tone (that I took as condescension), "didn't you pack any necessities?" "Of course, I did!" I shot back. "I'm not a child—I've been just fine on my own for years!" I assured them that I'd brought my contacts, retainer, and ADHD medication; my social security card, birth certificate, and tax documents; money in my checking for now, a savings account for tuition next term, and a credit card for emergencies; records of my updated shots and referrals for local doctors, and so on.

"But besides, fitting in at college," I argued, "wearing the right clothes, looking like I belong here—that's a *necessity* too." "Dammit Ceci, no one's denying that!" Pop not only swore but also shouted to make his point clear (and it worked, I was stunned—he rarely did either). "We just wanna make sure you have towels and sheets and stuff like that!" "Oh," I said, turning bright red. "N-no, I guess I d-don't," I stammered, suddenly feeling very stupid. "Looks like we've got shopping to do," Momma Jean chirped and jumped up, trying to lighten the mood, "and we'll get room organizers, too—see if we can't get your whole wardrobe in here." "Thanks, Momma Jean," I muttered and followed them out with my eyes fixed on the ground. When we got to the truck, I whispered, "I'm sorry," then hugged her and said, "I love you." "I love you, too," she said, pulling me closer. Then she stepped back, took me by the arms, looked me dead in the eye, and said, "Don't you *ever* forget it."

My alarm went off at seven the next morning and sent me jumping up and down on the bed. It was finally Wednesday, September 19—a date in my planner twice circled with colored markers and marked with a bold, black zero denoting the last of my one-hundred-day countdown. "Move-in Day!" I shouted out loud each time I bounced until I collapsed, breathless about ten minutes later. When we pulled up to Sage at 7:45 a.m., we were the very first to arrive (and for the very first time, I was glad to have grandparents who were *always* fifteen minutes early). By the time my roommate Jessi and her family showed up to move in, we were on our way out. We shared a quick good-bye lunch on campus then walked out to the truck and Pop pulled out a gift bag—amid all the excitement, I'd nearly forgotten that I was turning nineteen the following day. But, of course, Momma Jean always remembered everyone's birthdays. I pulled out a pair of wool-lined and accented lace-up sheepskin boots—the same ones I'd been looking at online. I don't know how she knew, but I did know it was her way of (reluctantly) giving me her blessing to live in the North (for a period of time not to exceed four years).

That night was the Lawrence University Class of 2011 Dinner. I arrived, late, as usual, to the Memorial Chapel on campus, to find some professor in an outdated suit already mid–welcome speech. I whispered for directions ("McMillan, Cecily") then tiptoed through the other four hundred or so alphabetically seated students to the "M–MC" table in the middle of the room. When I finally found my name card, I sat and smiled apologetically at the seven others in my circle then noticed the rolled-up kelly-green T-shirts in front of them. I looked around for my own but couldn't find one. The bookish-looking girl with unkempt hair and tiny black glasses sitting beside me leaned in and instructed, "You get them at check-in—over there," she pointed. Looking over, I noticed the whole room was decorated in the same color as the T-shirts: banners, streamers, ribbons, and confetti. "What's with the green?" I asked her aloud, forgetting the man speaking. Several students shushed me, and I blushed, lips pursed and eyes bulging. She choked back laughter, picked up a pencil and wrote her response on the back of an envelope: *It's our class color.* "Ooooo-hhh," I mouthed. "Thanks!" But I was still too distracted to listen to speeches.

Attempting to avoid eye contact with disapproving peers, I scanned the table and noticed the two throwback Polaroid cameras in the middle. Surrounding them was a ring of green *class of 2011* pencils further encircled by envelopes. I flipped the one in front of me over to find it labeled with both my name and student identification number (L00884621), so I opened it up and took out the single sheet of green paper inside. Predated *September 25, 2007,* to coincide with the evening, it was a template for *a letter to myself to be opened when I am ready to graduate.* Because I'd already attracted several side-glances for just opening, I figured why the heck not go ahead and fill it out:

I believe I will graduate with a major(s) in Government and Philosophy, a grade point average of 3.8(ish) and a long-term career goal of Plan A: Educational Reform, B: Criminal Defense Attorney.

As Welcome Week and my orientation to campus life are ending, I still feel "new" because I don't particularly feel "new."

If I could change one thing about myself as I begin college it would be better use of commas.

I feel most confident in my ability to formulate and relate in depth opinions.

My biggest apprehension at this moment is comma usage.

I think my college nickname should be unfortunately it is already "Cecilia." [The boys in the dorm next door had taken to getting drunk and shouting the Simon & Garfunkel lyrics at me, "Cecilia, you're breaking my heart!"]

One strength I bring to the Class of 2011 is honest conversation.

When I look back on my college years at Lawrence, I hope to be able to say "That this 150,000 dollar education has prepared me for my future endeavors."

Love,

Cecily McMillan

Me

Just as I scribbled my signature, the room burst into applause. I turned around and clapped along liked I'd been listening the whole time. "Did you actually hear any of that?" my neighbor asked. "Not a word," I said, folding up the letter. "I can't really focus on two things at once." "How're you gonna handle three classes?" she asked. "I'll be fine—" I said, stuffing the sheet back into the envelope (with some ribbon and confetti for good measure), "—as soon as I figure out those damn commas." "You're crazy," she laughed like I'd said something funny. "You're boring," I mumbled as I walked off in search of my roommate. "Cecily, over here!" I recognized Jessi's thick Chicago accent, but at five foot nothing she proved difficult to find in a crowd—then *poof!* Just like that, she popped out from behind some giant, hockey kind of guy holding one of the Polaroid cameras provided. When you could see her, she certainly was something to look at: she had long, layered blonde hair with bangs that framed her big, brown eyes and was otherwise busty with a healthy bottom to boot. She waved me over. "Let's take a picture together!" We pushed our faces together and puckered our lips. "Aaawww!" she said, shaking the image into focus, "our first roomie selfie!" A few seconds later, she showed it to me and squealed, "This is gonna be the *best year ever!*" I couldn't believe how happy I looked, *how happy I was*—my childhood and everything it had and hadn't been seemed so far away. "You mean, the best *four years* ever!" I squealed too then put the picture in my envelope before sealing it. "We're gonna laugh so hard when we see this at graduation!"

One month to the day later, I sat alone in my dorm room and wrote in my journal: *I'm ready to go home.* I'd come to college looking forward to the bastion of liberalism and racial utopia the North was supposed to be. Instead, I found a student body that was largely apolitical and overwhelmingly white—in fact, it was the whitest place I'd ever been apart from Texas. My peers were quick to draw distinctions between where they'd come from (mostly suburbs in the Midwest or, otherwise, Northeast) and the "backwardness of the South." At parties, though, I heard the same racist jokes and homophobic slurs from my childhood, but they'd say it was different and somehow okay: "He's not serious—just drunk and joking around." I got the feeling that "liberal" meant little more than "normal" and that the only reason they weren't racists (in a strict sense) was because they'd grown up largely apart from other races, making it easy to say, "I'm colorblind." "And anyway," I was told, "we're not here to talk politics. It's a party!" So I stopped going to them. I hadn't come to Lawrence to party anyway; I'd already done that in high school. I'd expected intellectuals and disciplined artists, serious students committed to learning in order to create a better society—why else would anyone go to a liberal, arts college? I felt so stupid when I learned, a couple of years later, that there was never any comma intended or implied: "liberal arts" was nothing more than a fancy term for "general education," a distinction from technical or professional schools—a misconception that pretty much sums up how painfully unprepared I was for Lawrence.

When I got my midterm grades, I booked a flight to Atlanta. For Thanksgiving, I said, but considered the possibility of going home for good. I'd gotten a C- in Freshman Studies, a D in Government, and was failing Philosophy, which I promptly withdrew from, at the insistence of my advisor, to salvage the other two. I'd never worked so hard to fail so miserably at anything—worse still, I couldn't think of anything I *could* do differently. I went to class every day and studied or wrote every night until I passed out (sometimes at my desk, face down in my work), but it wasn't enough. There was always too much material to cover, too little time to turn papers in, and sometimes I didn't understand my assignments to begin with. My classmates, instead, made it all look so easy (and seemed to make a show of it).

Adam was the only kid in my freshman studies class who didn't make me feel like a complete idiot. When the other kids, like predatory animals, sensed that I was weak, they began circling—it was open hunting, and I was in season. They pounced, it seemed, at every opportunity to make themselves look smarter at my expense. Of course, it didn't help that I'd get defensive and make myself look dumber. I think Adam felt sorry for me, but, whatever his reasons, he refused to partake in the bloodbath and, instead, invited me over to study; trying not to let on how stupid I was, I didn't let him help me much, but I did like reviewing the readings before class—it helped me anticipate the oncoming attacks. Most of all, though, it was nice to have another friend—before him, it was mostly Jessi and me hanging out in our room, when she wasn't on the phone arguing with her long-distance boyfriend.

Before long, I was hanging out at Adam's on the weekends, watching football or playing poker with him and his friends. Then, just after midterms, I noticed a new guy hovering in the corner of his room. He looked like no one I'd ever seen before, clearly white but sort of exotic: he was five foot nine (maybe) and pretty slender—the opposite of the stocky, towering figure of my father—but sturdy, no less, and somehow (I searched for the right word) debonair; his skin hinted of olive like my mother's, but he definitely wasn't Mexican—his nose was prominent, like mine, but sharp with a curvature instead of Irish-wide and a little crooked like maybe it'd been broken once. "Twice," he'd correct me later. "Ice hockey." He watched me through familiar eyes—ice blue and endless like every McMillan before me—that were angular, Asian almost but not quite, either. I found him difficult to take in entirely; altogether, his features were both bewildering and disarming—was it love at first sight or lust? Maybe I was just drunk and not seeing clearly. "Hey, you!" I demanded. "What's your name?" He turned his chin ever so slightly and fell on me with piercing eyes. "Andy," he all but whispered. I fell into them and—for God knows how long—sank deeper and deeper until I breathlessly (but reluctantly) emerged for air. "Cecily," I replied. I could look at him forever, I thought, then felt flushed and tried to save face. "You gonna hide out all night—or join us?" He flashed a half smile and sat down beside me. I don't know what we talked about or where the night went, but I woke up in his arms, more comfortable than I'd ever thought possible—as if I'd never been more seen, more heard, more known by anyone before that lazy, hazy autumn morning.

On the surface, Andy was everything I wasn't (and had grown up with everything I hadn't): he was an upper-middle-class suburban kid who grew up in the best (and richest) school district in Wisconsin and had later attended boarding school where, long before he arrived at Lawrence, he'd read nearly everything on the Freshman Studies syllabus as well as many of the "great books." For all our differences, though, we were "bound together," he wrote, "by an insatiable curiosity of the human condition, and of understanding our contribution— personally, and historically—to it." When I read his note—scribbled on the back of a hasty ink-drawing of his left hand—I swooned: to me, it was poetry, and the first anyone had written for me.

We'd talk a mile a minute for hours on end, without pause; even when I didn't know a word he used—"intrinsic," "platonic," "dogmatic"—he'd just say it a different way and keep going, so I would "get it" without feeling stupid for asking. I soon found myself, though, wanting to be able to speak like he spoke, know what he knew—not because I thought I was beneath him but because I wanted others to think more of me. I wanted people to listen to me when I spoke like I listened to him: with respect and consideration (instead of just waiting for me to mess up). If it hadn't been for Andy, I probably would have succumbed to humiliation, dropped out after fall term, and given up on college altogether—*but he inspired me.*

I took to reading Andy's copies of our assigned texts—all highlighted and annotated—teaching myself to read and think the way I was supposed to have learned before coming to college. And when I finished my readings, Andy—true to his childhood nickname, the Professor—would quiz me on each: Plato's *Republic,* Max Weber's *The Protestant Ethic and the Spirit of Capitalism,* Chuang Tzu's *Basic*

Writings (which, I might add, are by no means *basic*). Question by question, in apt Socratic fashion, he walked me through each until I felt confident enough to join the discussion in Freshman Studies and subject myself to the highbrow hazing of my pretentious peers.

That first term, and Freshman Studies in particular, was a harrowing experience (by design, it seemed). An intellectual boot camp of sorts, meant to break us of the idea that we already knew everything (or anything, really), then rebuild us to think correctly. The goal was to strive above all for "light, more light!"—the dying words of German poet and philosopher Johann Wolfgang von Goethe and the Lawrence University motto, urging students onward to ever greater knowledge and upward to an ever better world. Talk about a tall order for a bunch of kids not even old enough to buy beer yet. Above all, though, Freshman Studies was a test: Were we ready and able to rise to the call of "the Lawrence difference"? By the end of the year, one in seven of us, on average, would go home, while one in five would leave by graduation. I could tell that most everyone thought I would probably end up on that side of the statistic.

I didn't necessarily disagree either, but I was determined to prove us all wrong. As such, it wasn't my classes so much as my classmates that inspired me to stay. Or, more specifically, the daily, stubborn, marching rebuttal against their outright refusal to see me as anything but the raw, fresh cut of meat delivered to them on a silver platter. It forged in me, at first, a false confidence. This fake it till you make it mentality was foundation enough to stand on, if uneasily, and stand up, if unwisely, for my still-undeveloped opinions. I once argued, "I think, therefore I am, so if I don't believe in z then it doesn't exist"—x being time, y being space, z was, therefore, gravity in the discussion of Albert Einstein's general theory of relativity. Needless to say, my position was quashed quickly, with ease, and with no shortage of laughter.

In my defense: I obviously *knew* that gravity was a real thing (the bruises on my backside from braving my first snow were proof of that!)—I just didn't get it in the way Einstein had intended me to, didn't get how he had actually proven it on paper. I only spoke up to begin with because it sounded like most of the class hadn't understood either. Nobody took the bait, though; within a couple of minutes, the conversation returned to the same couple of (mostly male) students who usually controlled it. They redirected our attention back to the "crux of the matter," a phrase they loved to trot out to indicate that they, and they alone, understood what was important. With that proclamation I was sentenced to an intellectual time-out for whichever unspoken rule of discourse I'd broken this time.

I may never learn about gravity, but I did learn something life changing that day: my peers had something I didn't, a certain control over conversation that afforded them power to inspire ideas (or extinguish them), to promote discussion (or censor it), to invite people in (or kick them out). Before that class, I'd never really considered what I sounded like when I spoke or what I wanted people to hear when they listened—but there hasn't been a day that I haven't thought about it since.

From then on, I started listening more to the language being used—in class, of course, but, more enjoyably, when Andy and I hung out with friends. My first major task was learning all of the regularly name-dropped philosophers. As people spoke, I collected the names they said and repeated them in my head over and over to commit them to memory: Descartes, Heidegger, Foucault—all old (dead?) white men by the sound of them. Later, Andy would tell me about them and give me their books, as if I didn't have enough assigned readings. More than simply learning the canon, though, I liked to listen to my peers debate and pick out their communication patterns. I guess you could say I was studying the mechanics of how to structure a convincing argument—which, I learned quickly, was not always the same as a correct one. My data suggested that *sounding* right was paramount to *being* right.

"There's no such thing as an objective truth," I'd often hear; I took that to mean perception is everything—now, that was a concept I was fluent in. Nyrobi always said that I "had the gift of gab," but whatever "gab" meant at Lawrence didn't translate into my native tongue, a delicate dance between fast and smooth to find the quickest, slickest angle to win over the listener to whatever story I happened to be selling that day. This gab, instead, was a stuffy and ornate maneuver, an uptight classical ballet to my free-flow jazz routine. People took turns talking at one another, waiting to say something rather than actually listening. And when people did speak, they were penalized for less than perfect pronunciation of foreign names and phrases while those who could read a text in its original language were automatically "more expert" than those who could not. When, at long last, the speakers did get down to arguments, an opinion "in it of itself" was denounced as "baseless" unless referenced in the context of a respected text. (How texts came to be respected, I did not yet know—and still don't know *really*; though I'm confident, now, that I could provide a "convincing" and well "referenced"—if only somewhat "correct"—explanation.) Finally, if all else failed, the argument devolved into "semantics"—or an intellectual draw, whereby the winner was determined (there must *always* be a loser) by a sudden-death match of who had memorized the most SAT words, eventually digressing, of course, into who had gotten the highest SAT score on down to ACT, IQ, GPA to—the very last and least—high school class rank.

In a very short time—three months alone!—I'd practically learned a foreign language *and* survived the revenge-of-the-nerds Freshman Studies experience, karmic retribution, probably, for being a bitch to their kind in high school. But then my grades went up, and I passed my two remaining classes, leaving me with a measly and mortifying GPA of 1.6. It was a long way from the 3.8 I'd predicted in the letter I wrote myself the night before classes had started, but, then again, I'd also listed commas as my biggest apprehension. Back then, I hadn't even known of this whole new culture I had since taken on—this brand new world I was now living in. I started to wonder *why* hadn't I known about it before then. Had my teachers in high school known about it? If so, why hadn't they taught me? If I had so much trouble catching up (when high school had been a cakewalk), then what did that mean for everyone else? Did they all have someone like Andy? If not, how would they make it? And if they didn't, would it matter? If so, how much did they stand to lose? How much did I stand to gain? I didn't know, yet, the value of the world I'd somehow managed to break into—how unique an opportunity it was for someone like me. But, for the time being, I was tired of thinking—tired of trying to be everything everyone expected me to be. Fall term was over, and I was looking forward—for the first time in a long time—to going back to Texas for Christmas, to going home to my grandparents. At Momma Jean and Pop's, I'd finally be able to relax—eat brownies, ride four-wheelers, watch football—and, you know, just be myself again.

WHEN I RETURNED TO THEM, though, I was no longer the same person they'd left at Lawrence. The person that I learned to be with Andy was now a part of me. And that person turned out to be someone my family didn't much care for. In fact, I wasn't so sure I liked her myself. When they asked about school, I couldn't talk about it without sounding like I was giving a lecture, without name-dropping philosophers and referencing their texts. Somehow it came off to them as disrespectful, although that wasn't my intention. "Ceci," Momma Jean said, "you've gone and gone above your raisin's." I didn't know what raisins had anything to do with that saying, but I understood the gist of it: I was acting like I was better than they were and talking down to my elders—therefore breaking two cardinal rules in one fell swoop. Because I couldn't find a nice way to say it—a third rule—I didn't say anything more on the subject. The world that I came from and the one I was just beginning to inhabit would have to remain separate until I figured out how to build a bridge between them.

After the holidays, I returned to Lawrence refreshed, eager to see Andy, and ready for a new start. I'd failed once, but everyone fails once. And so—evoking the words of my childhood heroine, Scarlett O'Hara, I vowed, "As God is my witness, I will never fail another class again!" I still felt inadequate, unable to clearly communicate my ideas, and altogether alienated from a huge part of my identity. At the start of Winter Term, it was clearer than ever that, just like I had to leave a part of me behind to get along at home, I had to leave part of me there to do well at school. But, just as in high school, I figured, it was just a matter of cracking the code—once I did, I'd not only be able to beat the game, I'd be free to play by my own rules, free from doing anything I didn't want to—there to get my piece of paper and get out! It wasn't a good plan, but at least it was *a plan*. The important thing was that I was starting to see myself belonging, starting to think of myself as a Lawrentian. I had a good feeling at the start of the winter term and was hopeful that, by the end of it, I might just be calling it home.

If I were smart, though, I think maybe I'd never say the word "home" again. Whenever I say it, whenever I begin to feel comfortable somewhere, something really bad happens. (How had I forgotten, so quickly, that feeling of the calm before the storm?) And so, two weeks later, something happened that was so out of context, so reminiscent of my childhood, that I never even saw it coming. I was staying over at Andy's and just before bed, I picked up my phone to find nine missed calls from my roommate, Jessi. I got up and got dressed, then ran out the door. Andy followed close on my heels, asking, "What is it?" But I didn't say anything, hoping that I was wrong about what I feared I would find when I got to her. I phoned Jessi four times on the way to our dorm, but she didn't answer. When I opened the door to our room, it was just as I'd expected. I calmly instructed Andy to call 911 and get me some water. Jessi's body was limp on the ground, surrounded by vomit, an empty bottle of Tylenol PM and another of vodka beside her. She was clutching what appeared to be a letter. I checked for a pulse—it was faint but there—so I lifted her up, stabilized her head and neck, and shook her as hard as I could, trying to wake her up. No success. But I could still feel a pulse, and her airway was clear. I knew CPR, but I really hoped someone more qualified would arrive before it came to that. Just then, Andy ran in. "They're on their way," he said breathlessly then handed me a half-empty glass of water. I splashed the water in her face—she murmured. "Good," I exhaled. "They might get here in time."

Why did things like this keep happening around me? My two worlds were colliding, my past was smashing into my present, and it had me questioning myself. I started to think that maybe, instead of my family, I'd been the problem all along. I'd gone from Texas to Atlanta to Wisconsin, and every step of the way it was the same old shit—everything changed, the only constant was me. Was I the carrier? Had I infected Jessi, and James before her, my mother, too, with the crisis virus? Thoughts like that sent me spiraling into depression. Eventually, I went into mental health services and met with a psychiatrist; he had me call mom to find out what antidepressants she was on—he said whatever worked for her would likely work for me. *They didn't.*

The first pill I took made me catatonic, the second manic, and the third made me gain weight so fast I stopped eating again. I felt empty and helpless and sad and scared and, above all, angry all at the same time. At age nineteen, I was becoming the manifestation of everything I had hated about my mother as a child, and now I resented her for it. She should have known better than to have kids, I thought, and pass on this mental disease. But, instead, she had two of them when she was only a couple of years older than I was then because she "didn't believe in abortion." All I could think was, yeah, well, now look who was paying for it. Look at James! Look at me!

I was thrown into chaos yet again, and again Andy was critical to my survival. As it turned out, Andy and I weren't such opposites after all. He was the only one who really understood what I was going through; he'd been diagnosed with clinical depression at sixteen and had been hospitalized once for suicidal thoughts and again for social anxiety. I trusted him more than I'd ever trusted anyone; I gave myself over to him entirely and let him help me. He moved into my room, filling in for Jessi, and we mostly stayed there, and to ourselves, until I "got better"—that phrase, I hated that phrase. How many times had I used it to cover up my mother's absence, how many times had I wished she had a disease—any disease!—that could be cured? "My mother's sick," I would say. "She's in the hospital until she gets better." (My mother's insane, locked her in the loony bin until she stops trying to kill herself.)

I wanted to kill myself—not then, exactly, it hadn't got that bad yet—but preventatively, so that I'd never have to suffer the pain, the embarrassment of being made to live when I wanted to die; so that my loved ones would never have to suffer the pain, the embarrassment, of keeping me alive when I wanted to die; so that both they and I would never have to suffer the inevitable resentment that came from it.

"I don't want to live like this," I told Andy. "Then don't," he said, and we listened to music. We played chess and cards, we read books and plays, we drew and painted—he wrote and I edited. "Use your pain to create," he urged, "to connect to a world of pain, to lend your voice to human suffering when most go unheard."

I thought he was full of shit. But when I saw art and literature through his eyes, I was reminded of the beauty of possibility, and my hopelessness, my fears, began to fade away. Eventually, they disappeared. Like most cases, my depression turned out to be situational, a temporary state brought on by Jessi (and, maybe, a delayed reaction to Mom and James). I had to drop another class, but I finished second term better than the first and went into the last one feeling inspired. That spring, with Andy as my guide, I finally began to connect with my studies and figure out my own voice (instead of just getting by and mimicking my peers).

Andy was the only person who'd ever inspired me like my mother had: he made me think I could do anything I set my mind to. In some ways, I think I was drawn to Andy because he reminded me of Mom, but, because he was like her, he also scared me: the social anxiety and oversleeping, the missed medications and passed deadlines, a general inability to cope with expectation, and an overwhelming lack of consistency—it was like Mom all over again. It wasn't bad, though, until spring term, and at the time, I worried he'd worn himself out taking care of me. I tried to be supportive like he had been for me, but he'd turn despondent and retreat. When I'd nudge him to go see the campus psychiatrist or therapist, he'd get resentful and sometimes shut down altogether. Nothing I did seemed to do any good, and when my frustration got the better of me, we'd fight; sometimes, he'd shout, "I can't deal with this" then grab his backpack and *just leave.*

It made me angry—or that's what it looked like to him. Really, though, it made me feel helpless: all of a sudden, something I said would set him off and there was nothing I could do to stop it. His instability (like Mom's) made me panic, and I compulsively tried to fix things. I'd go after him, apologizing or trying to calm him down, but it would just make him more anxious, and we'd end up in this back-and-forth cycle until I'd lose my voice and he'd run out of tears. By the end of summer, I realized that, for as much as he was like my mother, I was like my father. His running, my chasing . . . if we'd had two little kids to take care of, I'm sure our fighting would've escalated to the point of theirs. *Something had to give.*

I loved Andy, I didn't want to let him go, but I didn't want to stay together and have him hate me either; he felt the same way about me. What could we do? Stop clinging on for dear life when (clearly) neither of us was going anywhere: we promised to love each other *forever* but agreed to slow things down a little. Sophomore year, we decided not to live together. He joined a fraternity. I joined a sorority. But we did run a student theater company together called Artistic Masturbation, inspired by my youthful experiences at 7 Stages. He became best friends with Zach, *of course,* my first love from back home (who'd introduced me to Lawrence). I met Emily, my best friend from college, and rounded out her girl posse (well known on campus for bringing the party). Eventually, Andy and I grew into ourselves and outgrew each other. It took a long time, a lot of work (and no shortage of growing pains), but we came out on the other side, able to love each other better (and like each other more) than ever before. More than friends, we were *family* (still are, and will be "forever"—just like we promised). It didn't feel like it at the time, but Andy and I grew up, became adults together. Our relationship was the most formative experience of my life until that point, and before it ended, Andy had opened the door for my next great love: learning.

I no longer paged mechanically through texts, but dove deep into my studies, consumed by curiosity. Noting arguments, counterarguments, and relative theories, my thoughts overcrowded the margins, brushing up against words that changed the way I understood myself and the world around me. My passion spread like wildfire from subject to subject, setting the boundaries between them ablaze. Amid the ash, I could still recognize the great thinkers, but as the smoke cleared, I began to see, for the first time, the interconnectedness of their ideas.

I remember sitting in a Russian history class, discussing the role of the vanguard party in the revolution, originated by V. I. Lenin in *What Is to Be Done*. I had only just read *The Communist Manifesto* the term before in a government course but, nevertheless, found it difficult to reconcile Lenin's vanguard party with the teachings of Karl Marx: "The proletarians have nothing to lose but their chains. They have a world to win." Lost in a daydream, my thoughts transformed into a scene of Brechtian epic theater—a few peasants toiled away as a Bolshevik appeared, handing out literature. Illiterate, one peasant turned his paper upside down. The Bolshevik pointed to the sheet and shouted, "Workers unite!" In unison, the illiterate peasants repeated, "Workers unite!" as they marched upstage, then returned with a banner quoting Lenin: "Literature must become a part of the general cause of the proletariat!" An audience member called out, "What does it say!?" The peasants chanted, "Workers unite!" Laughable as the scene was, it starkly reminded me of a question posed by Paulo Freire in one of my education readings: "How can the oppressed, as divided unauthentic beings, participate in the pedagogy of their liberation?"

It was a question that came to consume me, became the center of my studies at Lawrence—and ever since, really. By then, of course, I realized that it was the same struggle that I was actively undergoing— one that I found as frustrating emotionally as I did intellectually, one that required both the guidance of a teacher and the tenderness of a friend to navigate successfully. That person was Professor Stewart Purkey, head of the Education Studies Department—my first, *real* academic mentor. I didn't choose him so much as he chose me (I disliked him immediately). Like Tina Fey in *Mean Girls,* Professor Purkey was "a pusher"—and, *believe me,* I could have filled a whole burn book with all the bitching I did about him. For starters, he actually expected me to show up on time and even docked my grades when, of course, I never did. Then, especially when I wasn't raising my hand, he would call me out, "Cecily, what do you think?" The impossibly dull (impossibly *stupid*) conversation would grind to a halt, and he'd *push* me to explain—"with evidence from the text"— why I thought my classmates were wrong. After which, of course, they'd attack me. Worst of all, though, Professor Purkey would fan the flame, forcing me to defend my position under fire from the entire class. Only once did I ever manage to best the whole lot of them. It was during a discussion on affirmative action, and I was already having a particularly bad day. One guy said, in effect, that poor people of color and first-generation applicants shouldn't be accepted into college unless they can compete and get in on their own merit— not because it would be unfair to more qualified white students but because it would be humiliating for them. They'd be unprepared, fail, and become resentful. Several other people agreed with him, and when Professor Purkey called on me I was so angry I could hardly speak.

I told them how I'd been to so many schools, I hadn't learned a skill set so much as how to play the system. I told them about Mom and me living on as little as $12,000 a year, about the time I'd lived with Nyrobi in Glenwood, and that I'd been living on my own ever since. "Let me tell you something about poor, uneducated people like me: No one gives a damn about us, whether we live or die—we survive on sheer will, not on Daddy's bank account. We make our own way," I told them, "and fight for everything we have: work hard or otherwise take it. Above all, we take nothing for granted: teeth cleanings, toilet paper, medication, you name it. It can get pretty ugly, yes, but it's not that people can't do better: it's that most are never given the chance—"Where I come from, people don't even know places like Lawrence exist—hell, I didn't even know what a liberal arts college was when I applied. But Lawrence gave me a chance so I took it. And, yeah," I said, "I was unprepared, and, thanks to kids like you with your bright ideas about people like me, *it was humiliating!* I failed that first year," I confessed, "had a breakdown, nearly dropped out—but I fought my way back. Now, I'm caught up to all of you," I charged, tears of rage spilling down my face, "but my little brother, oh, he'd be running circles around the lot of you, if he'd had the chance. But instead, he's in prison with all the other poor idiots we'd surely be undermining with a ticket to college."

And with that, everyone was silent until Professor Purkey said, "Class dismissed," then asked me to come to his office. "Are you okay?" he asked. "NO!" I shouted and burst into tears. He handed me a box of Kleenex, and after I'd used up about half of them, I calmed down enough to say, "Sorry." "It's okay," he said. "What's your brother's name?" "James," I said. "Baby James, we always called him—he's a year and half younger than me. It just isn't right that I'm here and he's *there*." "How long's he in for?" "I don't know, seven years maybe—drugs," I said, then paused to think before adding, "It's *always* been drugs." I thought out loud, stringing together what little I could remember, explaining to Professor Purkey, trying to figure it out myself: What happened to Baby James?

He started smoking marijuana pretty early in middle school, he said it made him "calmer, more at ease." He had more friends than me back then and got invited to a lot of parties where he started doing other drugs, I guess. Prescription pills, first, I think—he used to lace his joints with Xanax and trade his Ritalin for both. But by high school, he was selling weed, and—maybe that was it—he became a drug dealer and could never really shake it.

"I talked to him a few months ago," I said, "but he was barely there, barely human, even. I was so disgusted, I stopped talking to him. So when he called I didn't answer—*I didn't answer* the night he got picked up." "So you blame yourself?" he asked. "Yes, no, I don't fucking know!" I said, then paused to really think about it. "It's just . . . ," I began again, a little incoherently, "it's just that for as far back as I can remember, I've pushed him down to get ahead but he's always managed to catch up, get even—until now, that is." "What do you mean by 'pushed him down'?" he asked me. I told him the story of my first memory of James, the one of us as children fighting in the rain and said, "I've always been one step ahead, prepared to sling mud if necessary. I let the first fistful fly when I chose to stay with Mom and let him go alone to Dad's—I knew that he needed me, that he was struggling with their separation; I was, too, but I knew I'd be better off just taking care of myself. Without him to worry about, I took off running as fast as possible away from my family. I retreated into school, sports, clubs, and friends' homes I liked better than my own. I wish I could say, 'I didn't look back,' but I did. I saw him sitting with his face in his hands, sinking deeper and deeper into the mud. I remember looking into his empty eyes during hospital visiting hours; cleaning up the floor, his clothes the first time he vomited from 'too much vodka, too many pills'; my friends calling him to buy drugs before we'd go to a party; that summer before college, when his girlfriend called me screaming, 'He's not breathing!' At some point, I remember knowing that he was stuck too deep to get himself out. But I didn't go back to help him: I fled to save myself, and he stayed there and never got out. If I'd stayed—it's true—I wouldn't have made it to Lawrence. But if I'd stayed—maybe, just maybe—he wouldn't have ended up in prison. Why was it a choice between him and me? Between my world back home and the one here? He should be here with me—it's not fair!"

"No, it's not," Professor Purkey agreed, "and it's not your fault, either—it's a problem much bigger than you and James." He told me that the whole country was segregated, separated into the two worlds I'd been trying unsuccessfully to straddle, the line between them drawn up in the same way: the few who are granted access to colleges like Lawrence versus the many who don't know institutions like it even exist.

"Access," he explained, "is the dividing line between the haves and have-nots." "You mean, the rich and the poor?" I asked, thinking, tuition is expensive, sure, but Lawrence isn't exactly a fast track to Wall Street. "Yeah, but more important than money," he said, "is class." "You sound just like Momma Jean," I said deadpan. "She's always saying, 'Ceci, your life would get a whole lot easier if you'd learn to show a little class.'" He tilted his head and said, "Um, well, what I meant was"—"Gotcha!" I laughed. "Come on, Purkey, I know my shit!" "Yeah, *you do*. And you'd have an A to prove it, if you'd ever get a paper in on time," he lectured, then winked. As I made to leave, I beamed—it was the first time I felt I belonged at Lawrence. "Oh, and Cecily," he added, on my way out, "I *am* really sorry about your brother. And I think your classmates would sympathize, too, and would *certainly* learn a lot from your experiences if you'd share them in class like you just did with me—they *really* are the good ones; you'll see if you give them a chance." "Fine," I conceded, "I'll try to 'show a little class'—but I want my A."

Walking back to my room, I thought about what Professor Purkey had asked me to do and was reminded of Mr. Herrera, from high school, who'd challenged me to see the universality of my experience, to ask, "What's the bigger picture?" His voice came flooding back, and just then *it clicked!* The hand I'd been dealt in life wasn't personal; it wasn't, like I often felt, one big, cosmic joke against Cecily McMillan. But the deck *had been* stacked against me—*me and everyone else* who had the misfortune of being born of that second world, that same one that had recently seen James off to prison. As for Mr. Herrera's question, I understood now why I couldn't answer it before: just like you can't see your own face without a mirror, I had to settle into that first world, make it my home, and become a naturalized citizen before I got far away enough to see the world I'd left behind—*and far away it really was, what a jump!* The distance looked impossible to cross, yet I'd done it without intending to, not knowing it was there; like Christopher Columbus, I beat the odds and arrived alive in a world better than expected, one that would afford me endless opportunity. That was "the bigger picture." Now that I knew where it was and how to get there, I could show others the way—others, like Marco.

He was thirteen years old and in the sixth grade when I first met him. I'd been hired at the local YMCA as a tutor for underserved youth—Marco was my first "student." I thought he was quiet and distant at first but soon discovered he was neither. He didn't talk right away, I think, because he stutters and has a little bit of a lisp. But when I noticed the book clenched in his left hand, tucked closely to his side and asked him about it, I couldn't shut him up. I don't remember what it was, but it was an adventure story of some kind, and Marco described in great detail an unexpected hero, the many struggles he encountered leading up to his eventual victory, and the widespread praise he won. Despite his dyslexia, he flew through this kind of book in a matter of hours, longer ones, in a couple of days. He loved to read adventure stories, he said, because "in the end, the right people always win."

In school, Marco usually got Cs or Ds in English class because, as he told me, his teacher "marks off a lot for spelling." He claimed he didn't like to write, but his notebooks were filled with elaborate stories with detailed illustrations. He also hated math; "I'm just no good at it." But that wasn't true either, he had an exceptionally intuitive understanding of numbers, quantity, and space. If you gave him a problem, he'd quickly figure out how to solve it, but his final answer would probably be wrong. His dyslexia made numbers frustrating. He got anxious, rushed through steps, mixed up numbers, and ended up with a big red X. Because his fifth-grade teacher overlooked this problem, Marco was a grade behind in math, making the same mistakes all over again.

Francine was Marco's mother. She was frustrated with his teachers: "He just doesn't get the attention he deserves." Tears streamed down her face as she explained to me that "Marco's never met his dad. It's just him and me—and I take care of my mother too." As a single mother, she worked two full-time jobs to provide Marco with a comfortable life but was usually too busy or too tired to be a part of it. For as hard as she worked, she felt like she should be able to trust the school to do its job, to educate Marco, "but it's just easier to ignore him."

For years, I met with Marco twice weekly; he started out as my student, but by the time I graduated, I had learned as much from him as he had from me. We normally started sessions talking about the book he was reading. As he got more comfortable speaking, he slowly started to stutter less. Moving on to math, we structured a system for minimizing mistakes: (1) number and rewrite the problem, check that it matches the book, (2) letter each step in solving the problem, then circle the final answer, (3) rework the problem using the previous steps, and (4) if the final answer doesn't match, compare steps to find the mistake. Marco rarely made mistakes, though, so we worked ahead to future lessons. Over time he saw math as a puzzle and, recognizing his aptitude for it, began to enjoy it—so much so that he was back on track in less than a year.

To improve his literacy, I helped Marco workshop his original short stories. He brought new material to each session and read aloud to me. Marco was proud to share his work with me, and unlike class, the one-on-one setting allowed him to work on fluency without feeling embarrassed. When he finished, he corrected spelling and grammatical errors as he typed them into my computer. Clutching the first copy of his twenty-page "Tales from a Middle-Schooler," Marco mused, "Maybe one day, I'll be a writer."

At the same time, Marco taught me that while my primary duty was to "teach," to impart knowledge, I could not do so without first learning who he was as a student, where he was coming from, how he learned, what inspired him or otherwise caused him to shut down. What's more, Marco showed me that the more I knew about him as a *person,* the more I could motivate him as a *student.* Finally, Marco helped me define the kind of teacher I wanted to be—and decide, resolutely, that I wanted to be a teacher (*a real one*). I resolved not to be "sausage-filler"—a teacher who writes a bunch of crap on the chalkboard, then does "unit tests" to see if the kids memorized it. When I had my own classroom, I vowed to embrace the individuality of my students and inspire them to make connections between what they learn at school and the world they see around them. I hoped to be the kind of teacher who empowered students to reclaim the classroom, to take hold of their education and use it to reshape "the real world," not just fit into it.

By the end of sophomore year, I was halfway through the Lawrence University Teacher Certification Program (taking education classes by day and "practice teaching" with Marco in the evenings. Then, junior year, I was paired with a real-life high school class to observe, at first, and then later, try my hand at teaching. It was only a couple days a week and I only taught a few lessons, but it was pretty surreal to think of myself as Ms. McMillan, when only four years prior I was one of those kids, sitting at one of those desks, hating everyone and everything—especially all the misters and misses who thought they could tell me something! I said as much in my written reflection and was relieved to hear all my peers share the same sentiment at our weekly meeting.

Combined, the practicum and seminar made up the final stage of training for student teaching—a full-time go at leading several classes for *a whole semester*. Near the end of the school year, I found the prospect as terrifying as I did exciting—but I'm pretty sure "scared straight" was Professor Purkey's goal. "Teaching is *not* a part-time job," Purkey must have reminded us a half-dozen times, cueing up for his signature drill-sergeant speech. "Our teachers don't do summers off, they do research and update their lesson plans! We don't do bad teaching here; sausage-filling is not going to cut it—teachers are society builders, and we won't accept anything less. If you're not ready, that's okay—leave now, because you can't walk out on your kids. It's your job to be prepared and patient, to listen and adapt to their needs—to teach and raise the next generation. The future of our country depends on you." Each time he finished, I suppressed the urge to say, "Sir, yes sir!" I didn't dare joke around, though, for fear he might think I didn't take him or, worse yet, *teaching*, seriously. Purkey didn't fuck around, and, for the first time with school, I didn't either.

"Are you okay?" Grandmommy Kay asked, concerned when I told her I wouldn't be visiting that summer. "You usually *can't wait* to come home!" It's true. Atlanta had always been my soul mate. Each year, all the way back to pre-K, I'd count down the days to my visit with Grandmommy until I finally moved there permanently in high school. For two short years, I'd gotten to call Atlanta my home, but, in earnest, I hadn't lived there so much as *survived*. Still, though, it broke my heart to leave, but I promised to come home after college and had only made short trips since, afraid that I might otherwise run out on Lawrence and say, "To hell with Wisconsin!" The summer after junior year would be my third consecutive summer living on campus, but usually, like she said, I flew back after finals for two weeks of brunching, drinking, and all sorts of events with all my friends and family I was ready, *so ready*, to come home to. "Don't worry," I assured her. "I'm just getting ready for student teaching: I've got less than two months to plan three different subjects, and I'm starting to freak out, thinking, I can't believe they would *put me* in charge of a *high school classroom!*" I was starting to understand what my mother meant when she'd been afraid to take me home from the hospital. "Wow, Cecily! I'm so proud of you," she said. "I've never seen you take something so seriously before!" "Teaching is serious work," I told her, borrowing Professor Purkey's word. "We're society builders!" "Good for you, hunny," she responded. "Hold on, your grandfather wants to speak with you."

Especially now that I wouldn't be seeing him otherwise, he asked if I'd like to meet him in Detroit later that summer for the United States Social Forum. "What's that?" I asked. "A bunch of activists getting together, holding workshops and panels, talking about social justice," he said. "Looks like there's a ton of good education stuff for you, and I'll be there, of course, for WRFG." Or 89.3 FM Radio Free Georgia, "your station for progressive information." Atlanta's only community-owned radio station, founded by Granddaddy and others in 1973 as a platform for voices and music traditionally left out of broadcast media. When James and I were little, we'd go sit in the studio and "listen" to his Sunday program live; *Fox's Minstrel Show* was (still is) a mixture of music, of all kinds, and current events, too, both framed in the context of his overtly radical politics—a perspective I hadn't seen then, of course, because James and I were too busy playing cards or fighting over the mic when it came time to "say hi to the listeners!"

It was only then, looking back on that time, that I realized I *still* didn't know much about my grandfather's beliefs, where they came from, and how he went about them—I didn't know much, really, about who he was *as a person*. "Grandaddy" Harlon Joye was our step-grandfather, technically, but had been around all our lives and didn't have any children of his own, so the connection was as good as biology on both ends. He was always there but, also, always next to Grandmommy, the veritable monarch of social butterflies, who was *always* the center of attention wherever she went. Granddaddy, in turn, bore the distinction of being the sole "quiet guy" in our family and, therefore, was more than happy to be left alone to do his own thing while our beloved matriarch took care of everyone and everything else. Recalling my time spent in Atlanta, two images of Granddaddy stood out most: him sitting silently, reading the newspaper during family dinners or beach vacations while the rest of us talked loudly to, about, and over one another, and him and my grandmother dancing together at her big, blowout birthday parties, while an audience of some two hundred of us watched, mesmerized by their style and grace and, more than anything, that big, epic love they'd found in each other. "That's what I want," I said aloud each year. "Get in line," someone always said from behind me.

He'd always been sort of mythical to me: the one Grandmommy had taken as a husband when she could have chosen anyone else— he, alone, being *the one* who completed her. Now, God knows why, Granddaddy was taking a special interest *in me:* his invitation to the United States Social Forum was his way of reaching out. It was my chance, I realized, to get to know him better and figure out, for myself, what made him perfect for my grandmother. It was an opportunity too good to pass up, even at the cost of making me more anxious, still, of meeting my start-of-school deadline, so I said, "Sure, I'll see you in Detroit!"

When I arrived a few weeks later, along with 20,000 others, I found Granddaddy and gave him a great big bear hug and thanked him: "I'm so glad you invited me—I was going batty in that dorm room!" Since school let out, I *really had* spent every waking hour planning every minute of every day of every class I'd be teaching later that fall. "This has been the most uneventful summer of my life!" I whined, then scanned the radical paraphernalia papering the walls (posters for causes, photos of martyrs, information on organizations you could join to "make a difference," and notices for meetings and panels where you could "learn how!"). "But, maybe," I added, stopping at one about a group called the Democratic Socialists of America, "that's all about to change." And, though I did not know it then or even immediately thereafter, I was right: that trip would not only change the tone of my summer; it would set into motion the course of events that would not only change but come to define the rest of my life.

One thing became clear immediately, though: Granddaddy was something of a celebrity among this group. By the end of that opening day, in just the couple of hours we'd been there, no fewer than a dozen people came up, shook his hand, and said something to the effect of "*Harlon Joye,* the legend himself! *Still stirring up trouble,* I see! And in style, same as always—who is this beautiful young woman?" "My granddaughter, *you dog!*" he'd laugh, blushing a little. "My eldest, Cecily." "Woah!" one after another shouted in disbelief. "Harlon, a grandfather, who woulda thunk it? Nice to meet you, young lady! Boy, *do you have some big shoes to fill!*" Each time, I was left standing there speechless with no room, anyhow, to ask, "What was that about?" before the next one would jump in. As for me, I didn't see anyone I knew until just before we left. Someone called out, "Cecily?" and I looked around to find a slender, hipster kid asking, "Is that you?" "Yes?" I said tentatively, searching his face. "Hi, *you*—" "It's me, Andy!" he shouted. *Clearly he knew me* but, *still,* I couldn't place him—"*Oh Andy, from Youth Creates* . . ."—from six summers ago, when I'd stood center stage, wearing the flag like a burka, and belted the "Star Spangled Banner." "Funny running into you here, but I guess it makes sense!" Back then, in 2005, our joint outrage with the Iraq War had inspired that performance and, later, my brief role as a student activist, organizing the high school walk-out to the anti-Bush rally in Atlanta. "Me, too," he said. "Been fighting ever since! Right now, I'm working with the Atlanta Friends Service Committee to end it—*check it out!*" He handed me a shirt printed with lines of empty combat boots: "War Is Costly" was written beneath them; "Peace Is Priceless," it read on the back. "Cool!" I said, and pointed. "I'm here with my grandfather—he's the handsome one, right there, with the old-school glasses and the thick, silver hair." "Who, *Harlon?*" he asked, and I nodded. "That's *so cool*—he's like a living legend!" "I'm starting to get that," I said, then made Andy's evening by inviting him to join us for drinks.

Once we got settled at a nearby bar and ordered our first round, Andy asked, "So when did you first start working with John Lewis?" "Oh, let me think," Granddaddy said, then sipped from his Jack and water before continuing. "It would've been just after the Freedom Ride but before the sit-ins—" "Wait!" I called out, interrupting him. "Our *John Lewis* is *the John Lewis* from the civil rights movement?" He nodded. "*How did I miss that!*" "Probably, because you were busy throwing parties," he jabbed. Andy laughed and I took a swig of my beer. "True," I said, then tipped my bottle at him. "I could throw a mean party, though, and *only once* got busted by the cops. . . . Oh! Remember, that was the only time you ever yelled at me: 'The next time you go to jail, it better be for something you believe in!'" We all laughed, but I was *only just* beginning to understand what he had meant.

"Well, I'd been arrested several times," he said, "but always in protest." Then he ordered another round and told us about how he'd been "radicalized" in college. He was active in groups that were precursors to Students for a Democratic Society (SDS), of which he was also a foundational member (drafting, in large part, its constitution); he worked to see SDS rise to a national organization of more than 100,000 members, then saw it give way to the anti–Vietnam War student movements of the 1960s. "Did you know Jane Fonda?" Andy asked. "No, but I worked closely with Tom Hayden, who she later married," he said, motioning for another round. "And I did interview her once." Then he told us about the time he went to the White House with Harry Belafonte at the onset of student marches for desegregation in 1959; about the time the sun came up over the Washington Mall while he ran around trying to "fix the port-o-potty situation," his direct orders from Bayard Rustin, Martin Luther King's closest advisor and lead organizer of the 1963 March on Washington; and about that time in 1977 when he worked closely with the deputy mayor of Atlanta Maynard Jackson to support the sanitation workers strikes and, later, solidify collective bargaining rights for public sector workers in the city.

There were more stories, too, but by then we were on our fifth, maybe sixth, round, and after that, the details get a little hazy. When I crawled into bed that night and lay there incoherently reviewing the unbelievable day I'd just had, I determined that I knew two things, for certain, to be true: (1) No matter how long I'd been in a sorority, Granddaddy could drink me under the table, twice over, *with ease;* and (2) my grandfather was a *badass!*

Late the next morning, I dragged myself out of bed, took a long shower, ate three breakfast pastries, drank two cups of coffee in between *several* hotel cups of water, washed down two Advil, put on my sunglasses, then appeared before my grandfather and muttered, "I'm ready." "About time!" he said, far too loud and far too cheery. "I told Barbara we'd meet her at the DSA booth!" "DSA?" I whispered. "The Democratic Socialists of America," he clarified, and I cringed at what sounded, again, like a shout. "Oh, y-yeah," I stammered, painstakingly trying to recall where I'd heard of it before. "I r-read about them on the wall yesterday; they have a y-youth organization, too, that sounds a lot like the one you were talking about last night." "I don't doubt it," he explained. "Back in the sixties, two full decades before Michael Harrington founded DSA, he was one of the creators of SDS—but we gotta go," Granddaddy interrupted the story. "Come on, I'll tell you the rest on the way." He explained that Harrington had been one of a few present at a conference in 1962 that drafted *The Port Huron Statement*, a call to action that immediately gave rise to SDS and came to define the political agenda of the New Left. Harrington agreed with everything written but urged the group to include an explicit anti-Communist stance in order to protect itself and "the movement" from McCarthyism and its federal strong-arm, the House Un-American Activities Committee. When the majority voted against the addendum, he split from SDS.

"Look around," he gestured broadly, when we walked into the building then pointed out specific booths. "You can still see the lingering effects of that divisive time by how many similar organizations there are with only slightly different names." He was right, there were *so many* distinct groups: *International Socialist Organization, Socialist Party USA, Freedom Socialist Party, Socialist Organizer, Socialist Alternative, Socialist Action. . . .*

"It all seems so redundant," I said. "If they put their little differences aside and joined forces, they might actually be able to accomplish something big." "We said that in the sixties, too," Granddaddy responded. "But the stakes were higher. What's little now meant *everything* back then: a single word made the difference between signing up for a mailer or putting your name down to spend a long time—possibly, a lifetime—in prison." Fateful words that were closer to home than I, or anyone, realized. Fateful words that, then, fell on deaf ears.

A few feet away, Barbara Joye saw us coming and waved enthusiastically—no coincidence here, she still carried Harlon's name from their long-dissolved marriage; but no weirdness there either, she kept it for a perfectly sane reason ("that's how everybody already knew me"), and after the divorce, the two powerhouses had continued fighting the good fight, often side by side, "because things like WRFG and fair wages," Granddaddy explained, "were more important, *were bigger than us.*" Made sense to me, I thought; I always liked Barbara anyway. She was a tiny woman with a big personality, a hard worker who never took no for an answer. She was pushy and it was effective, she knew how to work an angle and I let her. "Hey Cecily," she said with a warm smile. "Harlon said you were coming and that you might be thinking of getting involved—what do you think, ready to step into those big shoes waiting for you?" She looked up at me with eager eyes and gently extended the clipboard toward me. "Just put your information down here, and we'll send you some information about joining up!" *Boy, was she good!* She already had me, so I glanced up at Harlon to get his approval. "It's your decision," he said, holding back a smile. Between his stories the night before and her excitement just then . . . "Alright," I agreed. "Let's do this!" Less than a month later, I was a card-carrying Socialist, and they even brought me out to New York (on scholarship, no less!) for their annual summer training and everything. There I met with other crazy kids just like me, and they *really, really* liked me: I was nominated, then elected an officer on their National Coordinating Committee. Then it was back to Wisconsin for a week of packing and off to Chicago to start student teaching—the unbearably slow "vacation" I'd begun was flying by so fast now, I couldn't keep up!

Then, all of a sudden, summer ground to a halt, and *BAM!* I was slammed face-first into the classrooms of the South Side of Chicago. Six magnificent white columns supported an ornate entryway into the desolate holding cell that is Hyde Park Academy. The ceilings of the rat-infested rooms crumbled as the doors closed. The water in the drinking fountain was contaminated beyond safe consumption, and the books in the library were locked up because of mold. (I think? God knows what else.) The student body was 99 percent African American; 96 percent were enrolled in free or reduced lunch programs. "Good morning," I said to myself on that first day. "This is your wake-up call."

I should have been prepared for it—I signed up the summer before, fully aware of what I was getting into. I knew then (and still, in that moment) that I resolutely *did not* want to teach in the overwhelmingly white schools of Wisconsin. Those weren't the kind of students I had in mind, the kind of students I wanted to reach when I got it in my head that I would change the world by being a teacher. In my fantasy, I'd get my degree and rejoin my high school debate teacher, Mr. Herrera, teaching students like me at Henry W. Grady. I'd signed up for Chicago knowing it was the training I'd need to return to Atlanta, just in time to connect with the younger brothers and sisters, cousins and friends of the kids I'd met riding the school bus when I lived with Nyrobi and Isaiah in Glenwood.

During the year I spent with the Glenwood kids, I really grew to like them and respect their resilience. I learned that the "cold and hardened" demeanor they put on for the teachers was mostly a front: "Growing up hard teaches you to act hard, keeps thugs off you and the man from getting you down." "The Man" was the topic of many conversations and one, to some degree, we understood in common: the teachers at school, the boss at work, the police officer on the corner, and so on. They had a strong sense of insecurity, a feeling that the systems put in place to help them were, instead, "a setup," a trap door designed to hurt them. So instead of showing up and wasting their time, trying to learn the rules of a game they already knew was rigged against them, they rejected it completely: disobeyed the rules, disrupted the order, and plotted ways to "flip the board," dismantle the game entirely. They believed it was stupid to do anything else, "like any of *those people* give a damn about *us*."

I wanted to work with kids like that. That's what I'd wanted, and that's what I got—but I wasn't prepared to be the kind of teacher the school expected of me, and I learned *really quickly* that I was never going to be. I also wasn't prepared to be the kind of teacher the kids needed from me. They seemed in need of something more fundamental than that: an advocate, a sister, a mentor, a friend—someone to listen and hug them, give them space to play and be children, while also recognizing the aspects of their lives that had forced them to grow up far too fast, respecting the part of them that was already adult. I was too busy trying to wear all those hats to really be the teacher I wanted to be, but I can say this: I gave it my all, and though they deserved more, I'd like to think they found our little detour as fruitful and beautiful as I did (admittedly more in hindsight than I did in the middle of it).

I soon found myself in an oddly familiar circumstance: in a way, the school itself reminded me of my old detention hideaway. And the kids—many of them gang members, drug dealers, teen moms, or runaways—were "problem kids," but they were *my* problem kids. In this scenario, I was "the problem *teacher*."

I refused to implement the authoritarian "three strikes" behavioral policy: teachers were encouraged to write up students for even the slightest infraction of the behavioral code; after three referrals, the student was suspended; after three suspensions, the student was expelled. Instead, when I saw my students breaking rules, I simply asked them, "Why?" Most of the time they had good reasons: they were late to class because they had to drop off younger siblings at school, their assignments were late because they had jobs and families to deal with. Most of the time we worked out a compromise: students would meet me during lunch to make up time they had missed in class or to complete assignments. They got good grades, and I got to know them better as people; they saw me as someone who was willing to work with them, someone who cared about them.

Instead of a traditional pedagogy, I tailored curricula to fit student interests. Rather than read the textbook version of *Romeo and Juliet* aloud from their desks, they took the stage as Antigone, Peer Gynt, and Willy Loman. As a final project, students wrote, rehearsed, and performed their own (uncensored) stories. We created a democratic community rooted in respect and empathy, aimed at exploring the idea of universal human struggle. Together we worked to examine the bigger picture: "What the *hell* is wrong with this world?"

Whereas my style appealed to these "problem kids," other teachers and administrators saw my unorthodox methods as acts of insubordination, distractions from the number one goal: improve test scores. I tried to explain that my style addressed the same goal: it improved reading and writing skills, expanded cultural knowledge, and improved self-esteem. But, really, that held true only within the walls of my classroom. Outside my classroom my students' work did not improve; they continued to disrupt other classes, resulting in suspension and, at times, expulsion. There was no transfer, because there was no community. Outside my classroom, my students weren't people—they were test scores. It was all worksheets, reading drills, practice problems in preparation for the next benchmark, the next standardized test. "You think you're so much better than us," my mentor sneered, "but you'll do the same thing when your job is on the line."

That's when I realized that the teachers weren't the problem, they were symptoms of a failed system. It was clear to me, then, that efforts to make our school more efficient weren't working: uniforms, rigid curricula, and standardized tests had left our kids behind because they didn't fit into the white, middle-class model. To provide these students with equal educational opportunity (which *was* the public school mission), teachers needed the time and resources to engage diversity and address learning differences. Finally, I determined, transforming children into marketable goods wasn't enough. I wanted my students to leave Hyde Park Academy with the ability to actively participate in democracy, the cultural life of their communities *and, above all*, with a developed sense of self-worth.

That was a pipe dream. But that was my standard, and I would settle for no less. Maybe Professor Purkey hadn't taught me well enough, or maybe he had taught me *oh too well*. Either way, though, it came down to the same point: I wasn't cut out to be a teacher in our public school system. Instead, I decided, my efforts would be better spent fixing the structural problems underlying it. I didn't know the way to go about that, though, so I went back for an emergency visit to Lawrence and asked my government advisor whether he could find time to meet with me. He was booked all day but said he'd be at the Viking Room, the campus watering hole, that night guest bartending. "Sure!" I replied. "Believe me, I could use a drink!" Over the couple of hours, I told him my Hyde Park Academy sob story and ran though my possible comeback story: "So I think, maybe, I'd like to work on welfare policy, but how you even get a job like that?" "Well," he said, pouring a shot for each of us, "graduate school would be a good place to start." I picked up the tequila and said, "Is there any such thing as a socialist grad school?" He clinked his glass against mine, and we knocked them back. "There's the New School for Social Research in New York City," he said, coughing. "It *used to be* something like that." "Thanks," I coughed back, then asked for my tab. "See you next term!" I shouted on my way out, then stumbled back to my MacBook. "Girl!" I chided myself for drinking too much as I struggled to type *"New School"* into the Google search bar, *"Get it together!"* Minding my own words, I shut one eye (to correct my double vision) and set to work, filling out my online application.

". . . and send!" I said, on January 15, 2011, at 12:55 a.m. "Woo hoo!" I cheered, breaking the silence of the student center and making the other late-night studiers jump. "Sorry!" I called out, but I couldn't contain myself. "I just applied to the New School with five minutes to spare!" "New York City?" whispered the guy two tables down. "Yep!" I whispered back, beaming. "That's where I'm headed!" "But why's the deadline 1 a.m.?" he asked. "The time change, silly," I laughed. "It's one hour ahead." "Exactly," he said, "it's 2 a.m. there." *Uh oh,* my smile melted away. "Fuck!" I shouted. "Fuck, fuck, fuck fuck, *fuck!* It's two hours late!" Everyone laughed and I hurried off a worried e-mail: I apologized "for my stupidity" and begged them, "Please forgive me," then lied through my freaking teeth: "I'm usually very punctual, I promise, and if you give me another chance, I swear I won't ever be late again!"

It turned out to be no big deal, though, according to the confirmation e-mail I received the next morning that went on to say, "We look forward to reviewing your application and we'll be in touch soon." *Whew!* With that done, I picked up a copy of the *New York Times* and sat down to breakfast. If was a first for me, but it soon became my morning ritual: it made me feel "cultured," like a *real New Yorker.* Every day, it seemed, there was a cool fashion show, a fancy restaurant opening, a brand new art exhibit, a big Broadway show: I found the hustle and bustle of it all enticing and started to imagine a life for myself there. The Sunday before Valentine's Day, though, I went to grab the *Times* but was drawn to the local paper instead: in big, bold letters on the front page of the *Post Crescent,* the headline read, "Watchdog Report: Wisconsin Teachers Feel Budget-Cutting Pressure." Below it, the article said that "on Friday," February 11, 2011, Governor Scott Walker "unveiled a budget repair bill that would require public state employees, including teachers, to pay thousands of dollars more each for benefits, limit wage increases and put an end to many of the collective bargaining rights that have long helped them protect their jobs." Given what I'd just experienced firsthand at Hyde Park Academy, I was outraged immediately. And the story that unfolded thereafter came to consume me completely and overwhelm entirely any plan for graduate school—or even graduation.

For the next few days, I watched closely as the events unraveled: scouring the Internet, devouring articles and blogs, following the scenes through news coverage and raw footage from YouTube. When the newly elected right-wing governor released the details of his bill, it was the shot heard around Wisconsin. "Union busting!" cried the Democrats and Big Labor, sounding the alarm for troops to start mobilizing immediately for the upcoming battle at the Capitol building in Madison. The following day, Saturday, February 12, union leaders started signing up workers to testify against the bill, while approximately 150 Wisconsinites demonstrated outside the Capitol in Madison and another 100 protested at the governor's mansion on Sunday. On Monday, protests escalated when Governor Walker formally announced his bill, publicly stating that it "would generate $30 million in savings before June 30th and $300 million over the next two-year budget by forcing state workers to contribute more to their pensions and healthcare." In response, hundreds of University of Wisconsin–Madison students and instructors walked out of their classrooms to stand in solidarity with unionized workers and defend their rights and benefits. By Tuesday, it became a mass mobilization with 10,000 rallied outside and 3,000 more inside the Capitol building, including some 800 high schoolers who walked in support of their teachers and hundreds of union workers, lined up to speak in an attempt to filibuster the Finance Committee's vote on the measure, most of them expressing a willingness to make financial sacrifices but not cuts in collective bargaining rights. Nonetheless, Republicans voted to approve the bill late that evening, passing it on to the Senate while protestors, in turn, set up camp overnight to await the next round. On Wednesday, February 16, Madison Metropolitan School District canceled classes when "more than 40% of its 2600 union-covered employees called in sick"—the crowd outside the Capitol swelled to 20,000 while the group inside set up an indefinite occupation.

Watching it all play out on the screen, I found myself thinking of Granddaddy's stories of the sixties and considered that there never would've been a March on Washington if everyone had stayed home, instead, and streamed it. I knew I should go, especially after student-teaching in Chicago: How would those kids, those communities, those teachers survive on *even less* than they had now? They wouldn't, I realized, *and that was the point.* Scott Walker was saying, "These people are disposable—*Let 'em die!*—they can be replaced." I had to go, I decided, and told my professors as much: it's not right to stay here, safe in the Bubble, while people out there are fighting to stay alive, people, I might add, who keep us alive: firefighters, police officers, nurses, and, yes, teachers too. If we don't stand up for them, who will take care of us? Who will Scott Walker come for next, once he's finished with them? "I hope you understand," I wrote, "but if you don't, that's okay too. This is something I have to do. I don't know when I'll be back, but I'm prepared to suffer the consequences." I threw a toothbrush and some clothes in a backpack, then ran off to join the movement!

I arrived in Madison in the wee hours of Thursday, February 17, or roughly the same time the fourteen Senate Democrats fled the state to temporarily block the bill and force Republicans to negotiate. That morning, as more than fifteen school districts closed, teachers from all over Wisconsin flooded into Madison and grew to 25,000 with me, among them, shouting, "This is what democracy looks like!" On Friday, many schools remained closed, and the number of protesters gathered in Capitol Square grew to an estimated 40,000—drawing enough people, finally, to attract national media attention and the support of influential people, like Reverend Jesse Jackson of the Rainbow PUSH Coalition and Richard Trumka, president of the American Federation of Labor and Congress of Industrial Organizations (both of whom I got to see speak!). But then, *on Saturday,* 70,000 people descended on Madison, and I was *literally* moved to tears by the deafening roar—the power of the people shouting, *"Kill the Bill!"* Admittedly, though, a few thousand there were Tea Partiers bussed in by the Koch brothers (and other uber-rich assholes) to protest *our protest:* "Pass the Bill," they shouted back—but, that day, our voices spoke louder than money, and we quickly overwhelmed them.

And there it was—*in action!*—the reason why we, the people, require the right to collectively bargain: with a lot of our government officials controlled by corporate interests, the only way for ordinary people to protect their rights is to stand together in common cause. The right to collective bargaining is as much a necessity for democratic self-rule as the right to vote on Election Day.

Everyone at Lawrence should be here to see this, I thought. It's a lesson more important than any other they were learning this instant. I kept calling all my friends, telling them, "Come up! Come up!" but they were stuck in the Bubble—they couldn't see what was happening outside of them, didn't know there was *a movement* going on. The Lawrence Bubble had a certain charm, I couldn't deny it: the seclusion intensified our learning and fostered a strong sense of community. But if it gets to the point that we become so self-centered, so wrapped up in our books, that we ignore the real world happening outside of us, the real people asking for our help—then what kind of citizen is Lawrence really teaching us to be? Not one I could be proud of, that was for sure, so I decided to go back to campus and organize a rally—if they wouldn't come to Madison, I'd bring Madison to them.

A few days later, I stood at the entrance of Bobst Library, in the center of campus, facing a crowd of about two hundred, and delivered my very first political speech:

I'm an out-of-state, full-time student at a private college. Last week, though, I went to Madison to join the fight for public sector workers. Standing alongside teachers, students, nurses, police, firefighters, and workers of all trades I shouted with Wisconsin pride—this is what democracy looks like!

Y'all are used to unions here, you've had them forever—to the point, I think, that some people take them for granted. I grew up in a world without unions, though, and I can tell you firsthand: it's a cruel one for workers. Georgia is a right-to-work state: public employee unions have no legal standing. They cannot negotiate contracts and they cannot go on strike.

Back in Atlanta, my grandfather works for the American Federation of State, County & Municipal Employees, a union originally founded here in 1936. For decades, he has fought day after day for worker rights, only to return home beaten and exhausted. Grandaddy is a good man, a smart man, but when workers are divided, the best he can do is beg for their rights. So, no, I am not from Wisconsin. I am not a member of a union. I do not go to a public university, but marching on the Capitol with tens of thousands of workers in Madison, I knew well the reality of the words: Union busting is Disgusting—for everyone's sake, let's kill the bill!

"Kill the bill! Kill the bill!" they chanted with such force it echoed off the buildings and rang out all across campus. Looking out at the students and professors standing side-by-side with workers and their families, I was awestruck by the simple power of solidarity.

It's not that people don't want to work together, I decided. *Politics doesn't have to be divisive.* If you just get people together, get them talking, and ask the right questions—I was convinced!—they'd find out they have a lot more in common than not and that they could do a lot more together than they could apart. I was also convinced that I'd finally figured out what I wanted to be when I grew up: a bridge between people, someone who helped others feel what I'd felt in Madison.

CHAPTER 4

Activist

*W*hether it was as a Democrat in Texas or a Socialist in college, I'd always been the most radical person wherever I was—that is, until I moved to New York City and joined Occupy Wall Street. Most of my fellow "Occupiers" shrugged me off as some sort of moderate; others saw me as a serious threat to the movement. The first time I spoke in a meeting, a girl in all black with combat boots commented, "Wow! You're a *huge* liberal!" "Thanks!" I responded. I had no idea she'd meant it as an insult.

IN AUGUST 2011 I LEFT the comfort of my grandmother's home in Atlanta to start my new life as a graduate student in Manhattan. But the master's program at the New School was just the legitimate front: with the 1930s in mind, I set off for the Big Apple with big dreams to start a socialist revolution (but that sounded crazy when I said it out loud). As a testament to this sentiment, my first stop was a summer socialist retreat two hours north of the city in the tiny village of Wurtsboro, New York. It was my second time attending the drinking-meeting affair hosted annually by the Young Democratic Socialists (YDS), the youth sector of the Democratic Socialists of America.

Surrounded by activists from across the country, I spent all weekend plotting my political takeover of the New School: (1) start a campus YDS chapter, then use it to organize a student worker union, (2) pack the student government, and (3) take over the school—let the students run it! Everyone was so excited by the prospect that I was unanimously elected the Northeast regional coordinator on the National Coordinating Committee. In addition to my own chapter, I'd be supporting all existing chapters from Washington, DC, to Maine and coordinating their efforts with a national student debt campaign. We had all the makings, it seemed, for a student movement just like the '60s; we just needed to stir the pot!

To any rational person, all that *and* graduate school might have seemed too much, but I had no intention of letting school get in the way of my political aims. YDS was my most serious commitment—that is, until Occupy Wall Street changed my plans entirely. Like every juicy love affair, I never saw it coming. A few days later, I found myself mesmerized; within weeks, totally infatuated; and in a matter of months, outright obsessed.

It all started like your typical blind date. It was Andrew Porter, the national coordinator of YDS, who was responsible for the setup. Though he was skeptical of those organizing the Wall Street encampment, he thought my new-to-New-York enthusiasm made me a good fit for checking out Occupy. To sell me on the idea, Andrew showed me a web page featuring an online call for the occupation by *Adbusters*, a radical Canadian magazine. An image of a ballerina perched atop the iconic bronze Wall Street bull popped up along with #OCCUPYWALLSTREET in bold black and yellow letters.

Beneath both appeared a question: "Are you ready for a Tahrir Moment?" And an answer: "On Sept 17, flood into lower Manhattan, set up tents, kitchens, peaceful barricades, and occupy Wall Street." The ad charged Wall Street as the "greatest corruptor of our democracy" and called on those who agreed to take to the streets by the thousands with "one simple demand in a plurality of voices." Andrew explained that a group inspired by the *Adbusters'* call would be meeting the very next Saturday, August 13, in Tompkins Square Park to plan the September encampment and decide what our "one simple demand" would be.

I was immediately intrigued. At the beginning of September, I'd be moving to Alphabet City (in the Lower East Side of Manhattan), and Tompkins Square Park was right in the middle of it. Worst-case scenario: no one shows, I check out my apartment and explore the neighborhood. Best-case scenario: I meet some interesting people and set up a base for YDS. I'd been on my fair share of blind dates, but Occupy was different. It certainly wasn't love at first sight, but it definitely made an impression. Midafternoon that Saturday I set off in search of the meeting. Naturally, as the rule goes, I arrived fifteen minutes late to ensure I had the chance to see them before they saw me; after a half-hour perimeter walk, I realized I'd made a big mistake. The homeless playing chess and the hipsters skating were easy to rule out, but the several groups of likely looking young folks resulted in a couple clumsy encounters. "Um, is this Occupy Wall Street?" I stumbled, met with, "Occupy what?" Apparently the international motley crew was a study abroad Meetup, whereas the well-tattooed bunch was a feminist reading circle. Walking away from giggled whispers, I realized I had absolutely no idea what this group of would-be Occupiers looked like. And then, *there was a sign*—a literal, multicolored sign leaning against a large tree that read, "#OCCUPYWALLSTREET."

I scanned the circle of fifty or so cross-legged punks and academics scribbling in notebooks or wiggling their fingers. I stood frozen for a minute, took a few steps forward, and asked, "What's with the jazz-hands?" Wrong move. They turned to look at me with scowls that nearly knocked the breath out of me—*Wow,* I thought, *these people are really serious.* A white, middle-aged, professorial type standing above the seated group moved to the center of the circle and smoothly stated, "This is our process." "Process . . . of what?" I stammered, barely audible over the collective groan. The Left (liberals, socialists, radicals, etc.) has a long history of scaring off those unschooled in their ways, and after such a pretentious introduction, I was ready to walk away myself. But the professor pulled me back in. With a painfully patient smile, he performed a well-rehearsed monologue on "the process."

Democracy in the United States, he explained, is a vertical system—a few people represent the many, and they alone make decisions that affect us all. Instead, he said, we are a general assembly governed by the principle of horizontalism—each person represents only herself, and together we make decisions that affect us all. To make the best decision for everyone, horizontalism is rule by consensus—*not* rule by majority. A majority is when at least 51 percent of voters ignore the values of the remaining 49 percent; or, worse yet, when 1 percent buys off both political parties, leaving 99 percent of Americans with a choice between bad and worse. Consensus is when the group as a whole reaches an agreement that addresses the values of each individual member. The hand gestures are a tool to guide the group to consensus on a solution to a shared problem. The discussion is organized by an agenda put together by working groups, which are made up of individuals invested in particular parts of the whole; in our case, he elaborated, we have Arts and Culture, Media, and Outreach Working Groups, with a Tactical Committee to figure out how to set up the occupation.

To address an agenda item, a participant "gets on stack"—or raises a hand to be added to the speaking list. As one member speaks, the rest of the group uses a variety of gestures to signal their level of approval or disapproval or to add or request information. A hand palm open toward the speaker with fingers up, wiggling, means "I agree." A hand palm down, horizontal to the ground with fingers up, wiggling, means "neutral" or "yeah, sort of." A hand, palm back from the speaker with fingers down, wiggling, means "I disagree." A single index finger pointed up means "point of information" or "I have an answer to your question/concern." A raised hand in the shape of a *C* means "clarifying question" or "I got lost and need you to explain something." Two hands circling one another, means "wrap it up" or "we get it, already." Two hands coming together in a shape of a triangle means "point of process" or, generally, "you're off topic" or have otherwise broken the rules of discussion.

A decision is made once *everyone agrees* to a proposed action; otherwise, discussion continues. When a time-sensitive decision must be made and reaching consensus is impossible, the facilitator—the person who volunteers or is otherwise chosen by the group to guide discussion toward consensus—will call for a "temperature check." Fingers fly all around and the facilitator takes count. With a predetermined majority the decision passes by "modified consensus"—unless there is a "block." A block is shown with fists balled and forearms crossed into an *X* at the chest and means "if this proposal passes, I *will leave* this group." Whoever "throws a block" is invited to speak on her position; in response, the group must decide whether it is willing to move forward without her.

" . . . and scene!" I thought to myself; it was like experimental theater (not unlike my star-spangled burka days at Youth Creates). Then, without missing a beat, the group resumed the discussion about what to call themselves. I didn't participate that first meeting, though; for the next few hours, I didn't really even listen. I just *watched* the ripple of fingers. The meeting came to a close with the "consensed upon" title of New York City General Assembly. I must've looked pretty lost, because the monologue man approached me, introduced himself as David, then asked, "Did you catch on?" Still entranced, I responded, "Sort of . . . ," just before a twentysomething, clean-cut guy in glasses jumped in—"Cecily?! I thought that was you!" I hesitated, unable to place him—or *anyone* I knew—in the context of what I'd just seen. "Justin!" he reminded me. "We did a Skype interview when you were protesting Scott Walker in Wisconsin." "Justin!" I squealed and hugged him. "I don't know about you, but I could *really* use a drink." And with that, I made my first Occupy friend.

Justin Wedes had been in New York City for three years teaching public school but had recently been "excessed," or laid off, in the latest round of Mayor Bloomberg's budget cuts. The experience had inspired him to get involved in activism and speak out for the rights of students, parents, and teachers of public education. At the time, Justin didn't identify with any of the "–ists" (socialist, communist, anarchist, etc.) but was introduced to Occupy Wall Street through a teacher activist network. He'd been there from the beginning but tended to observe cautiously from the edges; like me, he wasn't won over just yet.

Sensing that I felt similarly after my first meeting, he suggested we go to a nearby pub. I promptly ordered a gin and tonic, took a big gulp, and got down to it: "That David guy—he's the leader of this thing right?" "Well, no," he paused to think and sip his beer. "David is an anarchist, and anarchists don't believe in leaders." "Anarchist?" I frowned, "Like kids who paint their nails black and sport circle-A T-shirts?" He laughed, "That must've been a really confusing meeting for you." David *Graeber*, he explained, was an anthropologist and organizer who taught at Yale until, as the rumor goes, he was fired because his conservative counterparts didn't appreciate his anarchist views. In recent years, his writings had earned him a prominent position on the academic Left, and he'd become a respected activist through a decade of participation in anticapitalist demonstrations worldwide. This summer *Adbusters* published his essay "Awaiting the Magical Spark" on the same day it released the #OCCUPYWALL-STREET piece. It was unclear how much he influenced the call, but he was certainly ready and waiting when the group first formed to answer it. He and a handful of fellow anarchists directed the group away from the typical protest march into what I'd just seen: a general assembly that makes decisions to better all of our lives now, not to make demands for legislation to better some of our lives later. "So, he's not the leader," I strained to sum it up correctly, "but he is behind the whole horizontal-twinkle-finger thing?" "Sure," Justin smiled. "Got it," I lied.

It was all so confusing—almost deliberately so. All the hand signals, the jargon, it all seemed so silly, so off-putting. And yet, I could barely put Occupy out of my mind the next week. There was something going on there, something outside of the normal grind of politics, and even beyond radical business as usual. I had to see where it went. In my heart, I already knew I wanted to be a part of it.

Nonetheless, I was just as surprised as everyone else when I turned up the following Saturday. Feigning confidence, I strutted up in Jeffrey Campbell sandals and a Betsey Johnson sundress (before leaving Atlanta, I'd scoured all the secondhand shops to show up New York ready). I crossed my legs into the seemingly compulsory position—taking great pains not to expose myself or, more importantly, scuff my shoes—then looked up to find a girl with a half-shaven head and a clipboard towering awkwardly above me. I smiled and waved. She grimaced, "Are you here for Occupy Wall Street?" "Yep," smiling harder. "Should I sign that?" She hesitated, "If you want to be on the listserv." I extended my hand, "Thanks!" She looked me up and down, then reluctantly relinquished the pen. After she rejoined her friends, she muttered, "Paris Hilton" just loud enough for me to hear—they all roared with laughter. Welcome to Occupy Wall Street.

If I were the squeamish type, I might have left. But as politically intimidating as they might have been, no amount of girl-on-girl hate was going to send me packing—after three years in a sorority, this was child's play. I found the discussion easier to follow the second time around and even timidly twinkled my fingers alongside proposals for the encampment and plans to turn out the public and the press. But the meeting was nearly over by the time I finally raised my hand to speak. From those first words, I would be stamped by Occupy's inner circle as a hopelessly naïve and politically unreliable troublemaker—which would remain my reputation throughout the duration of the occupation. "Shouldn't we have a statement of nonviolence?" I stammered self-consciously when my name was called. Several hands shot up in response, one in the shape of a *C*. The facilitator, Marisa—a twenty-five-year-old innocuous-looking girl dressed in all black—called on the guy with the *C* first, "Clarifying question?" Turning toward him, I met a stare so sharp it seemed meant to pierce my soul. "How do *you* define violence?" "Like, hurting people . . . ," I replied. "What about property damage?" he retorted. "Definitely not," I retaliated, provoking the rise of yet more hands. "Given the response we're getting here," Marisa interrupted. "It looks like this ought to be on the agenda for *next* week."

The nonviolence debate became such a hot topic that, one week before we were set to occupy Wall Street, we had yet to reach consensus on it—but only because I kept bringing it up. By then, at least, people had gotten used to me even if they didn't particularly like me. But it wasn't until that day that I learned how deep our differences went—or how Marisa was likely *the least* innocuous person in Occupy Wall Street. When the issue of nonviolence came up on the agenda, I rose to present my most recent proposal but paused when I realized everyone was looking somewhere else. Following the direction of their heads, I found Marisa standing silently with her arms in the shape of an *X*. She was blocking the issue from the agenda, she stated matter-of-factly, because we had more pressing issues to discuss with the occupation right around the corner. I calmly placed my notebook on the ground, then mirrored her position: "I block the continuation of this meeting before we reach consensus on nonviolence." She argued that the decision ought to be determined by those at the occupation, that until we get there and see what we're up against we should remain open to a "diversity of tactics"—in other words, if it *really* came down to it, people unwilling to do everything necessary to start a movement should step aside and allow those willing to step up and do what needed to be done. Taken aback, I argued against the occupation altogether without a statement of nonviolence. It was the first and only block I threw during my entire time with Occupy Wall Street. Banging my forearms together, I bellowed, "If we don't take a public stance against violence, we invite and even condone it. We *will* reap what others sow; history is *not* on our side." A temperature check was taken, and the group overwhelmingly disregarded my block— "Sheer stupidity!" I seethed, before slinging my backpack over my shoulder and storming off. "I'm not going to jail for this shit!" And with that, I was no longer just the Paris Hilton of Occupy Wall Street, I was also the frigid Queen of Nonviolence.

It was a painful breakup. Even though we'd only been together a month, it tore me to pieces when the General Assembly agreed to move forward without me. Maybe it was too early for ultimatums, but I just couldn't jump on the "diversity of tactics" bandwagon; it felt like a rickety concept, likely to spiral out of control. Feeling uneasy, I called Granddaddy to get some perspective. "You did the right thing," he said, "Always go with your gut instinct. If you're wrong, you're wrong—you can always go back. But if you stay, you consent to whatever happens." Afterward he told me the cautionary tale of the untimely demise of Students for a Democratic Society in 1969.

That year, he witnessed the membership of 100,000 dissolve in a matter of months when a minority faction (the Weathermen) split from the group at large to launch guerrilla war against the US government. Granddaddy's former friends in the Weather Underground were responsible for bombing fifteen government buildings and banks from 1970 to 1974, in addition to one accidental explosion that left three of the Weathermen dead. The antiwar movement, which had once attracted a degree of popular support, became a source of public panic when the Weathermen turned to violence and became widely regarded as terrorists. In the end, Granddaddy argued, the Weathermen—and those like them—were ultimately responsible for the decline of the New Left and the progressive '60s and for the rise of the Reagan era and the conservative '80s—"everything they'd fought for, everything *we'd* fought for, got reversed . . . no, not just reversed, everything got worse."

The lesson I took from his story was twofold: whether tactically or morally, violence was not the way to go. Tactically, violence is a great motivator, but under threat of chaos people run toward order—even if it's a bad order. Morally, it's wrong to use violence to force people to do something—even if that something is the right thing. What really hammered the point home was the hypocrisy of an antiwar movement turned guerrilla war effort. To me, it was simple: a human life is a human life. When the Weathermen prioritized one over another, they crossed the same line as the businessmen and politicians they despised for using human beings as bargaining chips.

And so it was that on Saturday, September 17, 2011, the idea of Occupy Wall Street became a reality—without me. That morning, a thousand protestors (and just as many tourists) arrived at Wall Street to find it barricaded off by the New York City Police Department. The group spent several hours splitting into snake marches and reconverging at one failed contingency location after another: Chase Plaza (barred), the *Charging Bull* (barred), Bowling Green (barred). At about 3 p.m., the remaining few hundred finally made a home of the 33,000-square-foot park sandwiched between Liberty Street and Broadway, Cedar Street and Trinity Place in New York City's Financial District. The privately owned public space controlled by Brookfield Industries—one of the wealthiest real estate companies in the country—officially titled Zuccotti Park in celebration of its chairman John Zuccotti—was promptly renamed Liberty Plaza by its new residents, the Occupiers. Political motivations aside, "plaza" was certainly more appropriate than "park"; there was no grass, only concrete and metal with a few out-of-place trees. It'd been the site for a couple 9/11 ceremonies but was otherwise not all that interesting or inviting—a place for tourists and Wall Street employees to eat a slice of pizza on a warm afternoon. All that was about to change.

With great reluctance—and great resentment—I made good on my block and did not go down that first day. Instead, I did what most spurned lovers do: I spent all day Facebook-stalking the occupation and otherwise calling friends to keep tabs on it. It had an undeniable hold on me, but I didn't break—I kept reminding myself that I made the right decision for all the right reasons. By the second day, though, my mantra wore thin and I gave in. Besides, despite the many who believed in a "diversity of tactics," the street skirmishes on September 17 were nonviolent—at least on the part of the Occupiers. As would be the case throughout the entire Zuccotti Park occupation and its aftermath, the only violence would come at the hands of the police. Occupy Wall Street remained nonviolent in practice *and* the General Assembly publicly endorsed the strategy in its Principles of Solidarity: "Today, we proudly remain in Liberty Square constituting ourselves as autonomous political beings engaged in non-violent civil disobedience and building solidarity based on mutual respect, acceptance, and love."

When it came down to it, I was itching to go, and there just wasn't a good reason to stay away. But for all that excitement, my first trip to Liberty Plaza was beyond disappointment; I was outright embarrassed to be associated with Occupy Wall Street (definitely not something I'd bring home to mother). I approached the park from Broadway and passed between a big red cube sculpture and a bigger red stick sculpture, before heading down the rabbit hole. Making my way from one side of Liberty Plaza to the other, I found myself in *someone's* wonderland—just someone decidedly different from me. I hurried past a band of painted street performers, around a dozen "downward dog" yogis, and froze face-to-nipple with three sets of liberated breasts. Just then a bunch of kids in *V for Vendetta* masks ran by, and, trailing them, I got pulled into a very Hare Krishna experience. It was like a drum circle without drugs yet so oddly spiritual that everyone might as well have been high. After politely declining a tambourine and an invitation to dance, I crossed the sea of flying limbs and swinging instruments to the isle of castaway protest signs. Exploring the rows and rows of posters, I found the terrain shallow and rife with whimsy: "Shit is Fucked Up and Bullshit," "I'm So Angry, I Made this Sign." I was midway through an eye roll after "Kill All Pigs" when I tripped on a paint can and figured that was the universe telling me to put up or shut up.

I saw a cardboard box next to a nearby trashcan and tore off a piece; squatting next to the can I took the paintbrush in hand and, without thinking, wrote, "Power Concedes Nothing without a Demand." "It never has and it never will," a familiar voice finished the famous words of Frederick Douglass. I looked back to find the cheerful face of David Haack, a friend I'd made while planning the occupation. David, soft spoken and a deep thinker, was a twenty-six-year-old tutor by day and a punk rock musician by night; two years earlier he ran for City Council of his hometown, White Plains—an affluent suburb north of New York City—"to fight the corporate influence of Walmart." He found Occupy through a fellow musician and showed up to the second planning meeting. He sat through an hour of strategizing the occupation before raising his hand, "Are we gonna get to *why* we're here, or are we just gonna keep talking about how to do it?" The group voted against discussing demands—"We can figure that out when we get there"—and David walked out. But, like me, he couldn't stay away.

I hugged him. "I knew you'd come back," he teased. "Well," he gestured to Liberty Plaza, "what do you think?" The silly scene before me was a painful reminder of our failed attempt to make Occupy more accessible to serious political players like unions and community organizations. "I think the Outreach Working Group should've put up a bigger fight." We'd been part of the group that formed in August to turn out local leftist organizations to meet *Adbusters'* call for a 20,000-person occupation—but given the few hundred who showed up on September 17, we were far from it. Standing in the park that second night, David and I reminisced about how hard it had been to sell people on Occupy Wall Street. From the get-go, it was difficult to mobilize people without a clear message. Every time we told people about September 17, they'd ask, "Now *what exactly* are you occupying for?" Every time, we would answer the only way the General Assembly allowed us to: "Show up, and we'll figure that out together!" And *every time,* it was a nonstarter: "Hmmm . . . interesting. Get back to me when you figure out what you stand for." After a week of striking out, we tried drafting a mission statement the General Assembly could sit with. It took a dozen of us five hours to decide on a one-sentence statement: "Empowerment for all equals justice for all—the corporate domination of our economy and government is destroying our lives and communities, therefore we are calling a General Assembly on Wall Street on September 17th to achieve real democratic participation." It had been an exhausting but worthwhile endeavor; had the General Assembly approved the statement on the following day, August 20, we would have had nearly an entire month left to launch a solid outreach effort.

But, of course, it didn't get approved—and now, a month later, we were stuck with the circus before us. I was so frustrated with the groupthink mentality of the General Assembly. But, then again, I found it kind of incredible that, for all of our arguing, there we all were. "I can't believe we actually did it," I said to David. "We really are *occupying Wall Street*." "Yeah," David agreed, "looks like horizontalism works after all." I hated to admit it, but he was right: for as irritating as "the process" could be, I found it endearing that it prioritized inclusion over efficiency. Staring off into the mounting pile of sleeping bags, I came to the bittersweet realization that I was falling in love with Occupy Wall Street.

THAT FIRST WEEK AT LIBERTY PLAZA was a whirlwind. Most people think it was just a matter of setting up a few tents—but, as a matter of fact, there were no tents until September 20, the fourth day of the occupation. Lupe Fiasco, a politically progressive hip-hop artist, donated fifty family-sized tents the first day of the occupation; however, by the end of the third nightly meeting, the General Assembly remained gridlocked on whether to use them, and the issue was once again tabled pending further discussion. It wasn't a debate of personal preference—of course, everyone preferred sleeping in tents over sleeping outside—but of legal standing. The New York Chapter of the National Lawyers Guild, an association of activist lawyers and legal workers founded in 1937 in protest of the politically conservative American Bar Association, advised the General Assembly that sleeping in the park was a lawful act, but erecting structures was not. By putting up tents, we ran the risk of getting arrested and, more importantly, of losing the park. It had been so difficult to occupy to begin with that we knew once it was gone, they'd never give it back. We didn't find the decision easy to make, so a few folks took the initiative to make it for us.

On the evening of September 19, I joined the postassembly march, which took off toward Union Square instead of its usual loop around Wall Street. The police were so busy chasing us around that the park was left largely unattended; when we returned to Liberty Plaza several hours later, there were tents awaiting us. Well, I thought, that's that. It wasn't a matter of *if* but *when* the cops would come for us—just the day before, they had locked up a handful of Occupiers for the heinous crime of "defacing" the sidewalk with children's chalk. There was nothing left to do but wait. As the sun rose over Liberty Park that Tuesday, the full force of the NYPD rose with it. Occupy Wall Street awoke to find itself surrounded—well, *more* surrounded that usual. Justin Wedes, my first Occupy friend, was afraid the police were planning to incite a riot as an excuse to evict us; trying to prepare for the invasion, he mounted a ledge with a megaphone and called for an emergency General Assembly: "When the police come, we need to stay calm and hold our ground."

Just then, dozens of police rushed the park. A few dozen protestors raced to the tents, stood side by side, and linked arms around them. Two officers seized the megaphone from Justin, snapped him around, and secured his hands behind his back—something about a sound violation. A line of officers stormed a line of protestors, pulled them apart, put them in zip ties, and pushed them into a police van. In the minutes that followed, several lines of officers tore down all the tents and took seven of us away with them; at the same time, another set of officers picked through the camp and snatched up five kids wearing those *V for Vendetta* masks—unbeknownst to us, there was a 150-year-old New York State law banning masked gatherings (with the exception of masquerade parties). September 20 became a mile marker in Occupy history: we were shaken but had otherwise survived the first round of arrests in the park. As for me, that was the day I turned twenty-three—it was not yet noon, but already I could tell it was going to be a year to remember.

From then on, dealing with the NYPD became a function of everyday life at Liberty Plaza. Putting it nicely, they were our neighbors from hell. With a small battalion of vans, cars, scooters, and sometimes horses, the police shut down Liberty Street and set up their own occupation next to our own. The nearby McDonald's was a neutral zone serving all of our bathroom needs—during our time together, there wasn't a single occupier who didn't share a line (and a pee dance) with a uniformed officer. Most of the time the hundred or so officers just stood around and talked to each other or otherwise sat in their cars and ate fast food. And, of course, they watched us. And, of course, we watched them. When we moved, they moved. Sometimes they beat us back, but every time it backfired—we had a saying: "Screw us, and we multiply." On Wednesday, September 21, 2,000 people protesting that evening's scheduled execution of Troy Davis—a black prisoner in Georgia, widely believed to have been wrongly convicted of murdering a white police officer—marched from Union Square to Liberty Plaza. Much of the march stuck around for the evening General Assembly, and the meeting reached a record one thousand participants. By the end of the first week of the occupation, the influx of newcomers encouraged the daily march down a new path: "Off of the sidewalk, into the streets!" Five hundred people flooded onto Broadway heading toward Union Square, halting traffic

all along the way. A hundred police, probably more if you include un-
dercovers, surrounded the crowd and arrested eighty of them.

The mass arrest of peaceful protestors on September 24 marked
yet another milestone for Occupy; the event was captured on cellphone cameras and spread worldwide on social media, while the video
of a police officer pepper-spraying two sobbing women went viral.
Back at the park, we watched along on our phones helpless to prevent
the horror unfolding a half mile north of us. Over the next few hours,
people trickled into the park and silently waited for the arrestees to
return—we all needed to see for ourselves that they were okay. When
they had yet to arrive by the 7 p.m. General Assembly, the only thing
to do was worry together: "Where are they being held?" "When will
they be released?" "Do we have enough lawyers?" "Do we have enough
bail?" A calm woman with a clipboard and a lime green hat that read
"National Lawyers Guild" assured us that her colleagues were keeping
tabs on all those arrested and were trying to get them released by
nightfall. Still, we worried, and still, we waited—until every last one
of them came home. Late that evening, each arrestee returned to the
cheers of an assembly that totaled as many as a thousand. And the
next morning, Occupy Wall Street awoke with a camp that spanned
more than five hundred.

By the start of that second week, Liberty Plaza had formed into a
landscape fit for a growing occupation. Dead center of the park was
the People's Kitchen; north of it was the trash and recycling center,
east of it was the General Assembly meeting area, and the encampment bordered it to the south and west. In addition to housing overnight Occupiers, the encampment also included a medic station and
comfort center: the former was a first-aid post, the latter was a free
store that collected and distributed donated clothes, sleeping materi-
als, and toiletries. It stretched from the center of the park across the
entire southern perimeter and lined the stairs on the western edge.

The stairs were reserved for the almost continuous—and often contentious—drum circle. The northwest corner beside it was declared a sacred space for people to do yoga, tai chi, and meditate under the "Tree of Life"—a tree on Trinity Place standing short amid the towering cement jungle. Beginning there and running east alongside Liberty Street to Broadway, the entire northern border of Liberty Plaza was packed with a variety of workspaces and resources. Adjacent to the sacred space was the art space, a sprawling section set aside for creating protest propaganda and street theater. Next was the media space, where a bunch of kids on laptops coordinated the online spread of Occupy Wall Street worldwide through social media: the Facebook page (Occupy Wall St.), the Twitter feed (#TweetBoat), the Tumblr (99 Percent Project), the live-stream channel (GlobalRevolution.tv), the Liberty Plaza website (nycga.net), and the global movement website (occupywallst.org). The media space also included the information table to welcome newcomers and, more importantly, to liaise with mainstream press—or provide press correspondents with participants who were trained to say "the right thing." Beside it, the stacks of books rounding the northeast corner marked the People's Library. By day it offered Occupiers a wide array of donated and dumpstered reading material; by night it became a makeshift cinema projecting movies onto a bedsheet—one guy got the idea to set up a free cigarette stand nearby, and the whole affair became known as "Nic-at-Night."

Along with the landscape, new structures had similarly arisen to address the needs of a growing General Assembly. Instead of one meeting each week, there were two every day. The morning assembly was for camp-specific concerns, so the agenda came from the Food Working Group (of the People's Kitchen), the Sanitation Working Group (of the trash and recycling center), the Comfort Working Group (of the comfort center), and the De-escalation Working Group, recently founded to mediate tensions among residents of Liberty Plaza, as well as between them and the NYPD. The nightly assembly was for movement building: planning actions, mobilizing media attention, partnering with local organizations, and so on.

But no matter how it grew, the General Assembly stuck to the same twinkle-finger method. And to amplify the voice of one speaker to hundreds (eventually thousands) of listeners, we picked up the People's Microphone (or People's Mic). It's a pretty simple, but *very* slow, process: before you speak, you call out, "Mic check!" and the crowd responds, "Mic check!" Then you say a few words, pause for everyone to repeat them, and so on and so forth until you've said what you needed to; if the crowd is so big that people in the back still can't hear, then the People's Mic can be extended to three rounds—but even that's pushing it a little.

And so it was with the People's Mic that we echoed our way through that second week. September 25: "Mic check! Anonymous [the infamous hacktivist group] put up a video on YouTube threatening to take down the NYPD if there's any more brutality." September 26: "Mic check! Michael Moore [the leftist filmmaker] is in the park!" September 27: "Mic check! We're marching to join the postal workers' rally against the five-day delivery week." September 28: "Mic check! The Transit Workers Union just voted unanimously to endorse Occupy Wall Street," and later, "Mic check! Kelly [New York City's police commissioner] just announced that the NYPD cannot shut us down—the law says the park must stay open 24/7." September 30: "Mic check! Several hundred members of the Transit Workers Union and the Professional Staff Congress at CUNY [the City University of New York] are now at One Police Plaza protesting the NYPD's treatment of Occupy." October 1: "Mic check! The police trapped seven hundred people on the Brooklyn Bridge, and now they're arresting every last one of them!"

It was like clockwork: another Saturday, another march, another mass arrest—a bigger march, a bigger arrest, a bigger movement. Like every Saturday before it, October 1, too, became the stuff of legend. It was nearly 4 p.m. when a thousand or so marching from Liberty Plaza met the NYPD at the base of the bridge. A couple hundred headed up the pedestrian walkway while others held back and waited for the larger group to gather. Just as the crowd spilled into traffic, a call broke from the frontlines: "Whose bridge?" "Our bridge!" those behind them responded. As the chant rolled backward over the crowd to the bottom of the march, the march pushed forward into Brooklyn-bound traffic to the top of the bridge. The officers, in turn, directed traffic away from the march and silently walked it all the way up. But *the moment* it hit the middle of the bridge, the NYPD corralled the march into a massive orange net. It took hours, but everyone was processed by the line of officers ready and waiting with reams of citations and garbage bags of flex-cuffs—then *all of them* were loaded up and taken to jail. About half of those arrested that night belonged to a union, and *every one* of their unions took an injury to one as an injury to all.

Four days later, on Wednesday, October 5, 15,000 workers and students marched to Liberty Plaza in support of Occupy Wall Street. Coordinating with the solidarity efforts of the Transit Workers Union and the CUNY Professional Staff Congress, New York Communities for Change (a grassroots neighborhood, tenant, and worker organization) drafted a call to action: "Let's march down to Wall Street to welcome the protesters and show the faces of New Yorkers hardest hit by corporate greed"; together, the three of them then solicited every major labor and community organization in New York City to endorse the Liberty Plaza occupation and the Community/Labor March to Wall Street, and the Professional Staff Congress also liaised with CUNY activists who, in turn, called for a citywide student walkout to the march.

I went to class that Wednesday but didn't hear a word anyone said—I just sat watching the minute hand tick toward 3 p.m. By the time it arrived, I was already out of the door and into the hall, shouting, "Out of your desk and into the street!" About ten of us left school together and walked nine blocks south to join the students converging in Washington Square Park. Over the next hour, groups came from campuses all across the city: Columbia, Cooper Union, City University of New York, State University of New York, the New School, New York University, and more. At 4 p.m. hundreds of students headed south from Washington Square Park on a mile-and-a-half march to Foley Square. Marching with them, I was reminded of my first walkout in high school—the first time I'd felt the thrill—*the power!*—of standing up for something right, walking out against something wrong, and taking back the streets: for the people, by the people, of the people.

At the same time, thousands of protestors headed north from Liberty Plaza on a three-quarter-mile march to the same place. From opposite sides, the students and Occupiers arrived to a rally of more than 10,000 workers—fifteen unions and twenty-four community organizations had endorsed Occupy Wall Street, printed the call to action, and distributed it to their members. Around 5 p.m., an estimated crowd of 15,000 protestors marched down Broadway to Liberty Plaza. On what *Business Insider* called "the most important day yet of Occupy Wall Street," every major media outlet came down to the park—for most, it was their first time. In solidarity with New York City, people the world over posted photos of themselves with the caption "I'm the 99%" as part of a "virtual march" on MoveOn .org. A Rasmussen poll released earlier that day found that Occupy Wall Street enjoyed "a higher approval rating (33 percent) than does Congress (14 percent)." Keeping step with the shifting public opinion, several top Democrats publicly endorsed the movement, including

House Democratic Caucus chair John Larson (the fourth-ranking House Democrat), cochairs of the Congressional Progressive Caucus Representatives Raul Grijalva (D-AZ) and Keith Ellison (D-MN), and Representative Louise Slaughter (D-NY)—who referenced the Arab Spring in applauding the march as a sign of a coming "American Autumn."

It was nearly 8 p.m. by the time the People's Mic fell silent over Liberty Plaza; with sore feet and lost voices, hundreds of the remaining thousands began to trickle back toward whatever borough they called home. In one day we'd made 15,000 new friends and hit headlines worldwide. What more could we want? Wall Street. Liberty Plaza was wonderful, but we still wanted Wall Street—and some of us thought the time ripe for the taking. A couple dozen huddled in a distant corner and discussed the prospect. When I approached, a hooded man was talking: "We might not get this opportunity again—a crowd so big with so much clout." To everyone's surprise, I agreed. "It's the perfect time. With all the unions here, there's no way they'll arrest us—the blowback would make this march look like kindergarten shit. But if they're dumb enough to do it—all the better for us." A kid with half his face hidden by a bandana jumped in, "Look, people are leaving. So if we're gonna go—we gotta go now." Heads nodded all around. "Alright," I responded, "let's do this."

About thirty of us stalked off toward Broadway, hung a quick right and headed south three blocks. With hurried whispers—"Wall Street!"—we swept the crowds lining the way. Seconds later, we passed Trinity Church on the right and rounded left onto Wall Street with 3,000 at our backs. We intended to rush the intersection and storm one block east to 11 Wall Street—home of the New York Stock Exchange. Traders with hand signals, screens with numbers, the daily gamble of the stock market—it's what most people think of when they hear "Wall Street." If we got there, Occupy Wall Street would be more than a camp at a nearby park; it would *literally inhabit* the heart and soul of American capitalism. But, alas, the dream would go unrealized.

That night was our best shot, but it stalled out at the Broadway–Wall Street intersection—oddly enough, our plan was foiled not by the police but by our own. Blocking the entrance, a hundred or so sat encircled holding a General Assembly on whether to do exactly what we were already in the process of doing. Ted Hall, in his early twenties but a vision from the free-love '60s, stood up when he saw us coming and announced, "Everyone needs to be patient, and participate in the process to reach consensus on the march." I said, "We've *been* patient! And we *have* consensus—*everyone here* is here for Wall Street. Now join us or move along—the police are here and we're marching!"

Just then officers broke through the flooded sidewalk on the right—armed with a stack of barricades. Most of the circle rose and ran left—Ed ran to my left and linked his arm around my own. "Ready?" he asked. I nodded, taking the arm of the bandana kid on my right—"Everyone link up!" I shouted. I clasped my hands across my chest, locked eyes with the police captain in front of me and counted down: "10-9-8 . . ." the police filed in from the left; "7-6-5 . . ." they brought out the barricades; "4-3-2 . . ." they lined them up before us; "1!" they clinked the line into place *right* before we rushed Wall Street. Two dozen of us at the front of the line managed a few measured steps forward before the force of the march slammed us face-to-face into the line of officers. They threw their weight behind the bars, and we pushed forward a foot or so then fell back. "Again!" I yelled. And again, the human barricade flung me headlong into a police line now armed with pepper spray. Whatever ground we gained, we quickly lost beneath the toxic shower. "Again!" I yelled.

In the blinking haze, I saw batons swing out before my body banged into the metal. In that final attempt, our line held out against helpless odds. We neither advanced nor retreated but stood our ground until officers broke through the barricades and beat us down. The captain who had held my gaze from across the line side-stepped the bars and stood front and center, swinging his baton back and forth against the circle of protestors around him. A few feet away, Ed took one to the face and fell to the ground. "Everybody sit down!" I managed, before a blow to the back of my head knocked me clean off my feet. I crawled over to Ed and together we tried to recover the frontline into a sit-in: we crossed our legs, linked our arms, and formed our fingers into peace signs. All around us our friends dropped like flies, and faster than I could say, *This is bullsh*—a boot barreled into my chest and laid me out, too. I looked up to find the same captain towering over me. He reared back and flipped me over with a kick so sharp it cracked a rib. He wrangled my wrists together and clinked the cuffs so tight they broke the skin. He grabbed the chain by the middle and jerked me up so hard he dislocated my shoulder. Then he slammed me forward so fast it snapped back into place.

When my shoulder went *pop!* I burst into tears. The officer responded, "Shut up! You get what you deserve, cunt bitch!" I shot back, "I beg your pardon?!" It was the first time I'd ever heard the "c-word" firsthand—it was strictly forbidden in the world of southern niceties I grew up in. That final moment—head back, mouth wide open screaming with mascara streaming down my cheeks—was photographed and published in *Rolling Stone*. A month later it appeared alongside an article detailing my work with the Demands Working Group and our general role in the great debate of Occupy Wall Street: What changes, if any, should we demand from our government? But on the night that photo was taken, there had yet to be any real discussion of demands. Apparently, all it took was one night in a holding cell to light a fire under my ass. By the time a guard called my name, I'd come to an important realization: taking a beating for my beliefs was all well and good, but my suffering (or anyone else's) wouldn't stand for shit until Occupy Wall Street stood for *something*. The next morning I walked out of the precinct without any charges and was approached by a woman from the National Lawyers Guild. She had seen the captain beat me and suggested I file civil suit for excessive force; she also said I had been unlawfully arrested since they'd held me without charging me with a crime. Had I taken her advice, it might have saved me a world of trouble down the line—but I just couldn't be bothered. I was in a hurry to go home and sleep, so I could wake up and go back to the park—I was dead set on getting Occupy Wall Street to demand concrete political change.

By 5 p.m. that same day, I was back at Liberty Plaza and hard at work. I bumped into David Haack—who'd always shared my frustrations—and he agreed to help me. We put our heads together and figured that our best chance to do the most good was to advocate for and partner with unionized workers. Since 2009, Mayor Bloomberg had stranded one-third of the city's 300,000 employees with unsettled contracts, while his recently approved budget had left another 3,600 on the chopping block. City workers made up a majority of the march to support Occupy Wall Street; shouldn't we stand up for them? We could demand that Mayor Bloomberg stop firing city workers and stalling union contracts, or we could demand that Congress fund and create more jobs—or both! David and I then brought the idea to members of the Labor Outreach Committee, who had been coordinating the union solidarity actions. I suggested that we organize a Labor General Assembly of supportive union leadership to work out a shortlist of demands then have them march their members down to Liberty Plaza and ask Occupy Wall Street to endorse it—"It'd only be right, they endorsed our occupation." "But regardless," I explained, "the General Assembly can't face thousands of struggling workers and just say no. Even those unsympathetic will have to be strategic—it'd be suicide to turn them away. The fact is, union support *is* public support." Those I spoke to were intrigued but ultimately wary of such a calculated move. They worried that the Occupy leadership would accuse us of staging a coup, of allowing Big Labor to co-opt the movement. Instead, the few interested members of the Labor Outreach Committee opted for the path of least resistance: they put together a Demands Working Group of Occupy Wall Street and invited union members to join us at Liberty Plaza.

A few days later, on Monday, October 10, the first Demands Working Group meeting was called to order at 5:30 p.m.—although it was anything but orderly! From the very beginning to the bitter end, the leaders of this supposedly leaderless movement were highly resistant to even the idea of us *just meeting*. Not for lack of effort, there was little, if any, discussion of possible demands. Instead, that first meeting was sidelined by a debate absurdly reminiscent of our American forefathers: namely, on the freedom of press and the right to assemble in Occupy Wall Street. In good faith, I announced at the beginning of the meeting that the woman next to me, Meredith Hoffman, was a journalist for the *New York Times* interested in doing a story on the group. Almost everyone was happy to have her, but two people threw up blocks: "Press is handled by the Media Working Group. You're trying to represent Occupy, and you don't." I said, "Journalists are always here interviewing all sorts of people. Meredith, *these* people are the Demands Working Group. The views and values depicted here do not reflect all of Occupy Wall Street." The group bypassed the block and agreed to let Meredith stay. "Now that we know Meredith," I laughed, "how about the rest of us introduce ourselves." Round two: the same pair blocked again. "What?" I asked. "We shouldn't meet each other?" "No, *this group* shouldn't meet," one said. "Occupy isn't about changing the government." The other explained, "The system's broken and it *can't* be fixed—Occupy is about making solutions for ourselves. We are our demand—we're building a better model in Liberty Plaza." The general response was yes, but until the world catches up, we need political changes to help those suffering now.

The political debate went on for an hour, before I finally shut it down with "the process." I explained, "The General Assembly calls for working groups to form organically around a shared need for a solution. We all share a need for Occupy to adopt a political agenda, so we came together to draft demands. You can block our proposals when we bring them to the Assembly, but right now you're infringing on *our right* to meet." That should have put an end to it, but it was only just beginning. Those two, or others like them, disrupted every Demands meeting—mostly they'd just argue, but sometimes they'd shove cameras with bright lights in our faces. One time they filibustered the discussion for several hours to whittle us down and vote to dissolve us. Another time, they removed the group from the Occupy website we used to coordinate our meetings. They never did shut us down, though—the harder they tried, the closer it brought us together.

The Demands Working Group was a motley crew of more than twenty core members, with upwards of seventy attending our largest meeting. We were professors, political consultants, bartenders, former bankers, musicians, union organizers, and everything in between. Together we made up the Left and beyond; we were Democrats, socialists, communists, anarchists, and even libertarians. We were seventeen to eighty years old and came from the 1930s Silent Generation on through the current millennials. Like Occupy in general, we were mostly white—with a small but consistent black, Latino, and Asian presence that made us unique. For a short time, the Demands Working Group became my family—my home in Occupy Wall Street. After meetings, the younger crowd gathered at a nearby pub, and it was there that I forged my own little activist clique: Jake Stevens, the publisher of Verso Books; Susan Kang, a professor at John Jay College; Andrew Gimma, a computer programmer; Erek Tinker, a party planner and political consultant; Walter Adler, a paramedic; and Chavisa Woods, a writer who became my first anarchist friend. For the next month, we met twice a week and otherwise sent a contingent to nightly assemblies. About two weeks in, we took up the additional ritual of Friday Solidarity Drinking. About the same time we settled on our first demand and held two Saturday teach-ins, the first at the New School and the second at Liberty Plaza.

On October 30, the Demands Working Group headed to Liberty Plaza to present our first demand to the General Assembly. We neared the park, and it was already brimming with people. Caught up in my own little piece of the whole, I'd nearly forgotten how much the occupation had grown after the failed eviction attempt two weeks earlier: On October 12, Occupiers observing the Jewish holiday, Sukkot, erected a sukkah, or "booth" with four walls and a leaf-covered roof reminiscent of ancient Hebrew dwellings during their forty-year journey to freedom. The Occupy sukkah remained standing through the evening, untouched by the police, and became the first erected structure in Liberty Plaza. Hours later, we were given notice to clear the park by Friday, October 14, as it would be closed for cleaning. By 6 a.m., 3,000 union workers descended on Liberty Plaza to defend it; Brookfield Industries postponed the cleaning, and we started setting up tents. From then on, there were always around 1,000 people in the park and up to 2,000 attending assemblies each night. Now, more than ever, we *never* got through the whole meeting agenda—which was what the facilitators were counting on when they slotted our demand proposal for last.

"You're just trying to silence us!" I charged. Instead, they maintained that the agenda was set according to urgency. "Yeah, well, we *urgently* need demands!" I argued in vain, then stomped off to try another approach. I asked the other groups presenting if they'd let us go first, and to my surprise, all but two agreed. The two items had been allotted twenty minutes each, but two hours passed and we had yet to speak. At 8:45 p.m., the facilitators finally called on us, and we finally understood what they were doing: they'd given us a forty-minute bloc, then pushed us into the last fifteen minutes of the meeting. It was now or never, though, so I stepped in front of the assembly with the two others selected to read the proposal. "Mic check!" I shouted. "Mic check!" the crowd responded. "We are a delegation . . . ," I began. "We are a delegation . . . ," they repeated. "From the Demands Working Group," I continued—the crowd echoed on, and a dozen in front stood up together in a line of blocks. Marisa Holmes—the same woman who stopped my nonviolence proposal weeks before—spoke on behalf of the group. She said we couldn't present our proposal because our group wasn't registered with the New York City General Assembly. A friend of hers rushed up with a camera and blinded me from the thousands repeating her words three rounds back. My mind raced against their voices, then the whole park fell silent. "The Demands Working Group . . . ," I began, no clue where to go from there. "Is under the impression that . . . ," I stalled again. Then I shrugged my shoulders and said, "We are, in fact, a working group." When the crowd finished, there was a slight pause and then—everyone started laughing! Even those who didn't want demands couldn't take the petty, bureaucratic ploy seriously. Shouts rang out—"Let them speak!"—but it was already past 9 p.m., so the discussion was tabled.

I would finally get my chance to speak the following week. On Saturday, November 5, my toes were frozen and my nose was runny, my hands were shaking and I was terrified that my voice might fail me. For a moment, I felt pulled back to first term, Freshman Studies—that sensation returned of being raw meat served up to a pack of wolves on a silver platter. *Stop it!* I told myself, standing there frozen looking at them looking at me. *They are no better than you—you've learned their language, you've earned their degrees. It's your time to speak and their turn to listen. Now open your mouth and USE YOUR VOICE!*

"Mic check!" I shouted and startled myself with the power of the sound that came out. "Power concedes nothing without a demand"—I took ownership of those words as I said them then drove home the preamble—"'It never did and it never will.' Frederick Douglass." And, evoking his spirit, I steamrolled through our proposal for a Jobs for All Demand:

> We demand a massive, democratically controlled public works and public service program, with direct government employ-ment, to create 25 million new jobs at good union wages. This is to be paid for by new taxes on the wealth and income of the rich, financial transactions, and corporate profits, and reinstate-ment of the Glass-Steagall Act—as well as by ending all US wars, disbanding mercenaries, ending aid to authoritarian re-gimes, and closing military bases. The new jobs will aim to rad-ically expand access to education, healthcare, housing, mass transit, and clean energy—and are to be open to all, regardless of immigration status or criminal record.

Jobs for All, of course, did not get approved but was tabled indefi-nitely for discussion. Nonetheless, most of us saw it as a victory: we'd fought our way there, they'd let us speak, and now they wanted to know more. We had proposed the *first ever* demand to Occupy Wall Street and started the discussion—sooner or later we'd find one that really spoke to people. But, unfortunately, time wasn't on our side.

Ten days later, on November 15, 2011, Occupy Wall Street was evicted from Zuccotti Park. I watched it come to an end, the same way I saw it begin: on a computer screen. I had been called home to

Atlanta because my grandmother's cancer returned, but I was flying back to New York City that very same day. At 12:59 a.m. my phone dinged with a text message: "ZUCCOTTI PARK SURROUNDED. EVERYONE TO THE PARK NOW!" I jumped out of bed, flung open my computer, and joined the 60,000 others watching the raid on GlobalRevolution.tv—Liberty Plaza's twenty-four-hour live stream channel.

Barricades shut down streets all around the park. The streets were flooded with hundreds of police, and more kept spilling out of vans. Lights were plugged in, which made it look like a movie set, but terrified looks on familiar faces made it all too real. Some officers started handing out flyers while another yelled into a bullhorn, "You are required to immediately remove all property . . . [and] leave the park on a temporary basis so that it can be cleared and restored for its intended use." Around then the video cut out, so I switched to Facebook. For the next hour, my timeline was flooded with photos of protestors leaving with all their belongings on their backs. Why are they leaving? I called Jake, my friend from Demands, to find out. "Can you hear me?" he shouted over the chanting crowd. "Are you at Liberty Plaza?" I yelled back. "No! Everything is blocked off three blocks around—they won't even let press in." Screams broke out and I lost him. Next I texted Andy, also from Demands: "Are we losing the park?" "Yes," he said, explaining that a hundred key organizers left earlier to plan another occupation and never made it back. I switched over to Twitter and followed the last moments of Liberty Plaza through @JoshHarkinson, a reporter for *Mother Jones* magazine.

3:02 AM: Almost whole park is already clear except for food tent.

3:10 AM: Cops have a giant orange bulldozer that they've used to scrape everything up

3:17 AM: Sweaty guy in suit and neon vest ripping off signs: "I've been waiting a long time to do this."

3:35 AM: The riot police moved in with zip cuffs and teargassed the occupiers in the food tent

3:35 AM: Then they wrestled them to the ground and cuffed them

3:36 AM: Everyone I witnessed being arrested was resisting peacefully

Twelve hours later, I returned to the corner of Broadway and Cedar Street. "Mic check!" someone called. "We still need jail support for the 142 arrested this morning." Before heading down to 100 Centre Street to help, I glanced back one last time. The empty park was lined with barricades and surrounded by police—if not for them, you wouldn't have known that Occupy Wall Street had ever existed.

Me, about two weeks old and just a week out of the hospital, being held by my mother. You can still see the rashes on my face.

Atlanta family helping Mom and Dad when I was a newborn. Back row: Mom and Dad; front row (left to right): Uncle Kevin, Granddaddy Harlon, Grandmommy Kay, and Uncle Eric (1987).

Abuela, my maternal grandmother, and great aunt, Tia Magda, who came to visit and help out Mom and Dad just after I was born (1988).

Me on my first birthday in Beaumont, Texas, seated between Caca and Pawpaw, my paternal great-grandparents (1989).

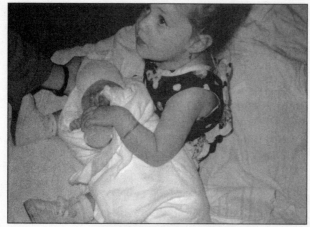

Me, almost two years old, holding days-old Baby James, born July 4, 1990, in Beaumont, Texas.

James and me "loving on" Momma Jean, competing for attention (Easter 1993).

Me and James "helping" Pop mow the lawn (1993).

Gymnastics meet at Béla Károlyi's ranch (1997).

Cheer Power USA, 2002, national champion—All Star Team, Cheer Express.

Nyrobi, taken just before I met her at the Youth Creates theatre program in Atlanta, Georgia (Summer 2005).

Me and Zachary Monteith, my first big love, at Six Flags Over Georgia (Summer 2006).

Isaiah, taken about the time I moved in with him and Nyrobi (Fall 2005).

Me and college boyfriend Andy Bauman celebrating his twentieth birthday (January 2008).

Last photo with James before long-term imprisonment (Christmas 2009).

Me posing with Kappa Kappa Gamma "big sister" Alyssa Bosse and "little sister" Katie Nelson (Spring 2009).

My first time attending the Young Democratic Socialists Summer Socialist Conference in Wurtsboro, New York, following the United States Social Forum in Detroit (Summer 2010).

Protests against Governor Scott Walker in Madison, Wisconsin (Spring 2011).

Occupy Wall Street planning meeting in Tompkins Square Park (August 2011).

St. Patrick's Day 2012 with college friend Lara Wasserman and roommate Gregory Montagnino.

Me, being led off the mass arrest bus parked on the Broadway side of Zuccotti. Seizing, while still in handcuffs, I fall forward as the officers lose their grip *(Credit: Stacy Lanyon).*

April 7, 2014, opening day of trial. Outside 100 Centre Street with legal counsel Marty Stolar and Rebecca Heinegg, I conclude the morning press conference with my one permitted line: "Thank you for being here today" *(Credit: Popular Resistance)*.

Second-round jury selection, sandwiched between Rebecca and Marty at the defense table—my assigned seat for the duration of the trial *(Credit: Popular Resistance)*.

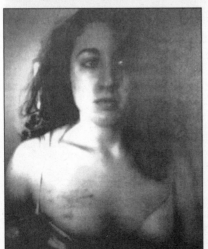

Photo from my medical records, taken the morning after my release from custody; blown up and mounted on a poster, the five-fingered bruise on my breast is displayed before the court as evidence.

May 9, 2014, Lucy Parks escorts Pussy Rioters Nadya and Masha to Rikers for my first scheduled visit *(Credit: Ash)*.

While I await sentencing, a crowd gathers in Union Square protesting police brutality and demanding my freedom *(Credit: Mickey Z.)*.

July 2, 2014, the Rikers Island Welcome Sign. Finally released, I deliver "We the Women of" to the press *(Credit: Pella)*.

CHAPTER 5

Victim

"Have you seen Jake?" I asked person after person, searching Zuccotti Park for my friend. "No, but ..." one after another Occupier replied. "Look at that outfit!" or "What are you wearing!?" I was wearing all green: shoes, skirt, shirt, tights, jacket, hat, scarf, gloves, and purse of shades ranging from lime to teal in mixed patterns of stripes, floral, and polka dot—and, of course, nail polish and eyeliner too. "It's St. Patrick's Day!" I shouted, already off to ask the next Occupier. You wouldn't know it, though, by the looks of this crowd, none of whom were dressed for the occasion. The park, nonetheless, was more packed than any bar I'd been to that night—and, to be fair—it *was* more of a party than a protest. But the hundreds gathered there were celebrating something entirely different, something "more important": the six-month anniversary of Occupy Wall Street.

Four months earlier, we'd lost the park. Our two-month occupation, though, had a lasting impact on US politics: income inequality was then a part of the national conversation in the 2012 election year.

The 1 percent versus the 99 percent entered into American consciousness. In that sense, Occupy Wall Street lived on—but only rhetorically. Organizationally, we were dead. Without the park, we had no central focus, no general assembly, no working groups, no way of holding onto public interest. When we held the park, everyone who was anyone came down to meet with us, some even joined us: journalists, writers, philosophers, musicians, television hosts, movie stars, community leaders, elected officials, union presidents. But by the time Occupy neared its half birthday and activists started planning the party—to reclaim our dignity more than the park itself—the bigwigs weren't interested in hanging out with us anymore. And why should they? The only lasting relationship was with Big Labor, which had banded together with Occupy to co-organize the upcoming annual May Day demonstration in New York City.

I'd never been an Occupy favorite, but I was definitely an Occupy diehard. I probably went to as many meetings and actions in the months that followed the eviction as I had in the fall of 2011, but there were fewer and fewer people at each event, and those organizing them seemed more and more on the brink of despair. In a way, we were political refugees: parkless, stateless, and impatient, aching to recapture a shared sense of belonging—searching desperately for a way to get back what the city had taken from us, searching for a way home. That was the lure of Zuccotti Park.

In fact, I ended up in another occupation just two days later. On November 17, 2011, the New York City Student General Assembly—a spin-off of Occupy Wall Street focused on higher education—had launched a student occupation at the New School. Because I was, at the time, enrolled in a master's program at the School of Social Research there, I helped to overtake the building initially and secure it while students arrived from every other major school in the city: City University of New York, State University of New York,

Columbia University, New York University, and Cooper Union. We set out to form a united front—bound by mutual conditions of rising tuition costs, low campus wages, and little to no say in our institutions—to systematically challenge the standards of higher education in New York City. We also hoped, in the spirit of Zuccotti, to inspire a string of campus occupations nationwide that would ultimately give way to a student movement like that of the '60s. Unfortunately, the Citywide Student Occupation gave way to infighting—mostly between private and public school kids along pretty distinct race and class lines—and subsequently fell apart within one week, inspiring no one.

I didn't give up, though. Instead, I worked right on through the holiday season, skipping the party circuit and leaving my family early to fly back Christmas Day to start organizing the next Demands Working Group meeting, fearing that if I didn't, people might lose focus over the holidays. And when it did fall apart just after New Year's, I helped organize actions for Martin Luther King Jr. Day, including a brief occupation of a Bank of America ATM center in Union Square. Following that, I organized through Valentine's Day for the Young Democratic Socialists' Winter Conference, "The Return of the Democratic Left: Building a Youth Movement for the 21st Century." At the same time, I turned my efforts to building a coalition for a 99 Percent Platform in the hopes of influencing the upcoming electoral season.

In other words, I hadn't had a freaking day off since August, when I had stumbled—brand new to the city—into the planning meetings of Occupy Wall Street. For the seven months I'd been living in New York City, I hadn't walked a single one of the bridges, gone to any of the museums, and had (maybe?) visited Central Park once. And, though I learned a lot about social movements from an independent study with renowned activist Steve Max, who was a founding member of SDS and had helped draft the famous *Port Huron Statement*, I hadn't attended many of my classes at the New School. Or, since coming to the city—seemingly teeming with infinite possibilities for romance—gone on a single date. Besides my roommates and my job as an Upper East Side nanny, my whole life revolved around "the movement." By that point, I figured I was long overdue for a little "normal" and had given up enough holidays already. They could have all the rest, I thought, but nobody was gonna stand in the way of St. Patty's Day—it was my favorite after all, and besides, I'd earned it.

My college friend, Lara Wasserman, was visiting from Iowa. It was her first-ever trip to New York City, and we were intent on recapturing our glory days as undergraduate partiers. When Lara arrived late that morning, we launched immediately into the all-afternoon affair of "getting ready" for our much anticipated all-night pub crawl from Chelsea to Alphabet City: picking out the perfect outfits, painting our nails, putting on makeup, and so on. It was already getting dark when we finally boarded the train, but all our hard work and preparation earned us no shortage of appreciation. Before we hit the first bar, though, I walked Lara through Zuccotti to show her where Occupy Wall Street had been. We left minutes later, eager to get our own party started and get out of the way of the police.

We kicked off the evening at a gay bar in Chelsea with a phenomenal drag set. "Queens in green!? I love New York!" Lara shouted over Lady Gaga between sips of her first cocktail. In retrospect, we both agree that we should have just stayed there all night, because as it turns out bar hopping on St. Patrick's Day in New York City is a sport neither of us was properly trained to compete in. At the next place we went—a sports bar, not even an Irish pub—it took thirty minutes to get a table and another fifteen to get a round of beer, but the beers were *green* beers and, therefore, well worth the wait.

As I took my first gulp, I suddenly remembered that I hadn't called Dad yet; it was kind of "our thing"—as far back as I could remember we'd always gone all out for the holiday. I called him promptly and proudly described every last detail of my outfit, my make-up, and *even my beer*—"Now, don't you get arrested in *that!*" he teased, somewhat seriously. "Oh Daddy, don't worry!" I promised, "No banners to-night—just beer!" When we hung up, I posed for a picture—the big smile, green beer in hand—and sent it to him, hoping to ease his worries (little did I know that would be my last celebratory photo of the evening).

True to my word, we only swung by Zuccotti Park briefly, around 11:30 p.m., to grab Jake on our way to the next bar—both Chelsea and the Lower East Side proved too crowded (and too crazy) for our taste, so we'd headed to Fi-Di in search of better company and some-thing a little less, well, "*PARTY!*" The plan was to meet Jake and his friends at the edge of the park, but traffic took longer than expected and he was nowhere to be seen by the time we finally arrived. We waited there while I called him a few times, but when he didn't pick up, it was clear that I'd have to go in to find him. There were probably about five hundred people in the park by then, but—at that point—it was still definitely a celebratory environment, even though it was surrounded by a couple hundred police officers. I explained to Lara that it wasn't an unusual sight, actually. "Still," she announced, "I am not, under any circumstances, going in there." Lara was supportive of Occupy Wall Street and had followed it closely—closely enough to know that many a protestor had been assaulted in that park (and to have promised her mother that she would *not* go near it). I, however, was used to it by then: there were *always* police whenever and wher-ever Occupiers gathered. Besides, I reassured her, I wasn't staying—I'd pop right in and be back in a second. What could go wrong? I headed into the park, telling Lara to go find us a good Irish bar (no shortage of those in the Financial District) where I'd join her, reinforced by Jake and others. As expected, I quickly found him and his friends Sarah and Kay—just minutes before the park unexpectedly became a war zone. In a split second, I found myself in the middle of *it*.

It is difficult to explain, impossible to see, unless you know it and have been in the middle of it. It's a vortex, one that I first experienced in September when the Occupiers had tried to take Wall Street with me at the forefront of the line. Individuals mold into a mass—arms link, legs cross, bodies crash to the ground—as voices cry out in unison, "We will not be moved!" The mass of protestors is mirrored by a group that is differently uniformed but similarly oriented: they move as one, refuse to budge, and attempt to corral their opponents. Cuffs clink, barricades scrape, sirens scream, and the bullhorn warns, "Clear the park or you will be arrested!" Those in orbit run to and fro, either tearing away from or getting caught in the vortex.

I glance at it then back to my friends. They're gone. Footfalls and flash-photography everywhere—I can't find them. I pull out my phone and type, "Yo! Where'd y'all—" "Miss, the park's closed for cleaning." I look up. It's an officer. Shit. I freeze—wrong move. He reaches out, grabs my shoulder and shoves me. "You have to go now!" I see the sidewalk a few yards away and rush toward safety. Almost there . . . five, four, only three more steps then—I'm snatched from behind, pulled up by the breast, and flung backward then face forward into the ground.

I AWOKE IN A HOSPITAL BED. Where was I? What happened? How did I get here? My head hurt. My chest hurt. Hell, my whole body hurt. Bumps, bruises, and scrapes everywhere. My tights were ripped at the knees and my skirt was bunched up around my waist. I tried to pull it down, but I couldn't. Metal clinked against metal—*Handcuffs,*

I'm handcuffed. My head throbbed as I turned my memory inside out looking for answers to the mounting questions—I found none. Only flashes: the feel of a grated surface beneath my cheek; the fear of suffocating, something covering my mouth; the force of white lights bearing into me; a bed (maybe?). Before it all—the concrete. *I crashed into the concrete—someone grabbed me!* Who? Why? I couldn't piece it together. Just then, I noticed the petite, black female officer peeking over the foot of my bed. *Uh oh, I'm fucked.*

But even that was an understatement. What happened, what *truly* happened—not the story the officers and prosecutors would later tell—was that I was assaulted then medically neglected for hours.

My attacker, as it turned out, was *Officer* Grantley Bovell. I'd never seen him before, never spoken to him. I never saw him coming. The exchange, incidentally, was filmed by Jake's friend Sarah, who'd made it safely across the same street I was heading toward when I was stopped short by Bovell. Turning her iPhone on the park, she'd intended to film what would later be described as "a police riot" and "the most violent night at Zuccotti Park." Somehow, I got dragged into the middle of it, and I'd watch Sarah's video hundreds of times trying to understand what happened to me and why.

The clip is unfocused and grainy, but (if I look frame by frame) I see Officer Bovell take hold of me with what I've since learned is a police tactic called a "seatbelt grab." He snatches me from the left side of my waist and rips diagonally across my torso (hence "seatbelt"). I watch him lift me off the ground and then slam me forward. I see my feet hit the ground and then watch myself take a few steps as I struggle to regain my balance before I double over in his grip. I hear my friend Sarah say, "Oh, there's Cecily," then I see him force me, face first, into the ground. After that, a bunch of officers swarm in, and Sarah asks, "Is she getting beat up?" Kay responds, "She's getting beat up right now!" A bunch of activists surround us, shouting,

"Shame!"—Sarah says, "Oh my God"—and yet more officers swarm them as others drag my seemingly limp body away: "Who is escorting her?" Sarah asks. "Cops," Kay responds, "and one guy not in a cop uniform who was probably—" The video ends abruptly. A second YouTube video, shot by a nearby protestor who narrowly escapes arrest himself, provided a little more insight: about half a dozen other officers appear to retaliate.

I don't remember what happened next, but from countless videos and firsthand witnesses I learned that the police beating triggered a series of seizures that lasted about fifteen minutes—most of which I suffered in handcuffs. For several minutes, my head repeatedly struck the ground while dozens of officers stood by idly; the surrounding crowd cried out, "Help her!" "Do something!" "The whole world is watching!" but the police ignored them and reportedly turned away paramedics. While I seized, a single, uniformed woman approached and knelt beside me; but, with the exception of holding my purse, it's unclear (from the videos) what, if anything, she did to help me. What is clear, however, is the image of me on my side, hands behind my back, in a hiked-up skirt exposing sheer, mint tights as my head bounces up and down—and there she is, kneeling beside me. See for yourself: just type "#OWS #M17 #OccupyWallStreet Girl Seizing Following Arrest, Cops Mishandle Her Situation" into YouTube. From there, you can find dozens of others if you feel so inclined—different snippets of the incident from a variety of angles.

What isn't clear is the *exact point* the seizures began. I do know for certain, though, that they were in full swing on the mass arrest bus. That night, the NYPD commandeered a city bus to transport arrestees to jail. According to Occupiers already there, I appeared to be seizing as two officers carried me onto the bus then—mistaking my condition as an act of protest—released my arms and sent me tumbling to the floor, where I continued to shake uncontrollably. At some point, though, I was moved to a bus seat where videos (shot through windows) show me seizing for some time before three officers struggle to haul me off, lose their grip and drop me into the street. Afterward, several videos capture my prolonged seizing in the middle of Broadway. Then I collapsed, motionless, and the crowd cried out, "Is she dead!?" (I shouted along with them, the first time I watched it: I couldn't believe that happened to her—*that* happened to me!) Of course, though, I didn't die. *Whew!* I rose up a few minutes later, only to suffer what looks to have been a panic attack: I gasped—and *gasped!*—for air. "She can't breathe!" the protestors cried. "Where are the medics?" Around then, the police medical team showed up (*finally!*) and put an oxygen mask over my face—yet, I frantically tried to remove it. (Thinking back to my brief flashes of memory: I guess *that* was what I thought was suffocating me.)

It's not any easier now than it was then to piece together everything that happened in those fifteen minutes. But what is crystal clear from the footage is that I never once looked behind me before Officer Bovell grabbed me, suggesting both that I hadn't known anyone was behind me and that I had not intended or prepared to attack anyone. Something else becomes clear: despite mandatory (if basic) medical training, no police officer ever came to my aid during the course of the several minutes that I seized—and, in fact, several observers noted that many police officers prevented licensed (and, sometimes, tearful) EMTs from entering the park and administering medical care—such criminal negligence being but one of *many* complaints in my pending civil suit against the City of New York. Everything that happened to me afterward would hinge on those fifteen minutes. They were the worst and, in some ways, the most important minutes of my life. And still I have next to no memory of what happened to me and absolutely no idea why.

Besides me, though, seventy-two others were arrested in Zuccotti Park that night, many of them badly hurt, several of whom are (still!)

suing the city. Among them was Cressa Perloff, who—during her arrest, for which the charges were later dropped—was similarly snatched by the breast by a different male officer entirely, the since-retired NYPD sergeant Joseph Catapano. In her civil suit, she charged that "the police department demonstrated a pattern of sexual misconduct against female OWS activists" and further noted that another police officer called her "an ugly cunt" after her arrest. In his deposition in the case, the sergeant accused of sexual assault declared that an officer was justified in grabbing "whatever means necessary to affect [sic] an arrest." In September 2015, Cressa won a $95,000 settlement from the city for her assault. My own case was introduced as evidence in her suit—but came out too late to factor into my own legal defense. Despite her vindication and the financial settlement, Cressa continues to suffer posttraumatic stress disorder from her assault. And, unfortunately, we have that in common.

Nonetheless, while Cressa and nearly all the other arrestees were jam-packed into holding cells, held together awaiting release on charges they expected would be dismissed in short order, I was totally alone, chained to a gurney. I was soon to encounter a brand of abuse unlike any I'd experienced before and one we think doesn't exist—certainly, I thought it didn't—in a democracy.

BACK AT BEEKMAN HOSPITAL, the police officer peeking over the foot of my bed was Lisa Waring, my official arresting officer. A few moments after we locked eyes, I collected my thoughts enough to speak and asked her, "Can I call my friends?" She said no. "What happened to me?" "You got arrested," she said. "Yeah," I said, attempting to lift my hands to the sound of clinking chains. "I got that impression."

When the doctor came around, she spoke to him (outside) before he spoke to me; my guess is that she led him to believe I was just some St. Patrick's Day hooligan—because that's pretty much how he treated me. He asked me questions mechanically and didn't seem interested in my answers; he didn't look me in the eye or, even, examine me properly. "Listen," I demanded. "Can I speak to you alone without the officer present? My mom's a nurse; I know that my conversations with doctors are supposed to be confidential." Even then, though, he totally ignored me, refusing to recognize that something was obviously off about the whole scenario.

When the doctor proved useless, I told Officer Waring that I wanted to speak to a lawyer, not that I had one, specifically, but I'd long since committed to memory the general number to the National Lawyers Guild. Calling a lawyer—far beyond "decency"—is a basic constitutional right. Nonetheless, she denied me that too. That, to me, was a warning sign: things could get really bad from here if no one knows where I am. I started shouting, again and again and again, "I want a lawyer, I want a doctor, I want a lawyer!" and in my desperation, I threatened to sue the hospital. Unbeknownst to me, Jake, Sarah, and Kay were at that very moment searching for me in the emergency wing—after my arrest, they'd gotten a tip-off that I'd been taken to the New York Infirmary–Beekman Downtown Hospital, on William Street in Lower Manhattan—and a nurse, breaking the rules, told them what room I was in. On their way there, though, they heard me screaming and ran after my voice. When they came in, I was there— tears streaming down my face—still shouting, "I want a lawyer!"

When I saw them, I broke into sobbing laughter and said, "But I'll take what I can get." Relieved, I asked them what had happened to me. They said I'd been beaten up really badly by the cops and had seized for several minutes—they'd followed me there to make sure I was still alive. "I *what?*" I said, but Officer Waring wasn't having it— she ordered them to leave, really mad at me for "calling my friends." (Like, what, I'd willed them there with magic?) Then, once they left,

Waring presented me with a medical release form; she said that if I signed it, we could leave now and get back to the precinct in time for me to be released with the rest of "my friends." Terrified and humiliated, I signed it, waiving my right to medical attention (a document, of course, that would later be used against me in court).

From Beekman, I was taken by police car with Officer Waring back to South Central Precinct police station. I still didn't know at that point what charge I was facing, although I assumed it was "disorderly conduct" because that's usually what the NYPD slapped us Occupiers with for daring to exercise our right to public assembly. Regardless, I was still asking for a lawyer; Waring, however, waved me off—assuring me I'd be released any moment, free to speak with anyone I pleased.

Once at the station, they put me in a holding cell with the other women arrested that night in Zuccotti Park. The women in the cell with me—some of whom I knew from Occupy—had seen me having seizures in the park and were very concerned. They wanted to know whether I'd been treated or even examined, and when I told them I hadn't, they were shocked and insisted that I go back to the hospital to have my head checked out. But I was just as adamant about staying there with them, terrified about being left alone again with Waring. At least with the other Occupiers I felt safe. And so the argument went on and on, as I kept passing out and they kept getting more and more freaked out.

Waring kept coming back every half hour or so to tell me I was *about* to be released. An hour passed, then two . . . then three. And finally, she returned with a definitive statement: I would not be getting out that night or anytime soon; Sergeant (or Captain?) So-and-So had ordered her to hold me, because I was being brought up on charges much more serious than a violation and would need to see a judge before I could be released, if I was going to be released at all. "I'm *what?*" I said, again. That's all the information she had, she replied.

Because I would clearly be there for a while and had become dizzier and dizzier, moving in and out of consciousness, I finally gave into the pleas of my cellmates and requested that I return to a hospital. I had no intention of dying in a jail cell. By that point, Waring seemed pretty pissed off—because she was my arresting officer, she had to follow protocol and stay with me, which meant she wouldn't be going home anytime soon. To make matters worse, I was right to be wary of relying on the NYPD to take my medical condition seriously. Besides being ignored, yet again, by another doctor, I'd also get a taste of what police can do to you when no one is watching. The second time around, I was taken to Bellevue Hospital, on First Avenue, and we got there at about 5:30 a.m. on Sunday by ambulance (which, by the way, showed up on *my* credit card bill—apparently, "that's the policy"—landing me in several thousand dollars debt for the ambulances that carted me around lower Manhattan that night).

At Bellevue I was brought into a special waiting room where I was placed on a chair to wait, once again, feet cuffed together and hands cuffed behind me. All the other "patients" were also handcuffed: homeless men in filthy rags, men and women going through drug withdrawals, a fellow Occupier, bloody-faced and defiant. The room smelled of urine and vomit and worse—my gag reflexes sent me dry heaving. The doctors and nurses who came into the room from time to time wouldn't look directly at us, like we were too far beneath them to notice or maybe too far gone to do any good. If there was a sadder, bleaker place in New York City, I didn't yet know it. Each time a nurse passed, I asked, "When can I see a doctor? A social worker, please?" (En route to the hospital the ambulance EMT advised me to speak to a social worker: apparently, two earlier ambulances had been called, and then turned away before he arrived and finally insisted I be taken to the hospital.) But most of these "professionals" pretended not to hear me while those who did acknowledge me did a double take when they saw me, as if to ask, *Are you lost—why are **you** here?* Waring was there all along, miserable about having to return with me to the hospital.

Finally, I heard someone call, "McMillan!" and thought, "Thank God—it's over." But then, it got worse. They cuffed me hands and feet to a hospital bed, then wheeled me into a little windowless room that looked like a storage closet. My skirt was bunched up around my waist. It was starting to feel like a horror flick, especially when I realized that that same tiny room doubled as the cellphone charging station for all the cops forced to work the nightshift with sick criminals. The door was left wide open, and every once in a while another policeman would come in, and they all seemed to know who I was. "Fuckin' Occupy cunt," one of them said, looking between my opened legs. "What you need is a good hard fuck." Another one came in and made a joke (or what he and his buddies considered a joke) about my "Occu-pussy."

Eventually, a social worker did visit me: a woman, but more importantly, a human being who treated me like a human being. I asked her for two things: a pair of sweatpants and to photograph my bruises. She brought me the sweatpants and even convinced Waring to temporarily uncuff me to put them on. After that, she took notes on my injuries and took pictures one by one of my bruising, including the hand-shaped bruise on my right breast, photos that conveniently went missing in the months that followed.

And then, at long last, the doctor! But, once again, he consulted Officer Waring outside the room first before speaking with me. And—*again!*—there was no examination: no CT scan, no x-ray, *nothing!* I couldn't help but wonder, don't these doctors take an oath to do no harm? Without receiving a proper examination or any medical treatment whatsoever, I was then rolled off to my third and final hospital:

Bellevue Psychiatric Ward. The only diagnosis I would receive that night, it seemed, was that I was criminally insane—rather than a victim of police brutality suffering from residual effects of a trauma-induced seizure.

For something like twelve hours, I sat (*still* chained) in the waiting room until I was finally called for intake processing to determine whether I was harmful to myself or others. Thanks to my mother and brother, I was all too familiar with this process. By then, Waring had gone home and I was transferred into the custody of some other officer (notable only in the sense that he, unlike Waring, did not insist on escorting me into the psychological assessment). And so, for the first time that night, I felt safe enough to tell the whole story of my assault. Unsurprisingly, after I'd been in custody for God knows how long, I was more than a little hysterical—exhausted, aching, and afraid that they were going to lock me away in Bellevue Psych and I'd never see the light of day again.

As I spoke, the young male psychiatrist opposite the table between us just nodded, checking boxes on the computer, nonplussed by my account of the night, it seemed. In that moment, I knew that I had to find a way to convince him that I wasn't a paranoid schizophrenic—that the police really were after me—so I choked back my tears, inhaled deeply and said as calmly as I could, "Look, I'm an Occupy activist. I got attacked last night, the police have been targeting me ever since my first arrest; it was featured with a photo of me in *Rolling Stone* magazine—you can Google it. *Please sir,* you have to believe me!" He replied, "Okay, sure—wait here, I'll be right back," and left me sitting there thinking, *Yep, he's definitely coming back with a sedative and straight jacket.* But instead, he came back in with the printed article—*Oh, thank Jesus!* He agreed to release me immediately. From there, I was driven once again back to the original precinct; it must have been sometime Sunday evening, but I'd been up so long I couldn't even tell you. Whatever time it was, all the other Occupy women were gone by then.

Surely, I thought, they have to let me go soon. I *still* didn't know what my charges were, and the officer who booked me said he didn't know either. "Can I call a lawyer, now?" I asked for what felt like the millionth time. I got the same answer: you'll be released soon and can talk to him then. This time, though, it seemed like it might be true: a couple of hours later, I was loaded alone into a police van and driven to the "Tombs," the holding cells under 100 Centre Street, the Manhattan criminal court building. But when I arrived, the officer in charge there refused to take me; she read my name "McMillan" with a concerned tone and then looked me over with an air of suspicion. What did she know that I didn't? Whatever it was, she said, "Oh no! We're not holding her here!" So, from there, I was escorted through a series of tunnels to some obscure unloading dock where I was loaded up, once again, into a van, but this one was black, unmarked with tinted windows. Once in, we tore west across the Financial District then north past the Meatpacking District, Chelsea, and Hell's Kitchen to the Upper West Side. Where were they taking me? After a series of turns that had me flopping about—I was still handcuffed, in the backseat without a seatbelt—we screeched to a stop outside yet another police precinct. But why *this* one? My question was soon answered: I was walked into the back past several single cells holding prisoners who appeared to be exceptionally damaged (emotionally, mentally?) before being locked into one myself. I had been transferred, I realized, to some sort of solitary wing for "mental inmates." As usual, my first question was, "Can I call a lawyer, now?" This time, I was told, "You don't get phone calls here." "Well, can you tell me what my charges are?" "You know what you did!" was the only answer I got. "No, I really don't," I shouted. "So that's your defense, huh?" an officer sneered—and that was the last time they spoke to me until the next day. All they said was "Let's go" before driving me back to 100 Centre Street.

When I arrived for the second time, it was early Monday morning—more than thirty hours since my arrest. I'd been awake (except when unconscious) since Saturday morning, so forty-eight hours. I was exhausted, I was hungry (all I'd had was a couple of milk cartons at Bellevue), and I was teetering on the brink of despair.

Finally, that Monday afternoon—forty hours after my arrest, three police stations, two hospitals, and one psych ward later and *no fucking call to a lawyer*—I was escorted to a bench outside a courtroom where a woman introduced herself as Megan Maurus—my lawyer. She said that she was with the National Lawyers Guild and that *everyone* there had been so worried about me, that *everyone* had been trying to find me for the last forty hours. I burst into tears, heaving, "I've . . . been asking . . . for a lawyer . . . for *forever—I need a fucking cigarette!*" She ran to find one, then walked me just outside the courthouse door before lighting it and putting it in my mouth (I was still handcuffed, of course). Then she told me what I was being charged with: elbowing a police officer in the eye.

Minutes later, I was brought before a judge. She read the criminal complaint and announced that I was facing charges of felony assault in the second degree. When I heard the words, my legs buckled out from beneath me—groping at the defense table, I propped myself up, worried that I would be sent back to the hospital again. As if things couldn't get worse, the district attorney asked that I be held on $20,000 bail because I was a violent Occupy activist with dangerous friends who had already gotten hold of the personal information of the officer I'd assaulted and published it online, resulting in threatening calls to his house and one very terrified mother.

Megan pointed out that I was locked up when all that had happened and, therefore, could not—by any logic, legal or otherwise—be held accountable for their doings. As for me, I didn't know which was more shocking, that they had seriously suggested that I was in cahoots with Anonymous—*Who do they think I am?*—or that somebody might've actually called this guy's house, on my behalf, and terrorized his poor mother—*Who would do a thing like that?* Not me, Megan argued, I was a graduate student and a nanny with no criminal history, not even a parking ticket on my record! The judge looked at me, then the DA, then back to me—looking for, it seemed, the sense in this strange scenario—then ruled that I be released on my own recognizance. In other words, she let me go without charging me bail. *Whew!* For the first time in days, I felt hopeful that there was still some shred of decency and justice left in our otherwise crumbling democracy. With Megan's help, I staggered out of the courtroom and into the blinding sunlight—a free woman, at last. At least, for the moment.

CHAPTER 6

Defendant

On YouTube, there's a video from April 7, 2014, 9:30 a.m. of three people standing at the steps of a Lower Manhattan courthouse. One of them—hair blown out with newly manicured nails in a salmon-colored dress beneath an Ann Taylor suit coat—is me (or a version of me). The two people on either side are my defense attorneys: Marty Stolar and Rebecca Heinegg.

It's a cold day, allegedly spring but following a long snowy winter that seems reluctant to change its grayish color. I'm shivering a little, from the cold and, perhaps, because I'm nervous. It's the first day of my trial. We're getting ready to go in and make our way up eleven floors to Part 41—my courtroom. A dozen or so reporters and photographers surround us, and several dozen of my supporters surround them. Marty speaks for a little less than five minutes, outlining my defense: innocent woman, wrong place–wrong time, victim of assault, absurdly accused of being the assailant, concluding with, "Forward we go, I'm glad you're all here—come and watch the American system of justice hopefully work to render an innocent person nonguilty." A dozen or so reporters and photographers surround us, and several dozen of my supporters surround them.

Standing center of the round, I've been nodding my head throughout Marty's presentation, as if hearing it for the first time. I'm onstage, playing the role of the gracious, innocent (cheerful, even) Defendant. At Marty's direction, I beam and wave to reporters and supporters alike and deliver my one, permitted line on cue: "Thank you for being here today."

FOR MOST OF THE YEAR, Lower Manhattan is a tourist mecca, its sidewalks choked with tour groups, its streets with tour buses; apart from Times Square, the area is the biggest draw for visitors to New York City. Most of the action unfolds along Broadway, from Battery Park at the tip of Manhattan (where the Liberty Cruise boats leave for Ellis Island and the Statue of Liberty), moving northward past Bowling Green Park, the bronze bull that symbolizes the financial district, Trinity Church, Wall Street itself, St. Paul's Chapel, Zuccotti Park (a tourist attraction itself *now*), and ending up at City Hall Park (where, long ago, the famous ticker-tape parades would snake up Broadway for war heroes, sports champions, and other celebrities, concluding with the ceremonial presentation of a key to the city by whatever mayor was then in office). The whole length of Broadway from the Battery to City Hall Park, depending on the density of visitors on a given day, can be walked in a half hour. Head east from City Hall Park, and you'll wind up at the Brooklyn Bridge. Head northeast a few more blocks, and you'll find yourself in Chinatown.

But if you head due north from the eastern edge of City Hall Park, through Foley Square (dominated by the federal court house), you'll come to a street that rarely sees tourists. For the long city block heading north to Chinatown, the street is dominated by a gloomy collection of virtually windowless official buildings, visited largely by police officers, lawyers, and the unhappy-looking friends and relatives of criminal defendants. In the spring of 2014 I found myself spending most of my daylight hours in one of these grey monoliths, 100 Centre Street, which houses both the New York County District Attorney's Office and the courtrooms of the criminal division of the New York County Supreme Court.

In 2001, there was a short-lived A&E television series called *100 Centre Street*, a courtroom drama starring Alan Arkin as a liberal Jewish judge named Joe Rifkind and LaTanya Richardson as a conservative black (and lesbian) judge named Atallah Sims. When I went on trial at 100 Centre, I got neither Judge Rifkind nor Sims, nor their real-life equivalents—instead, I was assigned the Honorable Ronald A. Zweibel (as big a character as either, with real-life consequences).

When I first encountered Judge Zweibel he was supposedly approaching retirement (but has remained on the bench where, it seems, he will stay until his seventieth birthday and the end of his term). He got his law degree from NYU in 1965, two years before my mother was born, and had served as a judge in New York City since the year before she brought me into this world. In knowledgeable legal circles, he had long been tagged with a pro-prosecution reputation; lawyers dreaded being assigned to defend cases in his courtroom.

There is a website called The Robing Room, a sort of Rate Your Prof for New York State judges, and back in 2009, two years before Occupy and five years before my trial, an anonymous poster had this to say:

> I found Judge Zweibel to be very biased in favor of the prosecution. He made surprising rulings that seemed to deny some of the defendant's most basic constitutional rights. . . . He

continuously sustained the ADA's objections to the defense attorney's questions, and made the defense attorney sweat and suffer at getting in even the most basic material and relevant evidence. . . . I found Judge Zweibel to be unfair towards the defendant and his attorney.

And in January 2012, just two months before my arrest, an individual identifying as a criminal defense lawyer voiced similar frustrations in a short, two-sentence summation: "He is nothing more than a prosecutor with a robe. Believes that every defendant has committed the crime of the century and should [receive] the max." The former was to be the precise template for his conduct during my trial; the latter would inform his new nickname in the press: Prosecutor in Robes. Let's just say, whatever fates determined the assignment of judges were not on the side of Occupy Wall Street.

During my thirty or so pretrial court appearances, he made it abundantly clear that he didn't like me or my lawyers, and when my case finally did go to trial, in the spring of 2014, I imagine the thought of (alleged) retirement didn't exactly broaden his perspective. On his best day, he looked bored, with an air of having seen and heard it all. Most frequently, though, he greeted his felonious guests with one hell of a resting bitch face. He was living proof of the cautionary tale Momma Jean often repeated when James and I were children: "Better watch it, your face will get stuck like that." Remembering her words, it took everything I had *not* to shoot him a dirty look back, but, most of the time, I found it easier to not look at him at all. I don't know how Marty and Rebecca managed to do it—my lawyers were saints, for sure.

Oh, Marty—where to begin? When my case came to trial, he was seventy-one years old, slim, erect, with white wispy hair and a trim white beard, courtly and comradely—the people's crusader of justice!

He was (and is) my advocate, my friend, my model of what it is to live a life of political commitment and personal decency. Marty was past president of the New York City Chapter of the National Lawyers Guild, the left-wing legal organization that has been defending the civil liberties of organizers and protesters since the 1930s. He got his law degree from New York University Law School in the mid-1960s, was radicalized by seeing the police violence at the Chicago Democratic Convention in 1968, and was soon representing Black Panther defendants in New York City courts.

He was one of hundreds of lawyers across the country who rallied for the Occupy cause in the fall of 2011, providing pro bono legal defense for the thousands of people arrested during the Occupations, in New York and elsewhere. And, since January, he and his co-counsel Rebecca (a younger version of Marty in her commitment to social justice and willingness to defend unpopular defendants) had been my lawyers, preparing to go to trial—first in February, then in March, both times postponed, and now finally in April.

And while Marty and Rebecca were busy strategizing my legal defense, a group of my friends were hard at work crafting a court support model for my political defense. By the time the trial started, #Justice4Cecily was a full-time organization run by a team of twelve activists and students working out of and, partially, living in my house. There was Yoni Miller, a fellow member of the Young Democratic Socialists who also participated in Occupy Wall Street, and our mutual Occupy friends Andy Gimma of the Demands Working Group and Stan Williams of Labor Outreach; there was Frank Coughlin, an ER doctor I met (strangely enough) through a student activist group, and NYU undergrads Caitlin Brimmer and Lucy Parks; with them came more students and nearly half the team: Bex Kuuleipoinaole, Drew Mitchell, Nanar Mowad, Lauren Wilfong, and Mariah Young-Jones. Among them, they developed a support network through a website, Facebook page, and Twitter; they coordinated an e-mail, call, and text list to keep supporters informed and involved; they cultivated a press list, sent out statements, and did interviews to generate media buzz; they organized online fundraisers and big events to subsidize court costs and team expenses; and, of course, they #PackedTheCourts—hosting pretrial breakfasts with updates and rules for decorum and conferences after, where Marty debriefed us on the day and answered people's questions. Let me tell you, it was a pretty freaking incredible endeavor.

You *would think* that between them and Marty and Rebecca, I would've felt totally prepared for court—certainly, I had a *helluvalot* more support than most people facing felony trial. But, no, it wasn't enough—and there's nothing they could've done better. There's not a single thing *anyone* could have said or done to prepare me for the indignity of the trial, the psychological warfare "the People" would wage against me, and the role I'd feel forced to play in order to *defend myself.*

A courtroom is a stage where actors (prosecutors, defense lawyers, defendants) each put on a performance to win over the audience (jurors) to their version of the truth. I knew a thing or two about theater, and I'd played many roles. This time, though, I was playing myself—or, rather, a character based on me intended to appeal to a mainstream audience. When my trial began, I spent almost every hour I wasn't in court preparing for it: identifying and refining the parts of me that "the People"—the judge, the jury, the press, and so on—would empathize or, at least, sympathize with and cutting out the complexities they wouldn't. What remained was Activist Barbie, a polished version of me that I could stand by—and one that I hoped would stand to challenge (or maybe even change) the characterization of activists as "dirty troublemakers" or, worse yet, "domestic terrorists."

To win the jury's sympathy, I needed to portray myself as an upper-middle-class educated white woman—congenial (but not saccharine), well adjusted (but not arrogant), concerned (but not emotional). It took every ounce of me to keep it together every day, so there wasn't room for much of anything else after the fact. By the time I took the stand, I could no longer sense the beating pulse of Cecily McMillan beneath the caricature that was but one side of the formerly three-dimensional me. And when the trial finally did end, there was nothing left but the void of the person I'd been before it—and the feeling that I'd never get her back.

My days began at 6 a.m. with a two-hour "Morning Routine" that was printed out and tacked to my bedroom wall (alongside my "Nighttime Routine" and above my "Weight Chart").

> Wake Up: stretch, run three miles, measure and record weight;
> Body: shower, shave, moisturize, deodorant, and perfume;
> Teeth & Face: floss, brush, and mouthwash (whitening strips weekly) then exfoliator, toner, moisturizer, pore minimizer, and lip balm (face mask, twice weekly);
> Touch Up Hair: straighten layer-by-layer, curl ends and bangs, set loosely in clipped bun and apply light hairspray;
> Makeup: primer, undereye/blemish concealer, face powder, natural blush (Marty says, "Not too dark!"), bronzer (cheeks/nose/eyes), mascara and eyeliner (top and bottom), brow liner (darken beauty mark), lipstick (blot and check teeth);
> Wardrobe: pantyhose, bra, dress (lint roll and fluff, as needed), jewelry, purse, shoes, and outerwear (coat, scarf, earmuffs, gloves, umbrella, as needed);
> Breakfast: protein smoothie, medications (Vyvanse daily with Allegra, Mucinex, Aleve as needed).

Around 8 a.m., I'd leave the house (smoothie in one hand, cigarette in the other) with Lucy, juggling a backpack full of court-support stuff, my back-up dress, and emergency kit: makeup, medications, stain remover, extra pantyhose, and the like. We'd walk in line (her up front, clearing the way for me, jumping puddles from behind) nearly a mile up Nostrand Avenue (the busiest street, at its busiest hour in Bed-Stuy, Brooklyn) to the A/C train station. During our fifteen-minute train ride, she'd take my lunch order and brief me on my evening schedule (appointments, meetings, calls, etc.) then we'd get off at the Chambers Street Station and grab coffee to-go at a deli and share one last cigarette before court (I wasn't sure if smoking would hurt my character, but I figured it couldn't help). Once in Manhattan, we didn't talk about the trial in case jurors or journalists were around, so for the ten-minute walk from the deli to the courthouse we got to just be friends. As the trial progressed, though, there was less and less outside of it to talk about, and by its end we walked in sober silence, both our lives reduced to the context of that courtroom.

Most days, we'd arrive outside of 100 Centre Street at about 8:30 a.m., and I'd take a few minutes to hug and thank each one of the growing number of supporters attending the daily #Justice4Cecily breakfast hosted by the Cargo Bike Collective and Occupy Guitarmy; afterward, I'd rejoin Lucy, who'd save my place in the security line, which at times stretched more than three blocks down. Once in, we'd go through x-rays and security wands wielded by officers who soon knew us by name (and later wished me "good luck!"), then head to the elevators. On the ride up to the eleventh floor, I'd hand off my coat to Lucy and trade in my flats (or rain boots) for heels then fluff out my hair and have her check my teeth. When the doors dinged open, I'd breathe in deeply and exhale into a smile, then thrust back my shoulders and step out with as much confidence as I could muster that day. Lucy would hold back, and I'd let the calming clickety-clack of my designer shoes carry me around the corner and through the flash photography of the paparazzi to Part 41, Room 1116—then back to elevator and around again (and, sometimes, again and again) as instructed by the men with the cameras that I had no intention of *ever* pissing off.

The way I saw it, if a picture was worth a thousand words, one had to be worth twice as much in witless, right-wing publications like the *Daily News* and *New York Post*—those most committed to covering my trial at its onset—or, rather, to assassinating my character as a symbol of Occupy Wall Street. I realized, of course, that I would never win over the minds of their readership, but I held out hope that hi-res shots of a nice-looking girl pictured beneath heinous, pun-driven headlines just might tug at their heartstrings. Most importantly, though, I believed that such displays of overt dissonance would attract broader media interest, drawing more journalists into the courtroom where their appetite for scandal would surely be whetted by the theater performance masquerading as criminal justice. Thankfully, I was right on both accounts. Each court day arrived with yet more journalists and concluded with more sympathetic coverage: most notably, Jon Swaine, who provided daily court reporting for the *Guardian*—and who, in fact, keenly noted the nuances of navigating a trial while given the title of "The Last Occupy Defendant."

Bolstered by her immaculate daily appearance in smart dresses, pearls and high heels, it seemed intended as the opposite of how a judge and jury would expect a violent protester to look and act. One morning early on, she startled a police officer guarding the courtroom by thanking him for his work. "Everyone says you have been so nice," she told him. Without fail, she stood to attention and smiled politely at the jurors as they entered and exited several times each day. A chic handbag sometimes rested on the table beside her.

My trial—*The People of the State of New York v. Cecily McMillan*—began on April 7 and ended four weeks to the day later, when the jury delivered its verdict on Monday, May 5. We met every weekday but Thursdays, Justice Zweibel's calendar day (where he presides over court appearances for all the felony cases he's been assigned), and three days that jurors had requested off. In real time, it broke down to twelve days in court. That doesn't sound like a lot, but it *really* was. At 9 a.m., I'd wave good-bye to the #Justice4Cecily Team and take my place between Marty and Rebecca at our four-by-three-foot table, an arm's length away from an identical one reserved for two women who desperately wanted to put me in prison: Assistant District Attorney Erin Choi, lead prosecutor, and her co-counsel, ADA Shanda Strain. "Don't look at them," Marty instructed the first day, "and try not to react to anything they say."

Court always began with the five of us sitting silently (occasionally whispering) at our separate tables—the lawyers arranging their evidence and files; me, my notes, Post-Its, and pens—until about 9:30 a.m. when Judge Zweibel would walk in. We'd rise, the gallery (of up to a hundred) would follow behind us, and Zweibel would say, "Be seated," then review the plan for the day and open the floor for discussion. "May I, your honor?" Marty or Choi would say, then request that some piece of evidence or testimony be allowed in or, otherwise, kept out; the other would argue against it, and the two would go at it; sometimes Rebecca or Strain would jump in, other times Zweibel would call them all up to the bench. Then Zweibel would rule, almost always in favor of the prosecution, and when he didn't initially, he would usually reverse it later. After a handful of rounds like that, sometimes lasting all morning, the trial would finally resume and slowly progress though jury selection, opening statements, prosecution then defense witnesses, closing arguments, and onto the waiting game: jury deliberation and delivery of verdict. With each step, Zweibel granted the prosecution greater latitude and gutted our case, forcing Marty and Rebecca to not only rework their legal strategy but fight for even the space to defend me. It was like watching firefighters trying to save a burning building, though not from the sidewalk or on the news—*but while I was in it.* I did my best not to fan the flames, to listen to Marty and not visibly react to the prosecutor's blatant lies and what I saw as the judge's total disregard for my right to a fair trial. And, otherwise, I tried to help stabilize the structure from the inside: I listened closely, took careful notes, and alerted Marty (on little pink Post-Its) to gaping holes and conflicting testimony. The uphill battle waged on every day from 9 a.m. to 5 p.m. with an hour lunch break at 1 p.m.—or lunch meeting, for us, with more smoking than eating as we strategized ways to regain whatever ground we'd lost that morning.

When court let out, Lucy would take me to alternating hair or nail appointments (to get blowouts every other day and a mani-pedi weekly) or otherwise wardrobe shopping as the trial dragged on longer than expected: dresses, shoes, blazers, pantyhose, and so on. We'd usually get home by around 8 p.m. for a quick dinner-debrief with the team, then they'd keep working to organize court support the following day, and I'd break off to get started on my "defendant nighttime routine." I'd spend about an hour answering e-mails and updating worried friends and family. Mom, most of all, who tried to play it cool—"I know you can take care of yourself, Ceci, you always have"—but, really, everyone was freaking out. Afterward, I'd pick out my outfit for the morning and prepack my purse and, finally, get ready for bed: set my hair, wash my face, brush my teeth, and stretch. Finally, about ten o'clock, I'd lie down and watch the worst rom-coms Netflix had to offer until I was distracted enough to drift off to sleep.

The night before my trial started, though, I watched several back to back, and it still didn't work. As such, I showed up to my

first day of court—Monday, April 7—hopped up on two large cof-
fees, "*super psyched* to pick out a jury!" Judge Zweibel, in turn,
seemed equally psyched to kick out my court supporters. When he
walked into *his* courtroom to find fifty of them with hot-pink paper hands pinned to their chests, by the looks of it, he nearly lost it.
The fuming judge ordered them to remove the "pink hands" immediately and banned future symbols of my "unsubstantiated assault"
from *his* courtroom. As he shouted, I watched droplets of spit fly
from his mouth and was distinctly reminded of being a teenager in
my father's house.

Marty might have let it go, and certainly would've liked to (not
wanting to "poke the bear" and all), but Zweibel had just publicly in-
validated the crux of my defense: the downward-facing, five-fingered
bruise (with scratch marks) on my right breast was the only injury
unexplained by the retaliatory beating following my exchange with
Officer Bovell and, therefore, had to have come from him. Marty also
pointed out that a video of the incident places Bovell behind me and
that the bruise (represented by the pink hands) was twice documented: by photos taken the day of my release and by medical records
of a physical exam performed the following morning—all of which
substantiated my claim that Officer Bovell had, in fact, assaulted me,
and not the other way around.

If that were true, Choi reasoned, someone like "Ms. McMillan"
would have filed a misconduct report with the NYPD Internal Affairs Bureau to have Officer Bovell investigated—as it stands, he
didn't come up in the March 17, 2012, investigation. It's not really
people's first instinct to report police to the police, Marty argued—
taking the words right out of my head. Zweibel, of course, couldn't
have agreed less: because my assault claim hadn't been substantiated
by the Internal Affairs Bureau, my side of the story was unsubstantiated, too (which in his courtroom, at least, was synonymous with

"untrue"). Anyone attempting to say or show otherwise would hence-forth be removed from the court.

Afterward—as if to underscore his contempt for my case and "people like me"—he handed down a devastating ruling that had the lawyers arguing all morning. Back in February, Marty had filed a pre-trial motion asking Judge Zweibel to review Officer Bovell's sealed personnel record and turn over evidence relating to my case—as Marty argued, I wasn't the first (or even the last) person to accuse him of beating them up then lying about it. From court records and fur-ther investigation, Marty discovered a laundry list of alleged abuse and corruption. In 2009, Officer Bovell arrested a man in a bodega and a physical interaction ensued where he can be seen on video sur-veillance apparently kicking that defendant while he was on the floor; Bovell claimed to have broken his ankle as a result of this interaction, although he denied kicking the defendant while down. In 2010, he was allegedly a part of a police action where a young man on a "dirt bike" was run down and seriously injured by an unmarked police vehi-cle in which Bovell was riding passenger, all leading to the arrest of the biker (who has since sued Bovell: the case was settled, the biker was awarded $85,000). That same year, Bovell was investigated and recommended for dismissal for his role in the Bronx ticket-fixing scandal but was kept on and disciplined instead. Finally, on March 18, 2012, seventy-two others at Zuccotti Park were arrested in addition to me. One, Austin Guest, filed a lawsuit against Bovell after he was allegedly observed "brutally treating [Guest] by bouncing his head on the bus's internal steps." In his motion, Marty argued that Officer Bovell's "prior questionable conduct has peculiar relevance to the cir-cumstances of the defendant's case."

In our view, Bovell had a habit of losing his temper then blaming the victim and lying to justify his actions—a trend that fit with my story and strengthened my case. Bovell said he took me into custody after an angry exchange, but I'd never spoken to or even seen him before. Then he claimed I'd seriously injured him, but Austin Guest was willing to testify that Bovell went on to bash his head in while I lay handcuffed and seizing in the street. The connection couldn't be clearer or the argument stronger, but Marty broke it down every which way you could. Zweibel wasn't hearing it, though. He not only denied us Bovell's record (in full or in part), he flat-out refused to look it over himself and decide firsthand if any of it were relevant. "Come on, Judge!" Marty cried out in desperation, "If he's done this before, the likelihood is that he did it again. The guy is a dirty cop!" Zweibel snapped, "He's not on trial—she is!" he shouted, pointing at me. "She elbowed him!" And with that began the trial-long trend of Judge Zweibel publicly proclaiming my guilt in court.

By the time it was over, the argument had dragged on so long that we never even got to start trial that day. When we were finally ready to go, the pool of potential jurors had already been depleted, sent home, or divvied up among other courtrooms. Trial—or whatever limbo we were in—was dismissed, and we were to reconvene at 9:30 a.m. the next day. Before I left, the court officer handed me (what felt like my billionth) court appearance slip, and I walked past the rows and rows of benches mumbling, "Here we go again . . . wake up, go to court, wait around, go home—same shit, different day." I felt like Bill Murray in *Groundhog Day*.

Nonetheless, I returned to court the following day, Tuesday, April 8, hopeful that our second attempt at jury selection couldn't possibly go worse than the first. Indeed, later that morning, when I stood facing a pool of eighty-four potential jurors, it felt like maybe our luck was starting to change. Things were starting to go our way. I should have known better. In Manhattan, where one in nine jobs is connected to Wall Street, Occupy Wall Street continued to be a flash point.

One potential juror, quoted in the *Guardian,* declared, "I'm involved in Wall Street things. I'm on the Wall Street side, not their side. They can protest all they want, but they can't brainwash my mind." Another admitted, "I like to think of myself as fair. But in terms of Occupy Wall Street in general, I would give less credibility to that group than average. . . . They seem to be people moving a little outside regular social norms and regular behavior. Therefore, I don't give them the same level of respect as people who follow the line." While a third asserted, "I used to live next door to Lloyd Blankfein, the CEO of Goldman Sachs. I'd come home and have them protesting, harassing the kids on the way to school. . . . Quite frankly, my view on the way it was handled is that the City did not do enough to stop it earlier." (And, honestly, they were just the tip of the iceberg.)

Of course, it was a good thing for us when potential jurors announced their disdain for Occupy; if they hadn't, they might've been seated. The prosecution, in turn, was on the lookout for anyone who might harbor a critical outlook on the NYPD. When potentially sympathetic jurors confessed that they were (even a little bit) wary of the police or, otherwise, condemned ticket-fixing as a strike against an officer's credibility (duh!), it was not to our advantage. And so it went that, by day's end, we had yet to choose a single juror. The following day, Wednesday, April 9, we managed to agree on and seat seven of the initial jury pool of eighty-four, then called in another sixty candidates to begin again. I don't know why I was surprised when it was just like before: one after another dismissed for being either anti-Occupy or wary of police. As such, the final five seats remained empty that day and, since Zweibel dealt with other cases on Thursdays, it was looking like jury selection might very well last all week. By lunch on Friday, though, we had our jury: eight women and four men, four of them employed by the financial sector and two of them people of color (a black man and a black woman). The demographics were a crapshoot—the silver lining being, it looked that way from both sides.

With the jury *finally* in place, the battle between prosecution and defense commenced in earnest that afternoon, when both sides presented their opening arguments. "'Are you filming this? Are you filming this?'" Choi said, "were the defendant's words right before she intentionally attacked Police Officer Grantley Bovell. According to her, I was "shouting, yelling, and cursing at a female officer" when Bovell, "seeing that [she] was alone, went to her aid." Apparently, I refused to leave the park when asked calmly to do so, twice, by Bovell, so he politely escorted me out "by placing his hand on the back of [my] right shoulder"—during which, acting out of hatred for "the system" and a desire for personal glory, I "crouched down and jumped up and struck Officer Bovell's left eye with [my] elbow." He suffered bruising and a cut, headaches and blurred vision. My alleged victim seemed to have had a singularly uneventful career on what are reputed to be the famously tough streets of New York City. "Officer Bovell was completely caught off guard," Choi told the jurors. "It was the last thing he was expecting to happen that day." There was no question of any other factor, say civil liberties, involved here: "Cecily McMillan thought she could get away with assaulting a police officer by shielding herself in the name of protest."

Of course, my defense counsel told a decidedly different story. Rebecca, presenting our opening statement, said that "March 17th, 2012 was St. Patrick's Day and Cecily McMillan took the day off from Occupy": dressed in bright green, I had friends visiting from out of town and had only swung by the park to pick up more friends and keep drinking. When a police officer asked me to leave, I tried to "immediately" but was attacked on my way out: "she was suddenly grabbed from behind and pulled up and back by Officer Bovell, grabbed on her right breast, grabbed so hard that it left a bruise in the shape of a handprint"—during which I incidentally elbowed him in the face. "Cecily did not intend to hurt him," she explained. "She did not even know [he] was a police officer. She just reacted." "And, ladies and gentlemen," she argued, "reacting to being grabbed by a stranger is not a crime."

So, basically, the whole trial—hundreds of thousands of tax-payer dollars and more than two years of my life awaiting trial to face another possible seven in prison—all came down to the question: Had I come to Zuccotti Park that night thirsting for revolutionary glory or as an accidental bystander in a green miniskirt?

Following opening statements, the prosecution offered its first two witnesses. From that moment on, I found myself relegated to the role of passive observer as my fate was being determined. It had been a long time since I'd bent over the principal's desk in Lumberton, Texas, and taken my licks for, essentially, insubordination to authority. But now, figuratively, and with much higher stakes involved, I was being made to do the same. I am *not* skilled at keeping my mouth shut and had always railed against every attempt to silence me. But until it came time to tell my side of the story—if, that is, Marty thought it best for me to take the stand—I was not to say a single word in my defense or even visibly react to anything the prosecutors or their witnesses would say about me, no matter how demeaning or untrue. My job was to remain a blank slate, except for when the jury came and went: I was to look at them directly and smile politely to remind them that I was a human being, not just a thing being talked about.

The prosecution's first witness was Doctor Eva Yan, a Bronx-based optometrist who examined Officer Bovell on March 19, two days after the NYPD's raid of the park. When he went in, Bovell indicated that he'd been "struck" in his left eye and had since suffered "a sharp pain" and sensitivity to light, as well as dizziness and headaches. Her examination confirmed that the iris of his left eye was slightly inflamed and that there was a small scar on his cornea. "In your expert opinion, [are] Mr. Bovell's injuries consistent with someone who was struck in the left eye with an elbow?" Choi asked. "It could be," Yan responded. My lawyers didn't dispute the fact that Officer Bovell had, indeed, been injured. Under cross-examination by Marty, Yan conceded that her records did not indicate any external injury at the time of his visit and that, given his age and the nature of his injury, his symptoms likely would have passed "reasonably rapidly." Finally, when asked, "If he was struck directly in the eye, would the injury have been more severe?" Yan responded, "Yes, it would be." So it was possible that the "slight flare" and "little bit of a corneal scar" had nothing to do with me while his supposed pain and discomfort should have passed pretty quickly (like, it seemed, his bruise and cut already had).

The next witness was Sergeant Joseph Diaz, who had little to say about me except that he saw me having difficulty breathing following my arrest. He testified that he and other officers had been instructed by their superiors to clear the park shortly before midnight—that it needed to be vacated for a scheduled cleaning. (*On a Saturday? A St. Patrick's Saturday!?* I scribbled, still flabbergasted by their flagrant attack on our right to peaceful assembly.) On cross-examination, Diaz was a study in vagueness, claiming he couldn't remember whether there were ten, fifty, or a hundred protesters in the park or how many of them were arrested. When Marty asked what the hundreds of NYPD officers surrounding the park had been doing prior to clearing it, he responded, "What every cop does, drink coffee, talk about baseball and not doing much." Not the most persuasive testimony (come on, baseball in March?), but it played well for the prosecution. Big, dumb, lovable cops, standing around drinking coffee—like Chief Wiggum in *The Simpsons*—the only thing missing was the donuts. What's not to like? And what kind of monster would run up and elbow one of those guys in the eye?

With him concluded the first week of the trial. We were dismissed for the weekend—booked solid with strategy meetings and styling appointments—then back Monday, April 14, for the second day of testimony. That morning my court supporters, thirty or forty of them, trickled in wearing pink paper hearts in place of the hands Zweibel had banned the week prior. I didn't dare turn around to see for myself, but muffled giggles in the gallery gave it away. I watched Zweibel catch one—wait, no, he missed it—yep, there it is. I watched his face turn double-take white to deep-seated red so fast it seemed to paralyze him. When he could speak, he ordered the jury "out, brief recess," then threw the closest thing you can to a tantrum while still wearing a robe. Okay, yes, they (we) were being provocative. And yet, where is it written that pieces of paper—paper conveying a message of support for a defendant otherwise being denied justice by the state—aren't protected by constitutional guarantees of freedom of speech? If an antiabortion protester were on trial for an equivalent offense—say, slamming a cop's hand in the door of a Planned Parenthood clinic while trying to chain it closed—would a judge bar supporters from wearing crosses around their necks? I don't think so.

In any case, the judge took it out on Marty and Rebecca: "I directed previously that nobody was to come in with pink parts on their chests," he declared. "I've seen hands outside the courthouse, and today it's hearts. If anyone comes in wearing something like that on their chest, they are going to be ordered out of the building and not allowed back." The way he shrieked I was reminded of Wonderland's Queen of Hearts. "You're looking right at me as if I'm somehow behind this," Marty replied. "And I'm not." (And he wasn't.) I kept my head down and intently sketched the mad queen screaming, "Diamonds shall not be worn at court!" Behind me, I listened to the polite, if slightly embarrassed, court officer doing his sworn duty to collect all the paper hearts. "You can have them back at the end of the day if you wish," he said. I felt a little bad for him, but I got my due: a bloody bottom lip from biting back laughter.

What started as a somewhat silly morning turned very serious, very quickly, when the prosecution called Officer Grantley Bovell to testify against me. It was the first time I encountered him face to face, the first I heard his voice—neither of which brought back the slightest memory of Bovell from that evening. Had it not been for the countless photos and videos, I wouldn't have even recognized him. Yet again, though, I found myself thrust unwillingly into him; and again, he had the upper hand and I was crushed beneath him—the weight of his words falling even more forcefully than his body had, two years prior. You'd think putting a face to the name would make things better, but it didn't: I just couldn't understand how he could look me straight in the eye and call me "Cecily," like we were old acquaintances or something—*like he didn't assault me.*

I had to hand it to Bovell, though, he was a sympathetic witness. Then thirty-five, he'd been a teenage immigrant to the United States from Barbados and had served four years in the US Navy before joining the NYPD, with nearly ten years of service. A loving son, he lived with his mother and a younger sister. He was soft spoken, smiled often, and wore stylish eyeglasses—nothing at all like a "threatening tough guy." It was like Dr. Jekyll and Mr. Hyde and, thanks to Zweibel, it seemed the jury would never see his bad side.

As the prosecution walked Bovell through his account of March 17, I listened closely for clues to expose his alter ego. He'd been redeployed from the Bronx to Manhattan early that morning, to keep tabs on St. Patrick's Day revelers. In the evening he was shifted to the Zuccotti Park detail. There he spotted me, flailing my arms and cursing at a female officer (I scribbled, *I'd love to meet her!*). He calmly approached me, informing me that I had to leave the park because it needed to be cleaned, but I'd be "more than welcome" to return once they were done. "I remember her yelling and screaming that she shouldn't be forced to leave, that she shouldn't have to leave," he testified. As he tried, patiently and peaceably, to escort me from the park, hand on my shoulder, I yelled to a man with a cellphone, "Are you filming this? Are you filming this?" And then, according to Bovell, I crouched down, whirled around, and hit him in the eye, "pretty hard," with my elbow. Then, he continued, I tried to run away. But, instead, he got me to the ground, secured me, and handcuffed me (*Saving the day, one Occupy-swine at a time!*). It was all nonsense, of course, but we'd have to wait for an opportunity to challenge Bovell's account of the night. Because of Passover, court was cancelled the next day and set to resume Wednesday, April 16.

That morning we arrived slightly better rested and more prepared. Unfortunately, we were met by an already enraged Zweibel, who came down on Marty with a gag order for "lying to the press." After court had adjourned Monday, reporters questioned Marty about Bovell's testimony. Of course, he explained that it accorded neither with my memory nor with the YouTube video, and that was enough to set Zweibel off: "This case is to be tried in this courtroom and not in the press, counsel." Choi chimed in, "I would like to point out that the quote that the Court is referring to was Mr. Stolar's statement saying that Officer Bovell's testimony was inconsistent with his client's version of what happened." How dare my lawyer proclaim my innocence in public, I thought. "That's his opinion!" Zweibel sputtered, once again questioning my innocence in court. "That's clearly Mr. Stolar's position, that's the defendant's position, and it can come in in its due time as there are witnesses and evidence, but that's not been on the record." Marty shot back, "Are you ordering me—" "I'm ordering both sides," Zweibel clarified but pointed only at Marty, "not to speak to the press!" I should introduce him to my mother, I mused; the few times I'd pointed my finger at her, she'd bitten it—apparently no one had ever taught him that pointing is just plain rude!

Since the jury was already out of the courtroom, the defense and prosecution went at it again, fighting over whether Austin Guest's suit against Bovell should be open for questioning. Zweibel, not surprisingly, ruled it inadmissible. Marty, in turn, called his ruling "a reversible error," or a bad ruling, proving legal grounds for appealing my conviction. (God forbid it should come to that!) Nonetheless, Zweibel stood by his ruling and—as if the morning were not already ruined—called the jury back in to see the famous YouTube video.

In a public hearing of about a hundred, I was forced to relive the night that Bovell grabbed me—grabbed me in a way no man ever had before. For more than an hour, my attacker repeatedly played his role as "the victim" while I sat there silently sobbing. I wept knowing that I shouldn't, but I couldn't help myself. The video was a litmus test for newspaper coverage. The city's two right-wing tabloids regarded it as incontrovertible proof of my guilt. The *New York Post* noted that the "footage was enough to make the defendant blubber in court" while the *Daily News called the scene "chaotic" and the video "grainy" yet, still, insisted that it showed* "Bovell walking to the back right of McMillan seconds before she popped him in the face and tried to bolt." Afterward, Choi questioned Bovell as to why he hadn't been listed as my arresting officer. "Because I was the victim," he replied, provoking suppressed chuckles from the gallery. To add (further) insult to injury, Bovell made light of my condition as he loaded me onto the bus: "She was playing dead. . . . Her legs are all the way out and she is just dragging, not using any motion to walk." After that, I started "shaking" and a group of officers carried me off—that was the last he saw of me. He remained on the bus to help transport the other Occupy arrestees to a nearby precinct then returned to the park about 2 a.m., where he reported to his commanding officer that he'd been assaulted.

Immediately after, Bovell recalled, "we went back to the precinct and at that time ordered an ambulance for my face." He was prescribed Neosporin and an icepack.

Marty's cross-examination of "the victim" began that afternoon and continued through the end of the week. He led with the 2010 Bronx ticket-fixing scandal, questioning Bovell about his involvement. The by-product of good coaching, I presume, he claimed ignorance of the law: "At the time, we didn't know it was the wrong thing to do." (*Oh, the irony of a cop "not knowing" the law!*) It was the one blemish on Bovell's personnel record that Zweibel had left open for questioning, but Marty used it as a springboard. In quick succession, he asked about the court records suggesting a history of excessive force but was answered only by the prosecution's objections, invariably sustained by Zweibel—who quickly ordered the jury out and shouted Marty down, threatening to hold him in "contempt of court" or to throw him jail if he "continued that line of questioning."

With the jury back in their seats, well insulated from the truth, Marty questioned Bovell about the night of March 17. If I had been so irate—"yelling and cursing"—and insistent on my right to remain in the park, "how did it come about," Marty asked, "that she turns around, right, so you can put your hand on her shoulder from her back?" "Luck of the draw, I guess," Bovell quipped. "And all of a sudden," Marty continued, "she goes from being quite angry to being quite cooperative?" "Well she wasn't happy," Bovell responded, "but she was walking in that direction." "And it is at this point," Marty clarified, "that you say Ms. McMillan says, 'Are you filming this? Are you filming this?'" "Yes," Bovell confirmed. "I turned to look, I [didn't] see anything and I put my face back and then she crouched down and elbowed me in the face?" *Whhhaaaaa!?* I thought, *That doesn't make sense on so many levels!* I went from irate to compliant to downright violent in a matter of seconds, and while he was looking the other way he somehow *also saw me* crouch down and elbow him in the face? *Bananas!*

Next, Marty brought out Bovell's testimony to the grand jury, where he had repeatedly stated he'd been hit in the right rather than the left eye and, therefore, suggested that the injury he sustained was not nearly as grave or memorable as his most recent court performance made it seem. Marty also grilled Bovell as to why he was so quick to assume I'd bluffed my injuries. He said he'd seen protestors play dead and fake seizures before, so "I told her, 'If you can speak to me, you can breathe.'" "And what medical degrees do you hold?" Marty shot back, provoking objections from the prosecution (sustained by Zweibel). Finally, Marty got Bovell to admit that he'd never searched for the policewoman in question. With the close of court on Friday, Bovell left the stand, and my life, forever. I never saw him again, but I haven't been able to forget his face, either.

The following week, beginning Monday, April 21, belonged once again to the prosecution. It had become tradition to start each week off on the worst possible foot, so, by the third one, at least, I expected it. In preparation for the following two witnesses, expected to testify on my condition while in police custody, Marty moved to enter a number of videos: a handful to clearly depict the severity and duration of my state, one of the violent beating I suffered beforehand and a couple more to characterize the general chaos of the evening. Justice Zweibel, of course, denied all but two: one of my seizing (he threw us a bone and gave us our pick) and the other of my beating (a short, shaky video taken by another protestor narrowly escaping arrest himself). Oh, but he ruled against audio: the jury would neither hear the fear of the Occupiers taking a stand nor the malice of the NYPD beating them down. The perversion of justice was so blatant, so overwhelming that I couldn't *not* react. Zweibel, of course, reacted right back: "Don't shake your head, Ms. McMillan!" He yelled at me like I was a little girl, and for one, weak moment I was reduced to one (resulting, of course, in a news line: "A visibly upset McMillan dabbed tears from her eyes with a tissue and left the courtroom"). At the end of it all, an exasperated Marty accused him of taking "the prosecution's side all the time—you never take mine!" "That's an outrageous statement you're making," Zweibel shot back. Marty threw up his arms, the gallery laughed, and I tried my best not to ruin my makeup *again* before the jury returned.

With half the morning already gone, the first witness to take the stand was Bovell's commanding officer, Sergeant Willie Briggs. Briggs testified that, around midnight, he saw Bovell, about fifty feet away, escorting a female out of the park in handcuffs. "She didn't seem to be complying with him, yelling and screaming and not really trying to walk," he said, and added, "He almost had to carry her [by] her arms [with] another officer assisting him out of the park." He also noted that his eyeglasses were askew, "tilted to the side." When he next encountered Bovell, it was 2 a.m., and Briggs noticed a "bruise on his face"; Bovell reported that he'd been assaulted and described the female officer who was allegedly present before our exchange. The two then spent the next ten minutes or so trying "to find her so she could be a witness in regards to his injury"; of the hundred or so officers present, Briggs said he questioned two women that fit Bovell's description—but could no longer recall those details, *at all.* In fact, he seemed to remember every detail of the evening—including the "body odor" of the protestors—*except anything relating to me.* Besides his fuzzy recollection of the female officer, when cross-examined by Rebecca, he could not identify much about Bovell's arrestee except "she was a female. She had hair." And, though, Briggs could remember that the woman was resisting arrest and screaming, he could not recall what color she was wearing. "So you don't know whether that person was the defendant here, do you?" Rebecca asked. "No. I do not." Briggs responded. *You killed it!* I wrote and passed her the note as she took her seat beside me.

When he was excused, the prosecution called, "Lisa Waring," and the very mention of her name made the hairs on the back of my neck stand straight up. Seeing my former arresting officer in the broad daylight of a public courtroom, without her uniform (or her handcuffs binding me to a bed in a closed-off storage closet), she almost looked nice, normal even. But then she took the stand as "Nice Ol' Granny Waring" and performed a well-rehearsed, fictional story of our time together.

She testified that she'd come to Zuccotti Park under the charge of Sergeant Diaz (the two had been in the same van). Unlike Diaz, though, she recalled that when she arrived around 5:30 p.m. there were 75–100 police officers and 200–250 protestors at the park. Around midnight, she (and about 100 other officers) had gone in to clear the park and, after warnings had been given, began arresting the 100–150 protestors who had refused to leave. Waring testified that when she first saw me I had already been handcuffed and loaded onto the arrest bus; from about five to ten feet away, she saw me through the window having trouble breathing then witnessed me being "brought out by one or two officers." Once on the ground, I started "thrusting" back and forth, and that's when she came over: "I just thought she needed help," she said. "I told her to just relax, everything's going to be OK, just try to breathe." While waiting with me, she testified that she "tried to give [me] aid": she adjusted my miniskirt to prevent my exposure and placed her coat under my "gyrating" head to protect it from the pavement. As such—under Choi's direction, she clarified—my head had never hit the ground, my eyes had never rolled back, and I never lost consciousness. After the paramedics finally arrived, she joined me in the ambulance, where I'd immediately stopped thrusting and gasping: "She was OK, once she got into the ambulance," Waring said. "I was surprised."

She accompanied me to the emergency room and remained with me the whole time, during which, Waring testified, I never once complained of any pains, showed any signs of cuts or bruising, or ever said anything about an officer assaulting me. Instead, I'd been "happy" and had even thanked her for being there. Later, when my friends stopped by to visit, she recounted, "Cecily was sitting up . . . was talkative, very good, very positive."

What a psycho! I wrote and passed the note to Marty as she was released for the day—who would be "happy" to be held prisoner in a hospital with a cop at the foot of the bed!? Marty nodded and, once the jury was released, communicated the same sentiment to Zweibel. He moved for a mistrial for the admission of hearsay—in legal terms, a statement offered in evidence to prove the truth of the matter asserted. In other words, Waring had presented statements to disprove my claim that I'd been assaulted and to prove that I'd faked my injuries to ultimately justify my assaulting Officer Bovell. Zweibel, of course, flatly denied the motion to dismiss the case and curtly reminded Marty that he'd have his chance to "impeach" (or discredit) Waring under cross-examination on Wednesday.

Marty replied that he'd be able to do just that if Zweibel would allow him to use the videos he'd ruled out that morning; he argued that the footage showed glaring inconsistencies in her testimony that she couldn't possibly back out of: namely, he explained, a couple of them clearly depicted my head repeatedly striking the ground and every single one suggested that I'd been unconscious for most, if not all, of the time in question. What infuriated me the most, though, was Waring's claim that she cared enough to pull down my skirt when every video I'd seen showed otherwise. Of course, she'd done nothing kind or motherly for me—but had, instead, neglected and humiliated me all night.

Choi, in turn, accused Marty of attempting to "manipulate the timeline" by "cherry-picking videos" to give the jury the impression that it "took a lot longer than it did" to have me arrested and taken to the hospital. I coughed in lieu of crying out *are you fucking kidding me?* Rebecca tenderly put her hand on my arm to calm me down while Marty tried a different route: he suggested that Zweibel show the videos to the jury and let them decide for themselves. If I'd faked the whole thing, Marty reasoned (now shouting, too), "she's a talent who deserves an Academy Award!" Zweibel shouted back (loudest of all), "I don't want you to win an Academy Award, either." With that, he reaffirmed his ruling against the videos and dismissed us.

On Wednesday morning, April 23, Choi continued her direct examination of Waring. I remained outwardly poised, but took to writing *I CAN'T* over and over in my notes. Picking back up at the hospital, she testified that I had been released pretty quickly because I refused medical care (which wasn't entirely true: *She told me if I signed the papers I'd be out in time to see my own doctor by the morning*—I wrote on a pink note to Marty). Afterward, she transported me to a detention center where I was "sociable with other prisoners in the holding cell." Waring reported that I remained congenial—"She was still bubbly, still in a good mood"—until she was informed by a desk sergeant that I was "not to be released because [I'd] assaulted a police officer in his precinct." She testified that I soured as soon as she told me: "She was amazed," Waring stated. "She said, 'If anyone, I was assaulted.'" After that, Waring said I was unfriendly to her: "Her demeanor toward me changed," she said. "It was like night and day." (*Liar! Liar! Liar! She never even told me my charges!*) In lieu of being released, she said, I demanded to go back to the hospital; once there, I objected to her waiting with me: "She didn't want me," Waring said. "She told the nurse, 'I don't want her near me. Can you take me to a room? I don't trust her.' Her whole demeanor changed towards me." "But I had to stay with her, she was my prisoner," Waring continued, "[but] I didn't have a conversation with her because she was so negative toward me." (That part, at least, had some truth to it: *I didn't want to "have a conversation with her" either!*)

Afterward, Marty cross-examined her, but without the necessary videos to provide context for questioning and with the rest of her testimony stemming from (alleged) conversations shared between only us—well, he was *still* able to impeach her twice! As directed by Choi, she'd testified more than a dozen times that I'd never said anything about a bruise on my chest or anything of the sort; she'd said otherwise, though, in a pretrial hearing. "Didn't [Ms. McMillan] tell the nurse at Bellevue that her chest was bruised?" Marty asked. "Not that I recall, no," Waring responded. After some argument, he recited her "sworn testimony" from the court record, and she reluctantly agreed, "Okay. All right. So if I said that, then that's what happened." That wasn't good enough for Marty, though: "She did make the complaint, correct?" he rephrased, and she answered, "Yes." "About her chest being bruised?" he clarified, and she took a beat, but *finally* said, "Yes."

The other discrepancy had to do with her report of my crimes that evening, the same report that had been used to bring felony assault charges against me. "Just so it's clear," Marty started in on her, "you signed an affidavit, sworn affidavit, that becomes a criminal complaint that said that you were told by Officer Grantley Bovell, shield number 17433 of the 40th Precinct, that while Police Officer Bovell was escorting an individual who was under arrest for an unrelated offense out of [Zuccotti Park] the defendant approached Police Officer Bovell and struck Police Officer Bovell's face with her elbow. That is the Criminal Court complaint and the sworn affidavit that you signed, correct?" "Yes," she said but explained that the only thing Bovell had ever told her was that he was struck in the left eye: "I got [the rest] from the desk sergeant. And at the time the—like I didn't have access to Officer Bovell because he had gone line of duty sick." Following a slew of excuses, Waring conceded that she should have included the desk sergeant in her report but testified that she did not know his name or where he'd gotten the story from. It all seemed *very* convenient—particularly, the fact that Waring was retired. Otherwise, her negligence (to put it nicely) might have carried professional consequences. As such, everyone escaped scot-free—Bovell, especially, with his story intact.

On that happy note, the fourth and final representative of New York's Finest walked out of the courtroom. For the first time since the trial started, I was finally able to breathe. It had been twelve actual days and eight court days of preparing for and listening to cops, cops, cops, cops. . . . My brave face had clearly begun to crack under the weight of mounting PTSD. Though I usually did well at pretending it didn't exist, the days of testimony had triggered a war in my psyche that waged on in my nightmares—because I couldn't control my thoughts in my sleep, the anxiety erupted into night terrors that had me jumping up and gasping for air every couple of hours, leaving me worse for wear each passing day. After that NYPD parade, it didn't matter who the prosecution called or what they said about me: as long as they didn't have a badge and handcuffs, I assumed I'd be just fine.

As it happened, the next witness was a nerdy kid with unruly hair and three-piece suit who looked younger than me—and, if you can imagine, more uncomfortable too. Poor kid, he'd made a wrong turn in life and ended up as a video forensic technician in the Manhattan DA's office. The prosecution called Jonathan Fong as their expert witness to substantiate the video of my exchange with Bovell. To be clear, though, their version of the footage was an edit in itself: the nineteen-second clip—starting with the sight of my silhouette and cut short of my being beaten—was taken from the original fifty-three second posting on YouTube (though they were loath to say it). As such, Fong presented their clip as "the video" and replayed versions of it for more than an hour, narrating different enhancements: he placed a spotlight on me to make it easier to follow "what happened," then presented the same video in slow motion to "show more detail." Finally, he walked the jury through a PowerPoint presentation of the spotlight video and attempted to explain, frame by frame, how I intentionally assaulted Bovell. And yet you still couldn't see much of anything really. For instance, you couldn't make out my face: it was just a little white dot. Honestly, had it not been St. Patrick's Day, I wouldn't be on trial—he would. Movement was indicated by contrasting colors, my green coat moving in front of his dark uniform behind me. Fong's "enhancements," as far as I could tell, didn't make things clearer: they just amplified my image (and therefore my actions) against the void of color around me. In short, all the digital remastering seemed only meant to enlarge my role in the incident, my culpability for trial. But, as Sarah Jaffe of *In These Times* noted, no one paid him much attention anyhow:

> What they don't tell you about court, what the courtroom dramas don't show, is how deadly boring it is. At one point during the testimony of the District Attorney's Office forensic video expert, explaining a video that allegedly depicts McMillan's altercation with Officer Bovell, at least one juror appeared to actually fall asleep. And yet as you sit there, watching, listening to the same question being asked over and over, you remember that someone's life is on the line, that the third repetition of a blurry YouTube video from the night of March 17 could make the difference between conviction and acquittal.

At the close of Fong's direct examination, we were released for the day, and I left not knowing whether to be relieved or worried—either way, there was really nothing I could do about it. So I did the only thing, it seemed, I could do: I got a manicure then went shopping on Madison Avenue, in search of the perfect LWD (little witness dress).

When court resumed that Friday, April 25, 2014, Marty cross-examined Fong, who testified to the degradation, distortion, and general low quality of the video evidence. A small victory, Marty got him to submit that the absence of multiple angles could compromise one's ability to accurately determine what happened and that when multiple angles are shown, they can give a different interpretation of the events. In short, the video provided shaky grounds, at best, for an assault charge—yet, apparently, the DA's office had staked its case on it within a few hours of the incident. From Fong, we learned that the footage had been downloaded from YouTube at approximately 6 a.m. Sunday, March 18, 2012. So, presumably, DA minions began scouring the Internet, looking for dirt, as soon as I was loaded into the ambulance. I scribbled off a note to Rebecca: *How creepy is that?* "Pretty creepy," she mouthed back.

After Fong, another representative of the Manhattan DA's office, stepped up to testify against me—or rather, was forced onto the stand by Marty's sharp, quick-step maneuvering (with little time for the prosecution's fine tuning). "In direct response to Mr. Stolar's missing witness charge," Choi called Hayley Cowitt, her former paralegal, to testify to the effort her office had made to locate the policewoman mentioned by both Officer Bovell and Sergeant Briggs but, otherwise, nonexistent. Cowitt recalled that she'd assisted with my case from June to July 2012: at Choi's instruction, she'd contacted NYPD Legal for "a complete list of officers who were assigned to Occupy Wall Street detail on March 17–18, 2012," then notified each of the seventy-five or so (sometimes twice over) to come down to the office and "tell their story of what happened on that date." Cowitt further testified that she'd been "present for some of the interviews" and "specifically remember[ed] that we were looking for a female officer." Despite their exhaustive effort, however, they were unable to locate the female officer who, according to Bovell, had served as the catalyst for my assaulting him.

Under cross-examination, Cowitt conceded that her so-called list was more like "a number of pieces of paper": of the names given, several were duplicates while others were completely illegible and, therefore, impossible to contact. Further, some of those she did contact never showed up. The list itself was decidedly incomplete to begin with: most notably, none of the officers who testified were on it, *including Bovell*. Worse still, she knew it and didn't do anything about it: "Did you ever go back and say, we got some more. Have you added somebody—and stuff like that?" Marty asked. "No," she responded, "It was past the date in question, so I went with the fact that I asked for a complete list, and this is what they provided me with." In essence, Marty got Cowitt to effectively admit that Choi did not exercise due diligence in validating Bovell's claims—*then, he swept the floor with it.*

"Based on the lack of credibility of Officer Bovell and his description of the events," Marty argued that the evidence produced by the prosecution was insufficient to prove its case. "The officer has not been produced. I don't think the officer exists, and I think the event did not take place. He doesn't remember going and searching for her even though Officer Briggs does. With respect to the video itself," he added, "it is not sufficient evidence. It's degraded, it's distorted, and it does not show . . . that she knew that there was an officer involved. The only way she knows there's an officer involved is if the incident were, [as] Bovell claims, that he's talking to Ms. McMillan and a police officer"—*the officer conveniently missing from the prosecution's case.*

"So," he swiftly concluded, "I think there is sufficient grounds for the Court to dismiss the case at the stage."

Choi declined to respond—why should she? The Prosecutor in Robes spoke for her: "What you are raising are questions of fact and those facts will be for a jury to determine, so the motion is denied." I can't say I was surprised. It was as satisfying an ending as I could have hoped for, but, alas, Marty's big moment wasn't sexy enough (or, maybe, simple enough) for the tabloids to cover. That's okay, though, I was impressed enough for all of us and told Marty so on a little pink note: *You're a badass! <3*

I was so lucky to have him: without Marty, I never would have made it through those two weeks of prosecutorial hell. Now, it was *our turn*. Marty and Rebecca would have to persuade the jury (or one juror, at least) that I was guilty of nothing more than being in the wrong place at the wrong time. I was worried, for sure. But I knew that if anyone could do it, it was Marty. I trusted him beyond a shadow of a doubt, I trusted him—still do—with my life. "The defense calls Jacob Stevens," Marty said, and I breathed a sigh of relief.

Jake, the friend I'd gone to meet that night at the park, testified that he'd known me since September 2011, when we were both part of the Demands Working Group. He said that our plans that night were to meet in Zuccotti Park and then "go out to get a drink." Those plans came to naught when, as he went on to testify, the police began to sweep people out of the park, with no audible announcement warning them it was time to leave. When Jake reached a safe place outside the police perimeter, he checked his phone to find a text message from a colleague: "We saw your friend get beaten up." He went to look for me, walking toward Broadway, and from a distance saw me on the ground, near the prisoner bus, seizing and left unattended by police. And then he recounted tracking me down later that night in Beekman Hospital, where he found me "very scared, very upset.

Traumatized, and bruised." He, Sarah, and Kay were told I was going to the precinct soon and would be released shortly after. The next he saw me was at my felony arraignment on Monday, March 19. My bruises, he testified contrary to Waring, were numerous and very visible, both in the hospital and at my arraignment.

When Jake finished, Marty called James McMillan—my father. Talk about a scenario I'd never in a million years imagined would happen. Jake's testimony had been dark and somber, but Dad struck a different tone entirely, and deliberately so: we called him to contextualize the absurdity of the charge, the silliness of thinking I'd set out that night to assault anyone. He told the court about our "family tradition" of celebrating St. Patrick's Day and about our jovial exchange that day: "She was very excited about a kind of costume she had," he said, then added, "I told her to be careful and not get in trouble, you know, to have a good time." Then Marty picked up a sheet of paper and said, "I'm going to show you what we'll mark [as] Exhibit T-1, [and] ask if you recognize it?" Before it got to Dad, though, Choi and Strain bobbled up: "May I see it?" both asked, in the same tone, nearly in unison. (*Eerie*, I thought. *Like Stepford prosecutor-bots.*) After they'd finished probing it, Dad took one look and, with a slight grin, said, "That's my daughter and that's the text and the picture I received." Marty, then displaying the screen shot on a big screen TV, pointed and (with great enthusiasm) asked, "And it says 'Happy St. Patty's!!!'?" Dad said "yes," turning red like he does when trying not to laugh. "Just to clear it up, let me show you another," Marty pronounced artfully and, once again, up Choi went, "May I see it?" She rolled her eyes: it was the same photo, just blown up (she was so uptight, he didn't even have to try to get her goat). Once again directing Dad's attention to the screen, Marty remarked, "She seems to be holding something in her hand." "A green beer," Daddy blurted, and stumbled to recover from what he mistook as a blunder. "I'm assuming, I'm sorry, a green liquid." Marty hadn't prepped him at all, but it was exactly what he was looking for: "A green liquid," he repeated, then asked, "St. Patrick's Day beer?" The gallery giggled and Dad, pink by now, joined them, "St. Patrick's Day beer, yes." A single word in my notes described my reaction to his testimony: "Fuuunny!" But, in earnest, I felt closer to Dad that day, and prouder to be a McMillan, than I had in many years. Choi declined to cross-examine Dad and, spared that small indignity, he was released.

On his way out, he mouthed, "I love you," and Marty called his next witness, Yoni Miller—the same from #Justice4Cecily who I'd known throughout Occupy and, before that, the Young Democratic Socialists. First, Yoni testified to my reputation at Occupy Wall Street as the "Queen of Nonviolence," known for my conviction that nonviolent political action was *the only way* to effect positive change. Afterward, Yoni described his account of March 17. Unlike me, he was one of about fifty protestors who intentionally refused the NYPD's orders to disperse that evening and knowingly risked arrest. At Marty's direction, Yoni explained that he and others stood their ground because "we felt that the orders for dispersal were unlawful": "Zuccotti Park is a publicly owned private space and part of its condition is that it's open twenty-four hours a day, seven days a week." In response to his passive resistance, Yoni said he was dragged into the street, arrested, and "hit multiple times in the back and neck area" by what he thought was either "a knee or a baton." Afterward, he was escorted onto the MTA bus where he first witnessed me that evening: "I saw several officers bringing Cecily up. She was flopping like a squirming fish and it was clear that she was not all right. People in the bus were shouting, 'Get her off the bus. Get a medic.'" And, so, they brought me off.

Whatever good Yoni had done me was swiftly undone in Choi's cross-examination, when she skillfully turned his words against me.

My reputation for and commitment to nonviolence, as attested to by Yoni, was "a fraud," according to the prosecution. As "proof," Choi introduced the fact that I'd been arrested eighteen months after the March 17 incident, in December 2013, for obstructing governmental administration, a misdemeanor crime: "Have you heard," she asked Yoni, "that this defendant interfered with police officers who were investigating two individuals for not paying their fare when entering the [Union Square] train station by grabbing one of the individual's hands and shaking it so that his identification card would fall to the ground and would be prevented from giving [it] to the police officer?" Marty objected: it was an open case and, therefore, mere allegation. Zweibel overruled it and, so, Yoni answered, "I have not heard of that the way you described it." "And have you also heard," Choi continued, "that this defendant followed police officers to the precinct and, when she was denied entrance to the precinct, she grabbed onto the door and kept shaking it and screamed her demand to get inside?" Yoni responded, "I have not heard that." It didn't matter how he answered, Choi got what she wanted by just asking the question: the implication that I had a habit of violently defying the police.

Besides being unproven, Choi's summary of the evening was (yet again) untrue. The two officers in question didn't present as such: they were undercover when they ambushed the Hispanic couple sitting next to me, demanding answers without presenting badges. The girl began to cry, the boy pulled her in, and the two seemed to panic—like, maybe, they didn't understand what was going on or, otherwise, were undocumented immigrants. They spoke quickly in Spanish, but (thanks to my mother) I got the gist of it: apparently, an MTA worker had waived them through the gate when their cards didn't work. As the couple searched their pockets, I cautiously turned on my iPhone video and commented, in English, "You don't have to do that, they haven't identified themselves." I hoped to cue the officers that someone who cared enough to say something was watching and I knew enough to know they'd broken protocol—the case would get thrown out, anyhow. *Woaaah!* the officers shouted (*finally* brandishing their badges) and demanded the couple to "come with us." There's nothing I could've done to stop them—and I didn't try to; that's not my style—but I could help them find a lawyer and provide a witness statement. They nodded, and I asked the officers permission to follow. "That's your right," one said—yep, it sure was. Nonetheless, the two were released and I was locked up, then, later, taken to Bellevue Psychiatric (*once again*). Why? I don't know. But on my way in, an officer taunted, "Choi's going to have a field day with this!"

When the misdemeanor case later came to trial, in October 2014, the charge proved so flimsy that, after cross-examining their witnesses, Marty (who also represented me then) didn't bother to present any defense witnesses, and I was promptly acquitted. Filming the police is not a crime or an act of violence, which Choi presumably learned in law school, but it was an opportunity to represent me as a psycho cop-hater—of course, she took advantage of it. More shocking, however, was that Zweibel had allowed her to do so when he'd previously denied my counsel the same courtesy, ruling Bovell's alleged violent behavior in other cases irrelevant and inadmissible. The final defense witness that Friday was Susan Kang, a professor of criminal justice at John Jay, who had worked with me in the Demands Working Group. She testified to my injuries following my release from jail the afternoon of March 19, 2012. Susan had been insistent on documenting my physical trauma and had taken photos that evening of the hand-shaped bruise on my breast, as well as other bruises on my legs, arms, rib, back, and face, that the prosecution had insinuated were somehow self-inflicted.

That afternoon was a nice reprieve, however short and constrained by Zweibel, from the prosecution's tall tales about me. It was a relief to listen to testimony of what had really happened that night—after two weeks to the contrary, I was starting to go a little crazy. *How could two sides of the same story differ so drastically?* More than anything, though, I was restless from sitting in silence, listening to everyone talk about me—I wanted to speak for myself. "*Surely,*" I urged Marty, "the jury will believe *me!*" Marty, however, wasn't so sure. "I still need to think about it," he said, but threw me a bone: since the prosecution had rested its case, he let me do an interview to tell the public, at least, *my side of the story.* Still though, it'd taken a remarkable writer to get Marty to even consider it: Chris Hedges, the Pulitzer prize–winning journalist who'd reported on global terrorism for the *New York Times* and had since become a columnist for the website *Truthdig.* Marty allowed me to meet with him on two conditions: that he be present for the interview and that I shut up when I was told to. We knew well, by then, how easily the truth could be misconstrued, and Marty wasn't willing to take any chances on my case. I wasn't either, so I readily agreed to his terms.

And so, Chris met me, Marty, and his wife, Elsie Chandler, at their Upper West Side apartment for dinner and a night off from the grind of trial preparation. I'd become accustomed to, by then, long nights in the living room spent building my case with Marty and Elsie: a relentless defender of underserved youth as senior trial attorney and director of the Youth Law Team at Neighborhood Defender Service of Harlem—yep, she was just as much a saint as Marty and, at five foot nothing, an even bigger force! That night, though, we made our way to the living room for after-dinner drinks; it was a nice treat and, despite everything, I'd really come to love it there. Raz, the black mixed-breed retriever-chow "man" of the house, immediately nuzzled into the place between the edge of the couch and my feet and began licking my knees from underneath. It tickled, and I giggled a little as I pointed out to Chris the creature comforts of that little oasis, the last remaining space that I felt safe and human in the unraveling tragedy of trial life. "Look!" I showed him the shelves brimming with law books, news clippings, and family pictures, the walls filled with mementos of Marty and Elsie's decades-long crusade to save humanity from the criminal justice system. "Enough," Marty laughed off my sentimentalism. "Get on with it, already!" Chris and I talked for a couple hours: him with the questions, me with the tangents, me burning cigarettes, him turning pages, Marty and Elsie following along, listening carefully, and censoring accordingly.

We talked about Occupy, Zuccotti, March 17 . . . about the trial in detail and prison abstractly . . . about who I was generally, and— most of all—where I'd come from and how I'd ended up smack-dab in the middle of this mess. Then he thanked me for my story, said it would be up by the end of the weekend, and left. As soon as he did, I started to worry: any misconstrued statement could land me in Rikers! Why had it taken me so long to get that? "Relax, you did fine," Elsie said, showing me out. "Get some sleep," Marty directed, "or you'll look like shit for the paparazzi." (He did always know how to motivate me.)

I awoke Sunday morning to find myself sprawled across the main page of Truthdig.com: my concerned face and outstretched arm at the head of an angry crowd beneath the towering red sculpture of Zuccotti Park. My stomach lurched, then back-flipped. "The Crime of Peaceful Protest," I read the title out loud to Lucy, but that's as far as I got. "You do it—I can't." My voice was shaking too much. By doing the interview, I'd hoped that maybe one of the jurors or someone close to them would read it—I know, the rules, but people *have to look*, they have *to know* before they send someone away, right? I thought, if they heard my story, the real story, they would know that I wasn't anything like the fame-driven, hot-headed revolutionary the prosecution made me out to be. They'd see that I really was just a twenty-five-year-old student-nanny-activist, not normal per se but maybe for the better: I desperately believed in our democracy and wanted to see the people come together and take it back for themselves.

I watched Lucy's lips moving. She was reading aloud, it seemed, but I couldn't hear anything she was saying. My mind was spinning, the worries swirled and stuck, mounting higher and higher until I couldn't breathe—they'd taken over, somehow, and now I was in a panic. You probably said too much, you got way too emotional—why did you chain smoke? And tell him about your family—really, *your family?* He probably thought you were crazy—*You are crazy!*—totally exhausting and incoherent, to say the least. He probably hated you—maybe not, but doubtful he liked you. "Oh my God! What did I do?" I said to myself (I think). "Choi is going to roast me on a spit—burn me in effigy, draw and quarter me . . . full-on character-assassinate me!" "Hey!" Lucy snapped, and the sound came back. "You listening!?" "Huh?" I murmured and blinked intently trying to bring her face into focus—"Listen!" she demanded. "Your last line—you totally nailed it":

Everyone should come and sit through this trial to see the façade that we call democracy. The resources one needs to even remotely have a chance in this system are beyond most people. Thank God I went to college and graduate school. Thank God Marty and Rebecca are my lawyers. Thank God I am an organizer and have some agency. I wait in line every day to go to court. I read above my head the words that read something like "Justice Is the Foundation of Democracy." And I wonder if this is "Alice in Wonderland." People of color, people who are poor, the people where I come from, do not have a chance for justice. Those people have no choice but to plead out. They can never win in court. I can fight it. This makes me a very privileged person. It is disgusting to think that this is what our democracy has come to. I am heartbreakingly sad for our country.

"Whoa," I exhaled. "Wait—I said that?" "Yeah you did!" Lucy beamed. "And, get this—Chris says, 'Being an activist in peaceful mass protest is the only real 'crime' McMillan has committed.'" Maybe, I thought—but dare not say it aloud—just maybe, I'll beat this thing after all.

WE HAD MONDAY OFF (because a juror was moving) then continued Tuesday, April 29, with a string of Occupiers to provide eyewitness accounts of the NYPD's forceful clearing of the park and testify to my reputation for nonviolent activism: Stacy Lanyon, Marisa Holmes, Amin Husain, Isham Christie, Joe Sharkey, and Zoltan Gluck.

Stacy Lanyon, a writer and photographer, joined Occupy Wall Street in October 2011 and documented its development both on her blog, *At the Heart of an Occupation*, and through several photobooks— including one entitled *Occupy Wall Street: Six-Month Anniversary, M17* (meaning March 17, 2012). Stacy testified that she'd been in the park all day photographing what, until 11 p.m., she described as a peaceful event. She was there when the park was cleared. And when she spotted me, postarrest, handcuffed on the ground and clearly in distress, she took a series of photos that Marty, over Choi's objection, was able to introduce into evidence. She pointed to several that showed an unidentified officer trying to move me: "I saw him trying to get her to stand," she noted, "and at one point in time her feet were actually off the ground in one of my photos, and she couldn't stand, and he then tried to get her to sit back down and that seemed even more difficult for her to do."

Up next was Marisa Holmes, a video editor at the City University of New York and my old sparring partner from all the way back to the planning stages of Occupy Wall Street. Testifying to our political differences, she said that I advocated for "voting for political parties and running candidates, trying to initiate some kind of small change to the system; not radical change, not anything having to do with fundamental revolutionary transformation," as she ascribed to. Contrary to the majority, Marisa said, "Cecily had no problem with the State. She had no problem with the police. She wanted to work through electoral politicians and legislative action. That's what the Demands Working Group was all about." For that reason, she concluded, "it was widely known in Occupy Wall Street that Cecily has a reformist position and a nonviolent position." I'd rarely gotten along with Marisa but had always respected her—that day more than ever. She didn't have to take the stand but had done so readily (and proved unequivocally the power, the camaraderie, of Occupy Wall Street).

Choi ignored everything she said, though, and, at the same time, dismissed it: "Are you aware that this defendant forcibly interfered with a police investigation of two individuals who had nothing to do with Occupy Wall Street on December 7, 2013?" Marisa said she wasn't aware of the incident, but Choi kept on anyhow, repeating the false allegations she had brought up earlier with Yoni. Each time, Marisa replied no and, finally, got fed up with Choi entirely: "I am not aware of [anything] you are saying, but you are not providing any evidence of it whatsoever, so how do I know that what you are saying is true?" And so it went. Each time another witness—Amin, Isham, Joe, Zoltan—testified to my nonviolent *bona fides*, Choi would counter with the December 2013 arrest. It was a master stroke. (One, it seemed, I might not recover from.)

After suffering the string of character blows, the defense called Riley O'Neill, a senior at NYU and our own video expert, to testify against the so-called irrefutable evidence of my guilt. Riley said that the video, although murky and ambiguous, provided evidence to suggest I was telling the truth about Bovell grabbing my right breast: "There's kind of a horizontal black line that you'll see, it looks like . . . there's still a black spot where it should be her torso." Marty asked, "Is the video clear about what the dark spot across her torso is?" "It's unclear," Riley replied, "but I can speculate and say it's whoever is behind her." Choi objected, of course, and Zweibel sustained.

Once Riley was dismissed, Marty announced, "We'd now like to call Cecily McMillan to the witness stand." It was a decision I'd spent weeks preparing for but one we'd only finalized the night before. Contrary to popular belief, defendants rarely testify in a criminal trial—that's what lawyers are for: to represent you. And that's why we have a Fifth Amendment right to remain silent: so someone who knows the law can represent you. Taking the stand leaves defendants wide open for attack with little room for lawyers to protect them when, legally, they don't have to prove their innocence—the burden of proof falls on the prosecution (hence the difference between "innocent" and "not guilty"). In short, a defendant generally has everything to lose and little to gain by testifying on her own behalf, which is why it's usually done against legal advice or, otherwise, as a last resort. In my case, Judge Zweibel had forced Marty's hand by preventing him from defending me himself. Nonetheless, the prosecution had probably expected it all along. After all, according to their story, I'd been angling for my star moment since the night I asked bystanders to film me at the very second I was psyching myself up to assault an officer. That version of Cecily McMillan would never give up her opportunity to take the stage, be the center of attention on the witness stand.

But for as famous—or infamous—as I'd become, I sure didn't feel like a star. *Believe me*, you wouldn't either if your name had been attached to some of those headlines. I felt small and vulnerable—at the whims of whatever forces were hell-bent on breaking me. Nonetheless, I took the stand determined not to let down Marty, my supporters, and my family—especially my grandparents, who feared further shame, and my brother, still in prison, who desperately worried about my facing that fate. More than anything, though, I resolved to stand strong as the (inadvertent) symbol of "the movement"—of Occupy Wall Street immediately but also of the long, proud tradition of the American Left's fight for social justice. Of course, our government has historically called that effort "subversive" and its proponents "traitors" and "terrorists"—criminalizing the very ethos this country was founded on. With that in mind, I willed myself to stay calm and steady my voice as I answered Marty's questions.

I talked about my background, growing up in the South, going to school in Wisconsin. I talked about my political involvement in high school and how in my senior year at Lawrence I had gotten involved with the Madison protests, stressing that in that situation, the police and the protesters were on the same side. "It was so incredible," I told the court. "The unions work with the students and the police and the firefighters and nurses . . . and even one time the police joined us in occupying the Capitol. So it is just a really incredible experience of collective organization." And then I talked about coming to New York as a graduate student in the summer of 2011. I talked about DSA and how I shared the group's priorities of "healthcare, jobs, free higher education, and workers' rights." I recounted the story of how I got involved with Occupy and the Working Demands Group. How, from the start, I urged Occupiers to make a declaration that they stood in the tradition of nonviolent protest. "From the moment I showed up, I was very concerned that there was not some sort of mission statement—who we are and what we stand for," I told Marty and the jurors. I explained why I hadn't taken part in the first day of the occupation, September 17, 2011, because I feared the possibility of violence. I talked about being an Occupier but an outsider as far politics went: "They called me a liberal, and I didn't know that was a kind of backhanded term." And I got a laugh, unintentionally, when I added that I was also sartorially an outsider in Zuccotti Park: "I was published in *Mother Jones* magazine as the Paris Hilton of Occupy Wall Street." Zweibel was not amused: "There is not to be any laughter in this courtroom during testimony."

While underlining the differences between me and some other Occupiers, I also came to Occupy's defense, because I knew the movement was as much on trial as I was. I didn't share the anarchist, off-the-grid perspective of most Occupiers, but I did find their intentions admirable: "I think most of the people at Occupy Wall Street really wanted to cut themselves off from a violent society and to create a society anew in the park. . . . They were not particularly interested in negotiating with what they viewed as a violent and decrepit and ultimately unsalvageable state." What I'd wanted to do, what kept me involved in Occupy despite our differences, was to take "this beautiful experiment" to the "biggest possible level, the national level," through coalition building and political involvement. Shortly afterward, the judge dismissed court until the following morning, Wednesday, April 30, at 9:30.

For my final day of testimony, I wore my chosen "Little Witness Dress": a rose pink, cap-sleeve, crochet sheath Anne Klein (with my mother's pearls, of course). Marty walked me through the night of March 17, what I could and couldn't remember. When he asked me about assaulting Bovell, I replied that "I have no memory of my elbow coming into contact with the officer's face," but I didn't deny it happened: "I'm really sorry that officer got hurt." From what I remembered, though, "all of the sudden I felt somebody grab me from behind, from my right breast and pull me backward. I was lifted in the air and then I felt my face slammed to the ground." Afterward, I testified about my time in custody (including the two hospitals) and how, when I was released on March 19, I *finally* received adequate medical care: I was examined for broken ribs and a head injury but, thankfully, had neither. The following morning, I went to my usual clinic, the Family Institute of Health, and *finally* received quality social services: a physician photographed and documented my injuries and a psychiatrist treated me for anxiety and PTSD.

About midday, my testimony was temporarily interrupted and postponed for Lara Wasserman, my longtime friend from Lawrence University, to take the stand. She confirmed my story of our evening pub crawl on St. Patrick's Day and the sequence of ill-fated events that left me a sitting duck in Zuccotti Park during prime Occupier hunting season.

When she stepped down, I stepped up for the prosecutorial showdown everyone had been waiting for. Choi grilled me on cross-examination about my medical records while under arrest: namely, why none of the doctor reports mentioned either seizures or sexual assault. I explained that I hadn't known about the seizures until the Occupy women at the precinct told me and was otherwise informed that seizures could only be diagnosed as they occurred, not after the fact; finally, I pointed to one of my medical records, "It says I was abused." Of course, not a single one of the doctors I'd seen had adequately examined me; if they had, they would've felt the bumps on my head and seen the hand-shaped bruise on my right breast—the bruise I reported to the nurse at Bellevue, the same that Officer Waring remembered me reporting but that nobody found important enough to note in my medical records. Still, I thought, the photo taken the following day at the Family Institute of Health said it all: there I stood, nearly naked and forlorn—humiliated really—folding my bra halfway down to expose the five-fingered, slightly yellowing bruise and accompanying red scratch marks on my right breast. If that doesn't convince the jury that Officer Bovell had sexually assaulted me, I thought, *nothing will*—and *nothing* would convince them of my innocence either: it would mean that they didn't see me as a person, a woman, but, instead, only as a symbol of the Occupy Wall Street movement. And that was *exactly* how "the People" intended to paint me. Pivoting for her final attack, Choi interrogated me on the only two interviews I'd given about the events of March 17, 2012: the first, two days after, with Amy Goodman on *Democracy Now!* and the last, of course, with Chris Hedges just a couple days prior. Nevertheless, she relentlessly insinuated that I was a fame whore.

On our last scheduled "day off" from trial, Thursday, May 1, I went to a May Day demonstration at Washington Square Park (surrounded by watchful friends to make sure that, even in the midst of that peaceful gathering, the NYPD wouldn't find a way to come after me). Then on Friday, May 2, I returned to court to listen to closing arguments. Marty confidently swept the stage with a cavalier yet conversational one-man show lasting nearly three hours. "There is no proof beyond a reasonable doubt," he told the jury. "So the only verdict that you can reach is not guilty." He pointed to the contradictions in Bovell's testimony. First I was screaming bloody murder at a female police officer, then calmly being led out of the park under Bovell's gentle guidance, before viciously assaulting him. And where was the mystery female police officer? How many female police officers were present that night? Why couldn't the DA locate the one person who would have perfectly corroborated Bovell's claim? "I suggest to you that if that female police officer existed," Marty insisted, "she would have been found." In fact, despite the hundred or more present, no other officer provided eyewitness testimony. All the DA had was Bovell's word and a grainy video clip, supposedly shot at my request. "By his testimony," Marty suggested, "the woman in the bright green dress, not someone hidden behind a mask, not someone who's wearing dark clothing, who stands out and can't be missed, says, 'Film this, I would like to have a record of me in my green dress committing a crime—that's what I want. Please film this.' That's his testimony. Does it make sense? Really not too much."

Marty also emphasized my commitment to nonviolence and electoral politics: "Everybody agrees that Cecily's position, and what she's known for, is being a nonviolent person, and not wanting to confront the state, but to work in collaboration with the state. That means you don't go around slugging cops. That's not how you make political change. She is not going to punch out a cop. It serves no purpose for her politically, it serves no purpose for her personally. She is not someone who goes around hitting cops. It just is not her."

In his final remarks, Marty urged the jurors to "send Ms. McMillan home. Send her back to school and let her finish her thesis and move on to become a teacher, a politician, or president of the United States."

After lunch, it was Choi's turn. Her melodramatic monologue brought to life my fictitious alter ego—Cecily McMillan, the publicity hound—and elucidated the inner workings of my diabolical mind. "This defendant wants to be the face of Occupy Wall Street. She decided to accomplish this by fabricating what happened on March 17th, 2012." Choi pointed out that I'd "conveniently" remembered every detail of the evening *but* my criminal conduct: "She remembers being grabbed, then *blank*. Is she trying to convince you that this breast grab caused memory loss?" Must be, Choi quipped, because I'd gone to four different hospitals, and "they all told me I had no seizure." As for the bruising, it didn't come from a police beating—it was self-inflicted: *I had assaulted myself.* "During the performance of her life," Choi explained, "she flopped around, slammed her body on the sidewalk multiple times, by herself." The bruise on my chest, instead, could have happened when I "fell on my right arm while trying to run away from Bovell" or, afterward, when I refused to give it over to be handcuffed. "Maybe," she said, and insinuated that I might have intentionally harmed myself to set Bovell up; but it couldn't have been him, she explained; he would have needed "razor blades for fingernails" and "a hot iron for a hand" to have caused my injuries.

"All we know," Choi pointed out, "is that [the bruise] wasn't documented in Beekman where she went within thirty minutes of the incident [or] at Bellevue where she was for two hours, and she doesn't mention this bruise when she goes to New York Methodist on March 19th"—all of which was to say, "this defendant definitely would've said her chest pain came from being grabbed by her right breast, but she didn't because she was not sexually assaulted." The (refutable) fact that I didn't report it was repeated thirty-four times throughout her twenty-five-minute speech as irrefutable evidence of my guilt and was, ultimately, the linchpin of her case: "This defendant has attempted to pervert this trial with grandstanding and outright falsehoods," she charged. "She assaulted [Bovell] and tried to exploit the situation by feigning that she couldn't breathe. When this didn't work she tried to run away, then feigned a seizure. When this didn't work, in February of 2014, on the eve of this trial, this defendant made horrific, baseless accusations." In fact, Choi asserted, my story was "so utterly unbelievable and ridiculous that [I] might as well have said that *aliens* came down that night and assaulted [me]. . . . She has no right to have you ignore the actual video evidence that shows her assaulting a police officer," she asserted, gearing up for her grand (if predictable) finale. "She made her decision and now the time has come to make yours. And based on all the evidence and common sense, that decision must be to convict this defendant of assault in the second degree."

Wooooooow! I thought, but was otherwise speechless. *Of course,* I didn't come out before trial and say what Bovell had done to me—I was under criminal investigation. *I wasn't supposed to.* My lawyers said so, it was Legal Advice 101: "Anything you say can and will be used against you in a court of law." And yet I'd been condemned for my silence because I dared to come forward and say what had happened to me. It was Victim Blaming 101: a smart, powerful girl like me couldn't possibly resist the urge to report Bovell immediately—since I hadn't reported, clearly I was "crying wolf" to get attention. How was it that my best traits were being used against me? Why would anyone want to be famous for having their breast grabbed? I didn't understand how someone who purportedly represented "the People," a woman no less, could get up there and say such heinous things. I was beginning to understand, however, why 63 percent of sexual assaults go unreported to police while, at the same time, one in two women fall victim to it.

That last weekend passed quickly. I met my close friend Maurice Isserman and his son David, both fellow members of the Democratic Socialists of America, for lunch on Saturday at a restaurant overlooking New York harbor, then took my first ride on the Staten Island Ferry. Looking out at the Statue of Liberty, for my first time really, I told Maurice, "There's *so much* of the city I still haven't seen yet!" "I'm not surprised," he said. "It's been a hell of a three years—you really *should* write that book." A renowned historian and prolific author himself, he'd been saying that since the first time he met me. "Don't be silly, I'm not a writer," I told him, as always. "I wouldn't even know what to say." Sunday, I met with a very worn-out #Justice4Cecily team (at their insistence) to finalize details for my victory party and (at my insistence) to draw up a contingency plan "just in case the worst were to happen." Everyone, it seemed, was more optimistic than me. "Stop it! Of course you'll get acquitted—or, at least, a hung jury and they'll have to throw it out."

On Monday, May 5, I arrived in costume (a white silk dress with plum Manolo Blahniks) to give my final performance as Activist

Barbie. The jury deliberated for three and a half hours while I sat in Marty's office, writing my "innocent speech." Then, just after 2 p.m., we were told they'd reached a verdict. When I pushed through the swinging doors of Part 41, I froze midstep. More than fifty officers stood armed and ready around the perimeter of the room, where every seat had been filled by supporters and reporters. All eyes were on me. "*Fuck,*" I mouthed. The jurors entered and, this time, not a single one looked me in the eye. *Well, that's that,* I thought. *At least it's over.* The foreman rendered, "Guilty." Marty muttered, "Oh my God." Zweibel dismissed the jury. Choi asked that I be held without bail until sentencing. "That's not appropriate," Marty objected. "Ms. McMillan has attended every single court appearance knowing exactly what the outcome could be. . . . She is not someone who's likely to cut and run." He requested that I remain free to get my affairs in order before the May 19 sentencing date. Zweibel denied his request: "The defendant is remanded." The courtroom erupted: "SHAME! SHAME! SHAME!" "Sit down!" police officers shouted. And I rose silently to be handcuffed and taken away.

CHAPTER 7

Prisoner

I unfastened my jewelry, unbuckled my Manolos, and undressed (ripping a seam without help from Lucy)—removed Activist Barbie and laid her to rest in the plastic Nordstrom bag I'd packed at Marty's instruction: "Just in case," he'd called that morning, "the worst were to happen." *Of course, with my luck,* I thought—pulling on the sweatpants I'd packed before throwing a hoody over my blown-out hair—*why would anyone have expected anything else?* Of course, this was opposite the sentiment of the polite Latino officer charged with booking me: he seemed both generally perplexed and genuinely concerned about my being there. He asked a lot of questions about my trial, before giving me a laundry list of things not to do in jail. I thanked him, as we walked deeper and deeper down winding, cold corridors and—just as I'd begun to worry about his being *too* friendly—he put me alone in a cell built for thirty and handed me "two rations" (of milk plus a mustard packet, baloney, and two slices of bread) so that I wouldn't get hungry waiting for the bus that was to come and take me away to

Rikers. Now that the anxious period of not knowing was finally over, I felt so tired. I stacked three plastic mats on the floor to make a bed and fell asleep, more deeply than I had in months.

"Time to go!" a distant, female voice pulled me awake. "Lucy?" I mumbled, confused—she didn't sound like herself. Blinking my eyes open, I squinted at the black woman in uniform standing outside the bars of the cell I was in. "Oh, right," I remembered, I'd lost the trial and was now bound for Rikers to await sentencing.

The East River is a salt-water tidal strait that flows northward along the eastern shore of Manhattan Island, then bends due east between the Bronx and Queens before returning to the Atlantic. Just past that eastward bend, with Queens to the south and the Bronx to the north, lies Rikers Island, a hard to get to (and harder to get out of) outpost of cruelty and misery, just across the water from LaGuardia Airport. The island is flat and treeless and surrounded by razor-sharp barbed wire fences; its only link to the mainland, the Elmhurst neighborhood of Queens, is a narrow causeway.

Rikers is called a "jail complex" rather than a "prison" because the inmates are confined there, supposedly, for a short time only. The majority of them are "innocent" (until proven guilty, theoretically), with a small population of "guilty" inmates (in other words, poor people of color who didn't have the time or money to take their case to trial) sentenced to one year in jail or less. In reality, though, those inmates awaiting trial—or, generally, the lowest possible plea bargain—are often held much longer than convicts. One man reportedly waited seven years on Rikers before being offered a plea deal by the Manhattan DA's office. More notoriously, Kalief Browder was arrested at age sixteen for allegedly stealing a backpack; after serving three years, two of them in solitary confinement, his charges were dismissed and he was released—his name cleared at the cost of his childhood and, ultimately, his life. Kalief, unable to overcome the trauma of Rikers, committed suicide two years later. As newsworthy as these stories may be, they seem to be more routine than anomaly: while in Rikers, I met more than a handful of women who had been in for as long as Kalief was and one, specifically, who had been imprisoned for five years (without, once again, being convicted of anything). In fact, now that I think about it, I saw no evidence whatsoever of this alleged "right to a speedy trial," and I never once met anyone who thought they'd get a *fair one.*

When Rikers Island was originally settled by the Dutch in the seventeenth century, it was only ninety acres. Then, in the early twentieth century, it was expanded to more than four hundred acres so it could serve as a landfill for New York City. During that period, it was also the allotted dumping grounds for its routine street sweepings. In the twenty-first century, the city still deposits its trash on the island—but now it comes in the form of human beings who, by the standards of our criminal justice system, are either undeserving of justice or are so poorly represented that their injustices will undoubtedly go uncontested. The island houses ten separate jails, all run by the Department of Corrections. If New York police officers are allegedly New York's Finest, the corrections officers who operated Rikers are "New York's Boldest"—at least according to the "welcome" sign posted at the Queens end of the bridge to Rikers. Their notoriously aggressive treatment of inmates at Rikers must have earned them that nickname.

As for me, I was headed for the Rose M. Singer Center, the only women's correctional facility, housing about 600 of the 11,000 or so prisoners wasting away on the island. For people not likely to ever find themselves inside a prison, not likely to know anyone who has ever been in a prison, their idea of what goes on inside of them is likely shaped by movies and television shows: *Escape from Alcatraz, The Shawshank Redemption,* and the like. While I was imprisoned in

Rikers, Netflix released its second season of *Orange Is the New Black,* the dark comedy adaptation of Piper Kerman's 2010 memoir of her year in a minimum security women's federal prison. The media storm resulting from my being remanded to Rikers would largely be informed, it seemed, by the already iconic image of Kerman. Save the color of our skin, though, neither my background nor my experience bore much resemblance to hers: first of all, I was a long way from being an upper-middle-class Bostonian and Smith graduate; second of all, Rikers is nothing like "Club Fed." Piper has acknowledged that she served most of her time in a comparatively cushy depository for white-collar criminals—the same kind of place women in Rikers indignantly suggested I should be, with other "white folks" like me. At the same time, I found it pretty laughable to imagine myself, the Occupy Felon, setting up camp in a 1-Percenter Prison—I was much better suited to the company if not the treatment of Rikers. (Though I guess I really wouldn't know. I've never seen the TV show; for obvious reasons, it wasn't my idea of escapist entertainment while awaiting trial, and, since living it, the thought of watching jail on Netflix very seriously makes me nauseous.)

My expectations of prison were better grounded than most, I suspect—largely shaped by my brother's experience and my efforts from the outside to win him decent treatment. But, even so, I wasn't prepared for the life (and, sometimes death) of Rikers. Movies and television make prison out to be tough and grim, to be sure, but also ordered and disciplined—a place of routine violence that you can anticipate, expect. Follow the rules, keep your nose clean, don't piss off the wrong people (or, otherwise, pay off the right people), and you'll survive. But that's not how things work at all, at least not at Rikers. Rikers is chaos. A maddening, totally unhinged state of chaos—you can't predict what will happen, you can't prepare for it. There is no reason, no "why?" or "because. . . ." *It just is.* That's how things work there, with or without your consent. You are at the whim of whichever guard is nearest at the minute, and the guards are at the whim of whichever captain is making rounds that hour, and the captains are at the whim of, well, that's where things get a little murky: either Commissioner of New York City Jails Joseph Ponte or Norman Seabrook, president of the Correctional Officer's Benevolent Association (the laughably named union), both of whom seem to be gridlocked in a struggle for power over what seems to be the uncontrollable, unforgiving force of Rikers Island itself. It's kind of like that TV show *Lost*, except everyone knows exactly where the prisoners are and what's happening to them—yet, there they remain, left to suffer and die. *That,* right there, is the *real* violence of Rikers: chaos on the inside and complacency on the outside.

When I went in, Activist Barbie (still entombed in the plastic Nordstrom bag) was taken from me and disposed of "in the back," where she was then exhumed and dismembered, according to the property receipt I received in exchange; that, in addition to my notebook (the one I was using earlier to draft my "innocent speech") were the only remaining records that she'd ever existed—that I'd ever been a person worth defending. Now, I was just a prisoner.

"STRIP," SHE SAID NONCHALANTLY, without looking up. The officer before me was slouched down in a chair, licking Cheetos off her fingertips. I stood there, like I usually do, with my hands on my hips, and responded, "Come again?" With that, she was up: "Oh hey, Miley Cyrus," she mocked me in a high-pitched voice. "Like, what do you think this is—a nightclub?" "Ma'am?" I questioned, trying to be polite. I could tell I was in trouble for something, but I didn't know what. "Ma'am," she repeated from behind me, continuing the charade as she made her way around. "A nightclub, guuurrrlllfrraannnd. You tryna pick up someone?" "No Ma'am," I said slowly, really confused. Before I finished, she was an inch from my face shouting, "Then put your damn hands down!" "Wha—oh!" I dropped them to my side and stood upright, "Sorry, I—" "Did I say you could speak?" I opened my mouth but closed it without speaking, realizing that was probably a rhetorical question. It wasn't. "I asked you a question," she shouted again. "Bitch, you better answer me." "No," I responded to her original question, but she misunderstood me: "I know you did not just say no to me." Daring not speak, I shook my head no and looked at her with beseeching eyes: *What do you want from me?* But she just laughed, clearly having fun at my expense, as she returned to her chair and said, "Come on, now, girl—strip."

I bent down and untied my tennis shoes, removed them and my socks too, grimacing at the feel of cold, dirty concrete beneath my newly pedicured feet; then I stood up and removed my hoody and sweatpants and stood there shivering, holding both in my hands so they wouldn't get dirty. No luck. "Put 'em down," she said, "and take off the rest." I paused for a minute, wondering if that were constitutional. "Let's go," she urged. "I ain't got all day." I uneasily removed my sports bra and my underwear then squatted down with my knees pressed firmly together and then stood with both my arms and legs crossed, trying to shield my body. Still, no luck. "Open up your arms, palms to me," she ordered, "and spread your legs wide." I cringed, then froze and shut my eyes, trying to disappear. "Come on, white bitch," she said, trying (despite her choice of words) to reason with me, "just get it over with—I don't wanna look atchu neither." Without opening my eyes, I spread apart my arms and legs. "Lean forward and shake out your hair," she instructed, and I responded mechanically. "Okay, back up—squat down. Turn around, squat again. Get your clothes and shoes. Put them in here"—she held out a basket, and I dropped my stuff in; she stirred it around with a stick and I watched, butt-ass na-ked; she gave me the basket, and I stood there holding it—"Go 'head, we're done." She picked up her Cheetos again, and I put my clothes back on.

Once dressed, I was sent to a desk in the center of the room other-wise lined with cells. "The Intake Panopticon," I called it, thinking back to sophomore year when I first learned the term reading Michel Foucault's *Discipline and Punish*—now look at me, I was living it! There, an officer with a Twizzler dangling from her mouth demanded, "State your religion." "Um, I'm agnostic," I answered, trying to avoid asking questions after what had happened last time. She took the candy stick out and pointed at me, as she questioned, "You know, that sounds Christian but you look Jewish—which is it?" "Neither?" I said timidly, trying not to sound like a smart ass. "Muslim?" she asked, with a puzzled look on her face. "No, definitely not," I declared. "But," I clarified, "I like Muslims just fine." "Just pick one already," she snapped, "or Ima put 'Christian.'" "That's fine," I said, and bit my tongue to keep from asking, *What's it matter to you?* "Step back," she said, and something flashed: the photo, apparently, for my inmate badge, which would also serve as my "pass for chapel," she explained, "but *only* for chapel." If I wanted to go to temple or mosque, I'd have to get permission to change my religion, which, she clarified, "could take several months." "Okay, thanks," I said, taking it—for my *chapel pass?* This shit is crazy.

Crazier still was my photo: it was almost identical to the pissed-off, pouty face of my Lawrence University ID. I'd made that face as a joke, to cheer up Jess when she'd gotten homesick the first week of school. I remembered that girl struggling to learn the language of power and thought of the woman I'd become since, able to "pass" with ease as upper-middle class, educated, and/or white (when I needed to). I learned the rules and mastered the game, all for what? *For nothing,* I thought. I ended up in the same situation as James, all that status didn't add up to enough, even, to afford me bail. It didn't matter that I dressed the part and played the role perfectly or that I took the stand and told the jury the truth. None of it was enough to win me the trial, to save me from the derogatory characterization of danger-ous "protester." And, though it had taken me seven years (and a quarter-million-dollar education) to build—it had been shaken down in a matter of minutes at Rikers. I'd soon learn that I wasn't entitled to anything in there, not even a name. That I was no longer seen as a woman anymore, not even a person—from now on, I was only a num-ber. Inmate Number 310-14-00431. An identity I might have to get used to for possibly the next seven years.

When Marty came to see me Wednesday, he did his best to con-vince me that no one had forgotten about me, that everyone was working to get me out as soon as possible. After he left me Monday, he had gone out to the court steps, to the same place this whole thing had started four weeks prior, where he was greeted by dozens of re-porters, several news cameras, and more than two hundred support-ers. He told them simply, "Cecily is not coming out." Since then, those devastating words had spread to many corners of the world, inspiring thousands of people to help me regain my freedom.

While I was locked in the tombs of the courthouse awaiting trans-fer to Rikers, hundreds of supporters had rallied at Zuccotti Park de-manding my immediate release and thousands across the nation echoed their calls on Twitter and Facebook. By the time I was being strip-searched, news of my conviction and imprisonment had brewed into a full-scale media storm: more than a hundred articles had been published nationally (including pieces in the *New York Times,* the *Wall Street Journal, Newsweek,* the *Atlantic, Reuters,* and the *Huffington Post*) and internationally (including in the *Guardian,* the *Voice of Rus-sia, Russia Today,* the *Turkish Press,* and *Prensa Latina,* the official paper of Cuba); my conviction had also been featured widely in the nightly news cycle (including segments by NBC, CBS, the BBC, *Democracy Now!*, and Al Jazeera); and had even been the topic of an eight-minute segment called "Justice for Some" on Jon Stewart's *The Daily Show*. At the same time, the #Justice4Cecily team—who hadn't slept since I was remanded—had been building both a leniency campaign (to get me out) and a jail support model (until they could): they had collected letters and circulated a petition asking Judge Zweibel for my release and had raised money for a jail fund (to cover commissary, phone calls, and court fees) and organized people to send me letters, books, and care packages. All the while Marty, in addition to helping out #Justice4Cecily, had been pursuing other possible routes to my release.

"I've got good news," he said, pulling out a thin stack of printed pages from his briefcase before folding it in half and passing it through the metal slot beneath the thick panel of Plexiglas dividing us. I opened it to find an article written by Jon Swaine, published the day before in the *Guardian*—I silently mouthed its title: "Occupy Trial Juror Describes Shock at Activist's Potential Prison Sentence." I paused, then looked up in shock at Marty. *What the fuck is this shit?* Still beaming, Marty pointed down and encouraged me to read on; I rolled my eyes and did so begrudgingly:

> Finally freed from a ban on researching the case, including potential punishments, some [jurors] were shocked to learn that they had just consigned the 25-year-old to a sentence of up to seven years in prison, one told the Guardian. "They felt bad," said the juror, who did not wish to be named. "Most just wanted her to do probation, maybe some community service. But now what I'm hearing is seven years in jail? That's ludicrous. Even a year in jail is ridiculous."

"Really! They thought, what—*we'd just hug it out?"* Marty threw up his arms, "Would you just read the damn thing?" I kept skimming and then froze on the paragraph, I suspected, Marty had wanted me to read:

> The juror said that an immediate vote after the 12 were sent out for deliberation found they were split 9-3 in favour of convicting. After everyone watched the clip again in the jury room, the juror said, two of the three hold-outs switched to the majority, leaving only the juror who approached the Guardian in favour of acquitting the 25-year-old. Sensing "a losing battle," the juror agreed to join them in a unanimous verdict. "I'm very remorseful about it," the juror said a few hours later, having learned of McMillan's potential punishment.

"Well, isn't that nice—she feels 'remorseful,'" I mocked, then cried, *"But it's a little too fucking late—dontcha think?* Hasn't she seen *Twelve Angry Men?"* "I'm tempted to ask *him* that same question," Marty said. "But now that he's gotten a large chunk of the jury to beg Zweibel to release you—I've decided to let him off the hook." "Wait—what?" I demanded. "This guy felt so bad, he reached out to the jurors he could find and now nine of the twelve have filed a letter with Zweibel requesting that you not be given jail time." "Oh," I responded. "Oh?" Marty asked, and I shrugged. "That's all you have to say—*really?"* "I, mean, that's good of him—*I guess,"* I rose to a low shout. "But I wouldn't need his stupid letter if he'd done the right thing to begin with!" "That's true," Marty said, looking a little sad now. "But I've never seen anyone do anything like this—at least he's trying to fix his mistake." The desperation in his voice made me realize that Marty was fighting like hell to put on a good face. I guessed then (and later confirmed) that the letter had been willed by Marty more than anyone else, so I said, "You're right, this is huge! But Marty," I added, "if I don't get out on May 19, I won't blame you—I don't blame you for anything, everything would've been so much worse without you." "Good, I don't blame you either," he joked.

Before Marty left, I asked him if I could borrow his pen, then I wrote a letter to my family:

> *James, Dad, Nyrobi, Mom (Celina), Grandaddy Harlon, Momma Jean, and Pop*
>
> *I love you. We talked about this and possible outcomes—I understand the consequences of going through the trial and stand by my decision and innocence.*
>
> *Marty is an incredible and loyal lawyer—he will help me through this troubled time. We will be trying to get bail through the appeals court (not Zweibel) and we're working on a letter-writing campaign to secure a low or probationary sentence.*
>
> *Also we're gonna work through appeals court for a retrial— Marty is confident that we have a strong case for appeal. So, I will write and call—but not bother you—because I am fine and I have friends that are here in NYC and Marty and his wife Elsie are going to fight like hell for me. Ok that's all. I love you and am sorry to cause you stress and embarrassment—just trying to do the right thing.*
>
> *<3, Cecily*

Following Marty, I was visited by two people who had likely written similar letters to their families during their own imprisonment. On Friday, May 9, my first alphabetically assigned visiting day, Nadezhda Tolokonnikova and Maria Alyokhina came to see me along with their translator, Pyotr Verzilov, who is also married to Tolokonnikova. Better known as Nadya and Masha, the two are the most famous members of the Russian punk rock collective Pussy Riot (while Pyotr is an accomplished artist and activist himself). The two women, about my age, served two years in prison for their 2012 performance art piece "Punk Prayer—Mother of God, Chase Putin Away" in a Moscow cathedral, challenging the policies of Vladimir Putin. I admired them and was shocked when they were arrested and charged with a crime far more absurd than my own: hooliganism. In May 2014, six months after their release, Nadya and Masha began touring the United States, where they'd since become pop culture icons of protest. During their travels, the two women learned of my conviction and got in touch with the #Justice4Cecily team to offer their support. Of course, I felt deeply indebted to my friends for suggesting the visit and honored that Nadya and Masha would take time to come see me.

And visiting someone on Rikers *does* take time—almost a full day. Traveling to and from the island takes two hours, minimum, plus three or so hours of visitor intake, which includes repeated searches (for my visitors especially, apparently). Then, finally, friends and family are escorted into a large, loud room where they are allowed a one-hour visit sitting across a small table from the prisoner they've come to see. But "no touching!" besides hands is permitted during the visit and a quick embrace before and after.

Nadya and Masha knew the drill, though. They handled the whole ordeal better than I would have, that's for sure, grumbling only jokingly about the extra-large T-shirts they were made to wear over their too-short skirts: "In Russia, they make us do beauty pageants in prison," Nadya said and Pyotr translated. As much as possible, though, we spoke directly: their limited English and my nonexistent Russian mitigated heavily through crude sign language (they're almost fluent now, though, and I've picked up a few words). They offered encouragement and support, and we exchanged jail stories and political views. Then, before we knew it, an officer barked, "Time's up!" and I hugged them good-bye.

At a press conference in Washington earlier in the week, they said they were "appalled and saddened" to hear of my conviction, calling me a "political prisoner." After their visit they told a reporter, "We got in prison for the exact same reason. We didn't want to accept charges. To see someone this brave who is ready to serve a sentence which might be longer than ours is very incredible." I didn't know if I was brave or just a little stupid; I had only been at Rikers for four days and didn't understand, not *really*, what staying there for a long time would mean. Either way, the bigger point was that their visit was emblematic of the privilege I was afforded to *feel brave.* Not only did I fail to grasp at that moment how a long sentence at Rikers would affect me; I also don't think I believed I'd actually be staying. After all, Pussy Riot's intervention on my behalf was unwelcome publicity for the politically minded and ambitious district attorney of New York County, Cyrus Vance Jr. (Erin Choi and Shanda Strain's superior), who would be determining the length of my sentence. Because of Pussy Riot, #Justice4Cecily, and the thousands of people I'd never met who signed petitions, wrote letters, and took other actions to support me, I had the safety of knowing I would not be forgotten. I could say things like, "My convictions are worth seven years in prison," in large part because I knew I probably wouldn't have to do them. Make no mistake, though: I believed in those words with all my heart then, and still do now. But when I met women inside who had *no one* outside looking out for them, I realized that it's easier to be brave with an army behind you, fighting to get you out.

Later that night, I stood in line for more than an hour to use one of the two phones provided to our dorm of more than fifty women; *My God!*, I thought, as I waited impatiently to call Marty. *How does anyone get through this without someone like Marty?* When he picked up, though, his tone that night was notably different from our last conversation. "I'm sorry," he said, "but the bail appeal didn't work out." "What's next?" I asked. "That's it, Cecily," he said, voice stifled. "There's nothing left that I can do, except prepare for sentencing." "So I'm here, until then?" I choked in disbelief. "*For real?*" "Yes. And," he took a breath, then exhaled, "Choi announced in court today that she's planning on asking for the two-year minimum."

With that, the loneliness of incarceration finally set in and I thought I might break that night. I lay on my mattress with the blanket pulled over my head, crying into my cupped hands. Blotting my wet face with the rags they called sheets, I heard a woman begin to sing softly:

In the jungle, the mighty jungle, The lion sleeps tonight

And by the time she got to the chorus ("Wimoweh, wimoweh, wimoweh, wimoweh . . ."), other women had joined in, and soon the whole room was singing, the first woman taking the lead and now belting the words unabashedly. I didn't sing. I still hid beneath the covers, still had snot all over me. But I stopped crying. *Okay,* I thought, slowing my breath. *I'm OK—I can survive this.* But I wouldn't survive it—not like I had everything else anyway: push forward, get through it, move on, and dump it. With help from the women of Rose M. Singer, I'd struggle with it, accept it, and live through it. I would come to find community in Rosie's, even family; a family that would not only sustain me, but also set me free.

I'm a talker. I always have been. But never before or since did I have conversations of the quality or duration I had in those months on Rikers. More than anything, though, in that first week I really learned to listen. I didn't meet a single other woman who'd actually been to trial—in that sense, I was the only convict in my dorm, the one who had actually been charged and found guilty of anything. No one I spoke to, though, ever had any intention of "blowing trial" and winding up with a heavier sentence, especially now that they'd met me: "If they sent you to Rikers," one said, "they'd give me the death penalty." Instead, nearly all of them were biding their time awaiting indefinitely postponed trial dates and hoping to strike a more favorable plea bargain. It seemed only a fraction of them would ever receive that coveted call with a lawyer. Other women waited in quiet desperation to be transferred for other warrants, or worse, to be deported to distant homelands.

Yet so many buried their fears for the future and continued to bear daily burdens on the outside: waiting in line for the phone, consoling someone on the other end of the line, listing instructions for an improvised caretaker, scribbling hasty letters to children, explaining the utility bill—in short, still running households and whole communities.

The shortcomings of men were everywhere, strewn about like the socks and dishes that were accumulating in the absence of women. This was the subject of endless conversation, the failings of men. They couldn't remember PIN numbers; they didn't know how to transfer money to an account; they didn't know how to run a household or care for children or negotiate with school authorities. "Without me, nothing gets done." When they were free in the world, these women were the ones who were keeping the fabric of communities together behind the scenes, ceaselessly providing for others: elderly relatives and neighbors, single mothers, the mentally and physically disabled. No matter what her supposed crime, every single woman was preoccupied with worrying about everything she must take care of on the outside, for her family and community. At night the dorm heaved with the worries of women, underpaid and undervalued, striving to do right by those they loved, those they'd been ripped away from.

At the same time, I remember a male guard lecturing us: "You women shouldn't be here. Jail is for men. It's a man's place. You should be at home taking care of your kids, your families. Not here." *You think we want to be here?* I scowled, but kept my mouth shut (for fear I might argue my way into solitary confinement). I didn't think jail was a place for men or women, but many of the women I'd met were in *because* they were women: victims of domestic abuse who fought back, sex workers supporting themselves and their families, and addicts crumbling under the pressure of a life bereft of the basic things we, *humans*, need to survive: food, water, shelter, work, community.

Never had I felt so conscious of the influence of women, nor so painfully aware of the universal plight that women often face alone. In that sense it was incredible to find such camaraderie in the most inhumane of circumstances. I had never talked about my body so openly, never talked about sexual assault and rape so readily. I don't think I had ever, before then, been particularly comfortable with the idea of being a woman (so much as thought of it as a sort of gender impairment). But *these women*, I liked the kind of women they were—and I came to really like being a woman with them. In all my life, before or since, I have never more routinely tapped into what it is that women do in our society—we are the organizers.

On top of everything else they had to deal with, though, they still insisted on contributing to my cause. On Sunday, May 18, the day before my sentencing hearing, a whole crew of them worked all night to recreate Activist Barbie (Special Rikers Edition). The women in 2 East-B were more impressive than any stylists I've seen since. The manicurist lathered my hands in medicated foot lotion and wrapped them in strips of torn towel wetted by the hot water canteen (for tea and instant coffee). While my hands soaked for an hour in the "moisturizing gloves," the hair removal specialist threaded my eyebrows with fibers from bedsheets while two hair stylists wrapped my locks around cylinders of rolled sanitary napkins, then tied them at my scalp with pieces of the protective wrapper (no fewer than fifteen pads were harmed in the making of my hair). When they'd finished, the manicurist gently exfoliated my hands with a (contraband) Brillo pad then used a plastic fork removed of all but one tooth to push back my cuticles and clean under my nails before carefully rubbing them against the grout between the cinderblocks in bathroom to shape them. Once their work was done, there was little left to do: I Naired my underarms and legs (the alternative to shaving, because razors are banned), showered, brushed my teeth, and applied my "combination oily face mask": lotion on the dry parts, toothpaste on the acne. Before bed, the laundress readied my dress (a hot pink Calvin Klein sleeveless number, mailed in by the #Justice4Cecily team): she removed the plastic mattress from my bed frame, put down four pieces of broken-down brown paper bags (from the commissary), and delicately positioned the dress on top; covering it, she put down four more pieces of paper bag then carefully returned my mattress to its place. "Don't move around too much tonight," she said, "and it'll be as good as ironed when you get up tomorrow."

Tomorrow meant 4 a.m., when inmates due in court are roused out of bed by cranky correctional officers at the tail end of a night shift. I promptly got up, washed my face, and put on my "makeup": "rouge" (congealed Kool-Aid), "eyeliner" (a golf pencil, softened by hot water), and "mascara" (instant coffee silt). I pulled up my pantyhose (also received by mail) and begrudgingly put on my "Patakis" (the jail-issued shoe, think geriatric Keds—apparently, you can't mail stilettos into prison). Then I pulled out my dress and found, to my great surprise, that it really *did* look like I'd had it pressed. When I put it on and let down my hair, I couldn't believe it but I really felt the power of that look return to me, again . . . until I looked down. I groaned. "Nobody's going to be looking at your feet, Cecily," I scolded myself in the voice of my mother. Today was not the day to psych myself out.

On Monday, May 19, I returned to the stage of Part 41 to deliver my big monologue—the sentencing speech—in the epilogue to *The People v. Cecily McMillan.* The curtain went up at 9:30 a.m., but, by the looks of it, tickets had sold out *far in advance.* When I made my entrance, I could see a mass of people behind the thick line of police officers but was quickly blinded by a series of camera flashes. I didn't need to see them, though, to know they were there. When I took my place beside Marty, I could feel the force of the crowd at my back— the heat of their bodies warmed me, and the volume of their white noise shouted, "We will not be moved!"

District Attorney Erin Choi recommended a "lenient sentence" of three months in jail with five years of probation and five hundred hours of community service to follow, plus a $5,000 fine and mandatory anger management therapy.

Marty argued that I be released with time served, based on my character, endorsed by the outpouring of public support for the leniency campaign: the crowd of friends and family that day in the courtroom and the hundreds more filling up the hallway, spilling over to the court steps outside; the petition signed by 150,000 people worldwide; letters submitted by elected officials, musicians, and celebrities alike, as well as the president of the school I currently attended and the president of the union I worked at prior; and, finally, the letter from the jury asking that I be given no jail time.

Then, it was my turn to speak freely, and *finally* on my own behalf. "Your Honor," I began, "I stand before you exhausted: I have spent thirty-five of the forty-two months that I have been in New York City trying to convince this court of my innocence. I have lost friends and family, school and work, and, most recently, my freedom. I have been exhausted of nearly everything that makes me, me—except, that is, my dignity.

When I was a young girl my mother told me, "Everything you see, your home, your loved ones, even your life, can be taken from you at will. But no one can strip you of your dignity without your consent." I did not know then what dignity was, but I understood it to be deliberate—something you had to define for yourself.

And though I am still young and still searching for answers, I have started down a path where dignity is derived from the law of love. And though it has been said that this trial is personal, not political, I maintain that the personal is inseparable from the political. Whereas nonviolent civil disobedience is the manifestation of my ideology, it is rooted in a love ethic that is central to my identity.

The law of love holds that all humankind shares one common life, that our existence beats with one common pulse—that as we listen to one another, learn from one another, love one another, we draw closer to one another and toward our collective happiness. Therefore, whether in resistance or in retribution, whether personal or political, violence is never permitted.

This being the law that I live by, I can say with certainty that I am innocent of the crime I have been convicted of. And as I stand before you today, I cannot confess to a crime I did not commit; I cannot do away with my dignity in hopes that you will return me my freedom.

However, that same law of love requires me to acknowledge the unintentional harm I caused another—for this accident, I am truly sorry. And in this spirt, Your Honor, I ask you to halt the violence here. Consider my words, as I ask you not to perpetuate one injury with yet another.

"Thank you, Ms. McMillan," Justice Zweibel said. Then, he issued his ruling: it may well be, he conceded, that I'm a good person who just made a mistake; nonetheless, I had been tried and convicted by the court, and, therefore, justice needed to be meted out accordingly. He sentenced me to three months in Rikers, with five years' probation and mandatory anger management therapy to follow.

WHEN I GOT BACK TO RIKERS, there was no time for tears. As a sentenced inmate, I was required to leave the detainee dorm "NOW!" The officer assigned to escort me was already there when I walked in. He ordered me to pack up my stuff immediately, before my little dorm family could even ask what happened. "I got three months," I shouted, frantically throwing my stuff on the bed. "It sucks, but it's not seven years!" All the while, he stood over me: tapping his foot, checking his watch, breathing down my neck . . . making me anxious, more and more by the minute. When it was all there, I grabbed up the corners of my bedding and tied two knots in the middle, making a sack of mythical proportions. "Done!" I announced to the smug officer, and demanded, "Happy?" "No, but I will be," he said, stalking off toward the exit. "As soon as I get rid of you." I hadn't moved—I tried to lift the bundle but couldn't. By then, I had received hundreds of letters, dozens of books, and had already filled a couple of notebooks: with notes and records, writings and observations, reports and campaign plans.

"*Hellllllooooo?*" he shouted across the room. "You coming?" I called back, trying to stay calm but also to be heard: "I. Can't. Carry. It. By. Myself." "I. Don't. Give. A. Shit." he responded. "Drag it, or leave it—I'm walking out, though, and if you're not with me, it'll be your good days." (Good days are the fraction of a jail sentence, usually one-third in Rikers, that can be taken off for good behavior; thirty days, for me, which was twenty-nine more than I needed to take him seriously.) "Bye everyone!" I waved, after I pulled and they pushed my stuff to the door. "I hope y'all get out soon!" "Bye Activista!" they called back—for everything I hated about Rikers, I freaking *loved* my jailhouse name.

I was assigned to the fourth floor, east wing, side A dormitory, or colloquially known as Room 4EA—my home for the next forty-four days. Before you move into a new house, the first thing you do is clean it. At Rikers, your bed is your house, but you aren't afforded cleaning supplies, so I did the best I could: scrubbed the whole bedframe and mattress (with five tubes of toothpaste), washed out my buckets and tied twine around the perimeter (to dry my wet socks and underwear); then made my bed military style, stacked my books ("have read," "to read," "am reading"), and organized my belongings into the two plastic blue buckets provided to each inmate: the first for clothes and food, the second for my piles of letters ("to write," "to read," "have read and responded") and other writings.

The whole process must have taken three or four hours, and then, as soon as I finally finished, sat down, and picked up Malcom X's biography to read, some twenty or so officers, some dressed in riot gear wielding giant wooden bats, came running into my new dorm room. Yep, that was my breaking point. I snapped, "What the fuck is this?" Don't ask, I've been told, if you don't want an answer: one of the white-shirted officers, a captain, came out of nowhere and yelled in my face: "RANDOM SEARCH! FACE DOWN ON YOUR MATTRESS!"

So I flipped over—*and fast!*—then laid there listening, not knowing what to do next. But then, I heard people getting up and moving around me, so I looked up and got it again: "FACE FUCKING DOWN ON THE MATTRESS." After that I didn't take my forehead off the mattress, no matter what I heard, until the girl from the bed beside mine was up and nudging me, "It's time to go to the bathroom." Outside it, a shrill female officer ordered us to "line up by bed order!" before marching us in and directing us *to the stalls!* where a whole line of female officers sat ready and waiting to force us to "*strip!*" So there I stood, *again,* butt-naked and spread-eagle, shaking out my hair, squatting forward and backward, this time with the new experience of being made to pee in a cup (which, it should go without saying, is not an easy thing to do with someone watching two feet in front of you). After that, we got dressed and were marched into the day room, used normally for "the feeding" (what they called meals there) but this time repurposed as a psychological torture chamber. For the time it took all fifty women to tinkle out our drug samples, we were forced to "stand, facing the wall!" But three or four captains kept calling out, "Hey miss, hey miss"—the way they addressed us when they didn't know our numbers, the female version of the derogatory "boy." So we all kept turning around, and they kept threatening to "take away our good days!" And then I got reprimanded for *not* turning around. One came up behind me and called out several times, but I ignored him, thinking it was a test. It wasn't. "Maybe she's deaf," I heard him say, just before I got hit by his tuna-breath. "Miss, turn *the fuck* around!"

I didn't think I had any left, but two little droplets fell out. He'd gotten me all worked up like one of those little yappy dogs and had actually made me piddle myself. Before it progressed any further, though, my neighbor (I didn't even know her name yet) broke into a full-fledged asthma attack. She wheezed, at first, then gasped for a while and started turning kind of bluish. By that point, all the captains were standing around her shouting, "Where is your inhaler?"

"Where is your inhaler?" *Really?* I couldn't stand there and watch any longer, so I ran to her bed and dug through her buckets, searching frantically for the inhaler. "Hey you!" one came after me. "What are you doing?" "Looking for—this!" I found it just in time—right afterward, she was sent down to medical for a steroid shot—but, even still, I got yelled at. "I don't care if someone *is* dying, don't you *ever* step out of line again," I was told.

God only knows how long I'd been staring at that pale blue wall before my line was finally called to march back into the dormitory. This time, though, we stood with our "*backs* up against the wall, facing the beds!"—it was a nice change of pace. But then we had to grab our mattresses and hold them folded over our arms while they picked up our buckets and dumped them out on our beds. So much for my new home. I watched the officer assigned to my bunk diligently remove every last letter from its envelope, look at it and toss it, without putting a single one of the four hundred back. To really twist the knife, though, one of the white-shirts took a running start and punted a pile of my books clear across the dorm room. I was speechless. But he came at me anyway, "Why do you have so many books?" "Because I'm a fucking graduate student!" I shouted with my whole body, so loud it bounced off the walls and everyone fell silent.

"You wanna say it again," he challenged coldly, then flipped up the inmate ID clipped to my pocket and read, "310-14-00431" Staring down, I recognized the book I'd been reading beneath his boot and took a moment to consider: What Would Malcolm Do? Then I looked him dead in the eye and said, "No, officer, I don't think I will." "That's what I thought," he responded, then stepped back and pivoted to send *The Autobiography of Malcom X* hurling toward the dayroom. "Next."

When all was said and done, I knew I'd made the right decision in that moment. I know that Malcolm probably wouldn't have done the

same thing in my situation, but I recalled his words "without education, you're not going anywhere in this world" and understood them
to mean "to take power, you have to understand it." I had learned in
college and, firsthand, through Occupy what power was on the outside, but this was a totally different animal. I didn't know enough
about it, yet, to wrangle it.

Nonetheless, while I circled the dormitory retrieving my scat-
tered jailhouse library, I couldn't help but daydream about *literally*
throwing the book at that officer. "I mean, *really*," I seethed, sweep-
ing up the dislodged pages of Toni Morrison's *The Bluest Eye*.
"What kind of person gets off on kicking books? Fucking sick son
of a bitch!" Right then, "¡Ay Dios mio!" a voice like Abuela's rang
out behind me. I jumped and spun around to find a middle-aged
beige woman with a short haircut talking to me: "¡Estás loca,
blanquita!" (You're crazy, little white girl!) I understood her perfectly, as it was something Abuela had told me many times. I guessed
that she was talking about the book showdown. "No siempre" (not
always), I said calmly, then paused to find the words to say what I
wanted to next. "Pero puedo ser, sí," I articulately deliberately, translated directly: "But I can be [crazy], yes." Really, though, I was letting her know that I was neither a bitch nor a dumb little white girl.
But somehow, she already knew that: "See, pendeja," she called out
to someone behind me. "I told you, she's not white!" An extremely
short but particularly tough-looking brown woman, presumably the
one she called "pendeja" (jackass), appeared at her side and demanded, "¿Hablas español?"

She was testing me. It was a test I failed many times in the classroom, unable to learn from a textbook that had seemingly been
banned from my household. But, this time, I needed to pass and—I
got the strangest sensation, though I couldn't explain it—it mattered
more then than ever before. "¡Gringa! Dije," she snapped when I

hesitated (Whitey! I said). "¿Tú hablas español?" "Sí, un poco, pero comprendo mucho," I said nervously (Yes, a little, but I understand a lot).

In broken Spanish, I explained that my mother was from Mexico City but I grew up in southeast Texas, where the people were racist, so she didn't raise us to be Mexican. "Claro," the second woman responded before turning to the second and saying, in effect, that explains why she acts white. As she stalked off, I rolled my eyes, and the other, to my surprise, comforted me. "Don't worry about Milly," she said. "Pinche idiota!" "*Now, that one,*" I laughed, "I *did* learn from my mother." "See, you are Mexican," she said, then held out her hand and said, "I'm Ida." Taking it, I said, "Nice to meet you, I'm Cecily."

It was an instantly warm connection—and the first hand I'd shaken since coming to Rikers. When she released it, I continued onto my bed, not wanting to overstay my welcome. "Ceci!" she motioned me over, calling me—from the first time she said it—by a name only my family had. "Move over here," she instructed, pointing to the empty cot nearby. "So I can take care of you, till you learn how to take care of yourself." And with that she became my protector and later my best friend and closest confidante. She was my jailhouse *madrina* (my godmother), and, to this day, I consider her family.

Once I settled in next to her, she walked me around and introduced me to the "neighborhood" (or the people that sleep nearest you in the dormitory): there were Flaca, Milly, Colette, Gumby, Hayes, and Diaz (their names a combination of first, last, and nicknames; though that's not the kind of question you ask in jail). Ida called it the "Upper West Side," on account of its physical location, but I thought of it as the "Latina District" (and was proud to be its newest resident). For the next forty-four days, that little corner of dormitory 4 East A would be my social center—both my home and family. Same as on the outside, there were jailhouse mothers and daughters, grandmothers and godmothers, sisters and aunts, and of course lovers, of all types, representing every gender and sexual identity you've ever heard of—and some I bet you haven't. Of course, not everyone got along, or even liked each other; but when push came to shove, we came together and stood up for one another.

With my new world in place, I finally settled into the reality that I was there to stay and set to work on a few things I couldn't afford to ignore anymore, namely medications that I needed to survive the rest of my time there. Since my intake exam, I had avoided doctors as much as possible. They'd been cold that first night; they didn't once look me in the eye and didn't speak to me but *at me* like I was a monster, incapable of being a person. They made me feel disposable, like trash—the same way the doctors in Bellevue had the night of my beating.

To get medical care on Rikers, you have to sign up for "sick call" the night before; if your name is not on the morning list, you're not allowed into "clinic" that day. "Whatever it is will have to wait till tomorrow." To go down, you have to be up by 5 a.m., but you could wait around till 8 a.m. for an officer to escort you there. If you show up that late, though, you probably won't get in: they only let in as many will fit on the four long wooden benches in the small waiting room overseen by a single guard at a desk. If they do let you in, though, you'll be last in line after thirty or so others, so you'll be there all day but probably won't see a doctor. "It's 5 p.m., the clinic is now closed— everybody out, better luck tomorrow!" You could be waiting for up to a week to be seen; the shortest time I ever got in was six hours. I sat there for three days before I finally saw someone who ultimately said he couldn't do anything for me but schedule a gynecologist appointment for the following week and, in reaction to my inconsolable sobbing, wrote me a mental health referral to see a psychiatrist. "Thanks," I said, on the way out. "You've been really *fucking* helpful!"

Truth be told, *I was losing it.* I hadn't been on my ADHD medication in weeks, and when I went to the psychiatric clinic, one after another psychiatrist had refused me my Adderall, all the way up to the director of the mental health clinic. At the same time, when I went to my birth control appointment, the doctor refused to prescribe my routine Depo-Provera shot (calling it an "unorthodox treatment") without a preliminary pap smear first. I told him I'd had one already this year and that he was welcome to check my medical records, but he insisted. Once in, he then pressured me into undergoing a cervix scrape that left me sobbing silently on the table and in pain for days after.

Afterward, I got dressed and returned "home" with a tear-stained face, fuming, "I'm gonna report that sick son of a bitch." "Yeah, that guy does stuff like that," Ida said. "But he's not as bad as the one that tried to cop a feel last week." "Yeah," Buddha added. "A lot of them do fucked up shit." "We should *all* write grievances," I charged. "Band together and take those motherfuckers down!" "That's not how it works," Ida explained, trying hard not to laugh. "You can't *grieve* doctors." "What?" I said, stunned. "*Why the hell not!*" "Listen, Ceci, to survive Rikers," she lectured tenderly, "you have to suspend your belief in the concept of 'Why?'" "That's bullshit!" I shouted. "They can't treat us like this—just wait till I tell my friends! They'll raise hell for what that guy did to me, *you'll see*, and I'll get my meds by the end of the week."

And so it went—just like I said. The next day, June 6, I was visited by Maurice Isserman (the same from my first Staten Island ferry ride) and our mutual friend Todd Gitlin, professor of journalism and sociology and chair of the Ph.D. program in Communications at Columbia Law. "She does not look well, seems anxious . . . ," they noted in their joint e-mail to the medical director of Rikers, demanding I get the proper medical attention and prescriptions I needed:

Most disturbingly, last week on two separate occasions, Cecily was coerced into undergoing what she described as invasive, painful, and humiliating vaginal examinations by a male ob-gyn, first as a precondition for obtaining a Depo-Provera shot, and second because the ob-gyn . . . thought she needed to be tested for HPV. Although she felt both examinations were unnecessary, she agreed to them and requested a female ob-gyn, but was told that none would be available for another week. Given that she has previously been the victim of sexual assault, her experiences with that male ob-gyn has contributed to her current high level of anxiety.

"*See,* Ida," I said. "That's what happens when you ask, 'Why?'" "No, that's what happens when *you* ask, 'Why?'" she responded. "Me? I've been asking, 'Why can't I see an oncologist?' every week since this lump in my throat came back—but that was six months ago, so it's probably too late by now!"

"Oh," I responded. There was nothing more I could say. Women die in Rikers from lack of medical attention. That is a fact. I saw it. Like the day I was waiting in intake to be transferred to my sentencing hearing and the unborn child of a woman died as she bled on the floor and her cries went ignored. Little illnesses, the kinds of things that mean nothing on the outside, can become life threatening on the inside. Like Diaz, who had a stomach ulcer and was called down a second time to give a stool sample when they lost the first one; frustrated, she declined and was made to sign what she did not understand to be a liability waiver in case "it bursts, leaking poop into your body," I explained, "which will cause you to go into sepsis and you'll die before they get around to treating you." "Why didn't they just say that!" she said. "I just figured I'd wait, since I'm getting out next week." And God forbid you should have something worse. I watched a woman with stomach cancer cry out in such unbearable pain for hours before medical support finally came to get her. When they did arrive, they refused to touch her and insisted that she climb up on the gurney herself. They wouldn't allow the rest of us in the dorm to help her either.

Fortunately, I was young when I got to Rikers and had no fatal pre-existing conditions, but Ida was right; even if something big did come up, I would be okay. I had resources unavailable to other inmates: powerful lawyers and friends, a whole team looking out for me, the public interest they'd drummed up, and now widespread concern for my well-being that had left the press wide open to me. They afforded me a certain safety that, I thought, should be afforded everyone—so I tried my best to extend that privilege to the women in my dorm and to use it to bring to light the plight of prisoners on Rikers Island, to expose the nightmare of it.

I recruited Paul Funkhouser, a recent NYU graduate and student activist I had first met at the New School Occupation, to join the #Justice4Cecily team and spearhead a new initiative: prisoner support. Lucy, Stan, Nyrobi, and others were fundraising for my phone calls and commissary, coordinating letter-writing events and visits from the press, and advocating generally for my well-being, but they were too busy taking care of me to take care of everyone else. Paul's job was to use the resources of the #Justice4Cecily team to extend to my Rikers family the same support I received. It was an impossible goal, of course, but he worked his ass off trying to achieve it. I would take a weekly order from the women in my neighborhood, and he would go shopping; then every Thursday he'd come to Rikers to see me and deliver our package: specialty notebooks, sports bras, pajama sets—whatever was asked for and the guards would let in. That was *huge* for them, and everyone came to know Paul, by name at least, while a few spoke to him directly and several had him talk to friends and families to connect them with legal resources and file complaints with the Board of Corrections.

For my part, I recorded the abuses they had suffered, and, besides sharing them with Paul, I spoke out about them to any reporter who would listen. "It's not like anyone in here expects to be treated like a human being," I told one reporter, Callie Beusmann, prefacing the fifteen-minute pay-phone interview on the plight of the women in Rikers:

My jailhouse Madrina, she came in here, and she had been in remission from throat cancer. During the time she'd been here, she developed a lump in her neck. The first time [she had cancer], it progressed very rapidly and they got it really quickly, so she was okay. She's been waiting for over six weeks to get a biopsy. . . .

Anna nearly lost her leg in another case where she didn't have her diabetes treated while she was in here.

Everybody falls in the shower here. It's really dangerous. The shoes they give us stick to the bottom of the floor, and you fall. . . . Alejandra fell and the captain said, "You look fine to me," and she woke up unable to move her neck and shoulders. When they took her to the hospital [six days later] . . . they were like, "You have a concussion."

This is normal. If there's anything wrong with you, you're fucked. My biggest surprise is that more people do not die here.

People are being denied their bipolar, paranoid, schizophrenia, anxiety medications. . . . The lack of stability of the medication, the lack of availability of the medication. It's governed by money. If your medication doesn't fit within their system, they don't give it to you, and they sedate everybody. It's terrifying.

> They'll also put you in isolation [if you freak out]. . . . There is a lady who has been in isolation for literally years, who takes her feces and stores them up, buckets and buckets at a time. . . . Smears them all over the windows so that nobody can see into her cell, smears them all over her body so that nobody can take her to court. She's been known to spit shit, eat shit. . . . There is something fundamentally and seriously off [when a] woman is so fearful and adamantly against having contact with people or guards or the courts.

I had a hard time summing up, in fifteen minutes or less, what I described as the "instruments of torture, humiliation and alienation at this place." But I was ecstatic to learn that, after I got cut off by the timer, Callie had transcribed the whole thing and published it in *Jezebel* as "Live from Rikers: Cecily McMillan on the Horrific Conditions Inside." It was a little victory in a sea of struggles, but it was a victory no less: I had finally managed to stretch my privilege enough to get the press to cover my friends, to get them to see the prisoners of Rikers as people, first and foremost, deserving of just as much public support and sympathy as I was receiving.

But all the while my privilege appeared to be expanding beyond the gates of Rikers, I was starting to see the limitations of it within them—learning, the hard way, that such privilege made me resistant but not immune to the daily disease of the culture of violence.

One day, I went down to the medication window to pick up my Adderall prescription that, yes, had been afforded me by great privilege and that the fates, in poetic fashion, were about to use against me to teach me lesson. I was talking to the pharmacist but couldn't hear him because the male CO behind me was yelling down the hallway, harassing another inmate. I waited patiently for him to stop, but when the pharmacist indicated he had to leave soon, I turned around and politely asked, "Excuse me, sir, but I can't hear what the pharmacist is trying to tell me." And, with that, the male CO stopped shouting at the inmate and instead turned the full force of his anger on me. "Who do you think you are?" he started in, and the pharmacist mouthed "sorry" before shutting the window. "*You will look at me when I'm talking to you!*" he shouted, and I meekly attempted to apologize, "Yes, sir, I didn't mean—" "Shut up!" he ordered. "See that's how things work here," he said smugly, rounding on me as I tried to back out. "You don't tell me to shut up—you're in my house, white girl, you do what I say." His chest was near enough to my face now; I glanced down ever so slightly at his badge and scanned it. Big mistake. He realized I was IDing him and roared, "Wanna report me, you fucking cunt, here—"He stuck his badge in my face and body-slammed me against the wall shouting, "Let me help you out, bitch, fucking report me." Fortunately there were two other officers in the corridor. A female CO stepped in between us, pushed me away, and screamed, "Get the fuck out of here!" Shocked, with glasses askew, I fled the scene (without any Adderall).

As soon as I got back to my dorm, I called Marty, crying, determined to file a grievance. But Marty talked me out of it. He said I had gotten off lucky, compared to many others, with no major harm done, except to my sense of personal safety. It was a random event, but to complain would only make me the target of further and especially targeted harassment. "You're right," I reluctantly agreed; I had enough of that shit to deal with already.

In step with my one-woman crusade against Rikers, I was met with the mounting force of a special brand of abuse, tailored just to fit me. When my visitors came to see me there was a note that said, "Call the captain." They were required to undergo special screening, including pat-down searches (usually reserved for people who set off the metal detector) and ion scans, a device that tests for the presence of narcotics and explosives on someone's clothing or skin. The guards had also started to censor my visitor packages, so that they could no longer bring in mail.

My team brought important documents in that way, because I was already fighting a daily battle to get my other mail in the first place. It seemed to undergo extra scrutiny or was just being withheld altogether. I asked the mail ladies (who were always very nice to me), and they said that a letter should take no more than three days from the time it is sent to when an inmate receives it. But on June 17, I got a letter postmarked May 22. *It. Was. Infuriating.*

To make a long story short, one day I *really* lost it: straight trailer-trash style, double middle fingers up, screaming at a CO, "Fuck you! I want my fucking mail!" Not my finest hour. But the women in the dorm thought it a fair point and were probably tired of hearing me whining. They all rallied to my cause, flocked to the dayroom, and stood there screaming and demanding, "You know she gets mail every day, stop fucking with her!" It worked.

I liked their style. It was the sort of dirty, "fist full of mud" direct action my clean-cut organizing was missing. We fit well together, and I liked being a woman in commune with them. There really was a sort of feminine beauty to the collective struggle of it all, and we came together to create a pretty impressive community. We shared and traded resources to solve problems and found ways to get what we needed by making do with what we had. The old-timers taught me how to make "burritos" out of crushed Doritos: add hot water, close the bag tight, roll it up in a newspaper, let it sit, and it'll congeal. They also made triple-layer cookie-cakes for people's birthdays, though I never did figure out the mystery of that one. And yes, there were the girls who could get you "anything you want, for a price," but the contraband most in demand were cigarettes, beauty products, and cleaning supplies; I saw drugs, weed, and crack only a couple of times and, just once, saw a razor. To be fair, though, it was one of those disposable ones that she claimed was "just for my legs, I'm allergic to Nair," as the turtles dragged her, kicking and screaming, off to solitary confinement, shouting out, "It's a weapon!" As for me, the black market was where I got *real pens*—so I was all for it!

Just like labor organizing or community building, living together in 4EA required problem solving and compromise to find the resources we needed to create what Rikers hadn't given us. Really, being a prisoner in Rikers required me to use every skill I'd learned as an activist on a daily basis: resource building, coalition building, marketing and messaging, leveraging and bargaining, campaigning and caucusing. All those things made me especially good at figuring out how to work with my supporters outside Rikers. The other women, instead, knew how to go through it and around it and sometimes, even, how to make that really tight system work for them. How do you visit your friend on the fifth floor when you live on the fourth and you aren't allowed into dormitories outside your own? How do you finagle a second hour of recreation or get an extra meal? They taught me.

In essence, what I experienced on the inside was everything activists worked every day to build on the outside: a working community, in its simplest form. But outside you have possessions and money and the façade of "choice" and "freedom" and "rights" to comfort you, distract you. The inside is just a magnification of the inequalities and oppression of the outside. Inside, though, none of us are treated like human beings: we're all numbers. And we're all worth about the same to society: nothing. Nobody cares what happens to us, so we have to work together to take care of ourselves. Each of us has our individual agendas, projects, and problems, but overriding it all is one singular collective problem: how to get by every day and make it out of Rikers alive.

And when the day came that one of our own looked like she might not make it, those complex social inner workings erupted into a full-scale mobilization to save her life. Judith, or Jackie as we called her, was a sixtysomething Puerto Rican descendent of the Young Lords tradition. She'd come to Rikers in May and since the day after, when she passed out and hit her head, she'd served her time bedridden in the infirmary. There she was given methadone pills, the same she had been prescribed, she'd later tell us, for a back problem; the same that had ultimately led to her arrest when police stopped and frisked her and found them stored in a weekly pill organizer, instead of the "required" prescription bottle. She tried to explain, but they ran a background check and found an open warrant and a prior drug charge, so they assumed she was lying and booked her.

As the reality goes for most women at Rikers, she copped a plea knowing it would be easier than fighting the charge and that she'd get out a whole helluvalot sooner. "So now I'm here," she summed up her story, then defiantly added, "but I'm not a junkie anymore! I'm only back on the fuckin' drip because they think I'll sell my pills in the sentencee dorm." "What's the difference?" I asked. Liquid methadone, she explained, is stronger and lasted longer, used as a heroin alternative so that addicts didn't go into shock and die without it—over time, it is administered in smaller doses to slowly wean people off of it and safely detox them. "I know all about it, I was on it last time I was here," she said. "But since I haven't done H in years, it'll be too much for me."

So she tried to go without medication altogether that first day, but her back hurt too much, so she joined half of my dorm in going down to the "methadone line" that next morning. Afterward, she nodded off, slept in most of the day, and commented, "I've lost my appetite." It was a surprising thing to say because we'd just gone to commissary that day, which, on Rikers, is the equivalent of coming home to a holiday feast. After her second day on the drip, though, she got *much* worse: she outright refused to leave her bed and cried, "Leave me alone, let me sleep," when we tried to get her up for the feeding. Later that night, she seemed delusional and incoherent, mistaking a storage closet once for a bathroom stall. And by day three, she wasn't even "there" anymore. She didn't act like she knew where she was or what was happening *at all*. Then, that afternoon, she started throwing up bile and dry-heaving; we assumed, at first, because she hadn't eaten in a while. People ran around trying to find something tasty enough to coerce her to eat, but still she refused. A few of us plotted ways to force her to come to dinner, but before it came time, she started throwing up blood.

At Buddha's insistence, the CO on duty called medical, and they said to send her down, but she couldn't stop throwing up long enough to do so. It continued for hours and soon became flecked with something else. Buddha announced, "That must be chunks of her liver or something, since we all know it's not food." With that, the whole dorm rose up and reinforced her demand to the CO: "Call the clinic! Tell them it's an emergency! She needs a doctor *now!*" "Okay," the CO said. "Be quiet, so I can talk to them." We all held our breath at once, watched her with worry until she restored the phone to the ringer and reported, "They're on their way." Then we collectively released a sigh of relief.

Our anxiety quickly returned, though, during the hour it took them to finally show up. "It's been four hours since she's been like this," we greeted them and showed them to Jackie who was, by then, covered in blood. They didn't say anything to us and asked her only one question, "Do you want to go to the hospital?" She responded with the only thing she'd been saying for over a day, "No, I just want to sleep." Thinking "that's that," they turned around and made to leave. We had no intention of letting them off that easy, though. The whole dorm flew into an uproar. "Look at her, there's blood everywhere! Come on, you can't leave her like this! *You're doctors, do something!*" "She refused medical treatment," they announced. "There's nothing we can do." "She's not fit to make decisions right now," Buddha pleaded. "You have to see that—you have to take her to the hospital, *now!*" But they didn't. They walked right out the door. And never looked back.

We all stood there stunned. But when the blood started coming up again, we knew what to do: take matters into our own hands. Buddha got Danielle to help her get Jackie dressed while the rest of us lobbied the CO: "You have to let them take her down." We didn't ask her, we told her. She wasn't going to stand in our way; she knew that if she did, we'd move right past her, and if she called anyone, we'd probably riot. So when Buddha said, "We're going down now," she just said, "Okay."

The two of them, alone, carried Jackie all the way to the clinic, and when they walked in, Buddha shouted, "This is a medical emergency!" "Ha!" the doctor took one look at the blood-spattered Judith and laughed, "You call this a medical emergency?" Unfazed, Buddha protested, "We're not leaving until you call her an ambulance." He did finally call 911, although he said nothing of her vomiting but told the operator instead that Jackie needed to be picked up because she was "emotionally disturbed." Either way, though, EMS arrived forty-five minutes later and took her away to the emergency room.

We thought we saved her, but unbeknownst to us, by the time she arrived at Elmhurst Hospital, it was too little, too late. She slipped almost immediately into a coma: the body tissue in her vomit (what we'd called "specks") and her disoriented and delusional state were textbook signs of acute liver failure—and her lab test immediately

confirmed that to be the case. For three weeks Jackie remained coma-
tose, hooked up to machines until the morning of June 25, 2014,
when she went into organ failure and flat-lined two or three times,
leaving her brain dead. At 9:40 a.m. her family took her off life support, and at 2:40 p.m. Jackie was pronounced dead.

Buddha found out from a nurse the next morning, and, when she
told us, we were all outraged. "They have blood on their hands!"
someone said. "We should out those doctors!" another one said.
"Yeah," another added, "and get them fired!" "Activista," Ida said,
"tell us where to start." "Well," I suggested, "my team is already organizing a press conference for my release in about a week; we could
tell her story there and expose the truth about medical care in here,
write up a list of grievances of things that aren't working." When
everyone got really excited about that idea, I wrote up a quick notice and read it aloud:

> Heartbreak today. Our friend Jackie was only taken to the hos-
> pital after coughing up blood for several hours, when the
> women in my dorm came together in uproar. We found out
> that she died this morning, she had undiagnosed liver cancer
> and Hepatitis C. I remain strong with my sisters. We are devel-
> oping a list of grievances that I will read at the gates of Rikers
> upon my release.

"So, what do you think?" I asked them. "Should I send it out?"
"Yes!" people shouted. "Send it, send it!" It was our first little declaration of war on Rikers, our way of saying Judith's death would not
be in vain. And with that, our mobilization became a movement.

The week before I was due to get out of Rikers, everybody knew
that I was preparing for this press conference for my release on July 2
and that I was really, really, really "tight," as they called it, about

writing my speech. I'd been writing drafts all week, writing about me—my gripes, my struggles during my time at Rikers—trying to figure out what I wanted to say. All week, I'd been reading them drafts. Whenever I wrote anything in jail, they always wanted me to read it to them. I'd sit on their beds and practice my speeches. They helped me figure them out: the words that were wrong, the pacing that was right, what I was saying, and what I really meant to say. I'd been reading them what I was working on, but I didn't feel really good about anything I was writing.

So I got frustrated and just started bitching to them about everything I thought was wrong with Rikers, and they were supportive anyway. They listened to me and tried to help me work it out—like in college, when I'd get stuck on a paper and go out to coffee with friends: at first I'd just whine ("I can't write this fucking paper!"), but then they'd become sounding boards, and by the end of my coffee, I'd have it all figured out.

It was much more urgent that I get it right this time, though. First off, these women weren't just my friends; they had become my family. Second, it was a press conference and not a midterm paper; I had one chance at getting it right, and it's not like I could request an extension or a do-over. But the day before I got out, it all came together. While I was bitching to Queen, I said something that really got her going, and she started bitching, too; then I was on roll, and then Buddha, Ida, Tiffany, and Collette joined in. Then everybody, it seemed, was hating on Rikers—4EA had become an all-out Bitch Fest (in the best possible sense) that might have turned into a full-scale Pussy Riot had it not been for whoever it was that asked, "If you could change anything, what would it be?"

Listening to them, I realized: *this* is the speech! These women were the experts—some had been there for almost eight months, most had been there before, and almost all of them had friends or family who had been in Rikers. I'd only been there for fifty-eight days. No wonder I hadn't been able to write about it—I was still figuring it out. *"Fuck what I think,"* I announced. Everyone fell silent and looked at me like: *White girl doin' her buckets again.* "No, no, no," I explained. "I figured out the speech! *This* is what matters: what *you* think, what *you* know—I don't know shit, I'm still learning. But who would know how to fix Rosie's better than you?" I was excited. "If you could change anything," I repeated, "about Rosie's, what would it be?"

They were excited too: the conversation kept picking up speed, and I tried to write down all their points, but I fell behind. Just to make sure I'd gotten everything, I asked everyone to write down the most important demand. Then Buddha and Queen went around collecting them and talking to people who hadn't shared yet while I tried to consolidate my notes. In the end the three of us compiled fifty-three points of change into three broad demands that the Rose M. Singer 4EA General Assembly adopted with full consensus.

ON THE DAY OF MY RELEASE, captains came to get me, which was the first sign that everything was probably going to go wrong. Captains do not talk to inmates. The captains make all the decisions, so if you want a decision you have to go through a CO to talk to a captain, and even then captains don't address you; they talk about you (in front of you), and then the CO tells you what the captain has decided. Usually inmates who are about to be released are brought down at 7:30 a.m. to be processed. That morning, though, I was passed through about a dozen captains starting at 5 a.m. People from property and people from medication had also been called in early that morning just to discharge me.

At 8:30 a.m. I was technically "released," and by that I mean put into an unmarked black van with a very nice CO. I promptly asked him, "Have you ever seen them try to get rid of somebody so quickly?" He said, "No, I've also never been ordered to chauffeur somebody off the island either." "Wait, what?" I exclaimed. "No, no, no, I'm supposed to go to the Perry Building," which is where people wait for inmates to get released. My friends were there. I really needed to meet them because I didn't have an ID or a phone or any money and nobody would know where I was. Thinking back to the last time I'd been disappeared for forty hours without any access to a lawyer, separated from all my friends and very nearly admitted to Bellevue Psychiatric Ward, I thought, *Oh God, what is happening here? What does "disappearing" look like for a prisoner of Rikers Island?* I was terrified. What was I supposed to do, tell this officer, "Thanks for the ride, but no thank you, I'd like to go back to my dorm now?"

I think he saw me freaking out a little. "Calm down," he said. "Let me talk to my captain." So he called the deputy warden over, and I promptly interrupted them and plainly stated, "I do not consent to being driven to an unknown location without ID, without phone, without keys, without talking to my friends, nothing. Once I have passed the gates of Rikers, you are no longer in charge of me—I demand that you afford me my constitutional rights, and let me go free."

After that, I sat there for about forty minutes, while I'm sure they followed the chain of command all the way up to Joseph Ponte, the commissioner of Rikers himself. Then the CO said, "I'm sorry, I have orders; my wife died a couple of months ago from cancer and I'm in charge of these two young boys and I can't lose my job; I can't lose my pension. If I disobey orders, I'm going to get in trouble. This is coming from all the way up."

He then drove me to God knows where and dropped me off with my MetroCard and my package (a big-ass brown bag in lieu of a suitcase housing all my Rikers belongings: books, letters, discharge papers, and my former Activist Barbie attire from the day I'd arrived two months prior). No house keys, no wallet, no ID—though he did wait around until I managed to find somebody with a phone before he drove off. Luckily, there was a young man who recognized my jail bag with my numbers on it; he said, "You look really distressed; did you just get out of jail? Do you want to borrow my phone?" and I said, "Please." I called Lucy and explained what had happened. "Wait, what? Where are you?" Lucy exclaimed. "I don't know!" I shouted. "Queensboro," my new friend said. "Queensboro," I repeated. "Where ever the fuck *that is!*" "You want me to talk to her," the guy offered, and I responded again, "Please." He turned out to be an activist for Chinese immigrant rights who was actually familiar with my story; for the next half an hour, he waited with me and we talked about my time in Rikers. "Are you happy to be out?" he began. "I don't know, yet," I responded. "Right now, I mostly just miss my friends." "They'll be here soon," he said. "No, they won't," I responded, knowing he meant Lucy but thinking about Ida. "And when I do see them, we'll be living in two separate worlds again—but today is the day I start trying to change that."

On July 2, 2014, after everything that had happened that morning, I arrived only five minutes late to the scheduled press conference. I strutted across the street, trying to psych myself up, yet again, for the oncoming flash photography; trying to put on, once again, that version of me that the public thought powerful, the one whose limits I now understood. When I *finally* did join the crowd, I hugged several supporters then posed (on command) for several minutes, and, before I knew it, several mics surrounded me demanding that I "Speak!" I summoned Activist Barbie, breathed in deeply and started in firmly, "Fifty-nine days ago, the City and State of New York labeled me a crimin—" I choked (literally) and coughed uncontrollably. Straining to speak, I tried to save face: "I haven't been allowed to speak for my-self—for a while." *Still coughing,* I turned my back to the watchful crowd and—*Thank God!*—someone handed me a water bottle. As I drank it, I took in, too, the Rikers Island "Welcome Sign." I looked at it, for the first time, as a "free woman."

In a split second the power of the previous evening washed over me. I remembered that it hadn't been my voice, my leadership, that had inspired the words on the pages I was holding—the power had come from the women, when I stepped down and they had taken over. For so long, I'd stood in their way, trying so hard, at first, to do the writing, to do the thinking for them. And then, sitting there listening to them, it had all become so clear: I'd been so busy asking, "Why?" for myself, when I should have been asking, "How?" for them. How can I help them bring their voices, their experiences, their *truth* to light?

It's true, Activist Barbie *had been* silenced by Rikers, but it had not silenced *me*. She was the voice, the performer, seeking a standing ovation from a sympathetic audience, trying desperately to prove "I am one of you." All those people hadn't shown up because I was just like them, though. They came out because I'd been through something decidedly different. I was a prisoner earlier that day. I was still a felon, for now. But no appeal could erase the effect of time served—I would forever be an ex-convict. And, thinking of Ida and Buddha, Judith, and Queen . . . that was something to stand by, something (given the company) I was proud to be.

I put the cap back on the bottle and turned around (with a smile, to let them know that I was ready). I began again, this time, filled with the spirit of the women in Rosie's: "Fifty-nine days ago the City and State of New York labeled me a *criminal*"—dignified yet indignant, I let it take me and carry me all the way through (without missing a beat).

Millionaires and billionaires who had a vested interest in silencing a peaceful protest about the growing inequalities in

America worked the justice system, manipulated the evidence presented and suddenly I became dangerous and distinguished from law-abiding citizens. On May 5th the jury delivered its verdict, the judge deemed me undesirable, and officers *drove me across that bridge and barred me within.* On the outside, I spent my time fighting for freedom and rights. On the inside I discovered a world where *words like freedom and rights* don't even exist in the first place. I walked in with one movement, and return to you a representative of another. That bridge right there, not only divides the city from Rikers Island—it divides two worlds. Today, I hope to bring them closer together. Crossing back over, I have a message to you from *several concerned citizens* currently serving time at the Rose M. Singer Center.

Incarceration is meant to prevent crime. Its purpose is to penalize and then return us to the outside world ready to start anew. The world I saw at Rikers isn't concerned with that. Many of the tactics employed seem to be aimed at simple dehumanization. In the interests of returning the facility to its mission and restore dignity to its inmates, we, the women of Rikers, have several demands that will make this system more functional. These were collectively drafted for me to read before you today.

First of all, we demand that we be provided with adequate, safe, and timely health care at all times. That, of course, includes mental health-care services and the ability to request female doctors if desired at all times for safety and comfort. We often have to wait for up to 12 hours a day for a simple clinic visit, and occasionally 12 hours a day for up to a full week before we see anyone. The women of Rikers feel a special sense of urgency for this demand because of a particular event that occurred recently.

About a week ago, our friend Judith died as a result of inadequate medical care. Judith had been in RSMC for a while, but was transferred to our dorm 4 East A, where I was housed, only a few days before her death. She had recently been in the infirmary for a back problem, and had been prescribed methadone pills for the pain for quite a while. A few days before she died, they decided to change the medicine to liquid despite her dissent. They gave her a dosage of 190 mg, which any doctor will tell you is a dangerous dosage, far higher than what anyone should be taking unless it is a serious emergency. Judith was not allowed to turn down the medicine or visit the clinic to get the dosage adjusted.

After three days on that dosage, Judith could no longer remember who or where she was and had begun coughing up blood, accompanied with what we believe were chunks of her liver. We attempted unsuccessfully to get her medical treatment for the entire day, at one point being told that this was "not an emergency," despite the fact that Judith was covered in blood. That night they finally removed her to the hospital, where she remained in critical condition before passing away a few days later. This was a clear case of medical malpractice, both with the ridiculously high dosage of methadone and the refusal of adequate treatment. Stories like this are far too common in Rikers Island, and we demand that no more of our sisters be lost to sickness and disease as a result of inadequate medical care.

Our next demand is that COs should be required to follow the protocol laid out for them at all times, and that at some point soon that protocol should be examined to make sure that all rules and procedures are in the best interests of the inmates. We also demand that we have a clear and direct means to file a grievance that will be taken seriously and examined fully, so that officers can be properly disciplined and removed from the area quickly when they abuse or endanger us.

Recently my friend Alejandra went to file a grievance about being denied access to medical treatment for a concussion until she awoke one morning unable to move. When she met with the captain after filing the grievance, she was presented with a different sheet and a different complaint than the one she had provided and was forced to sign it. Inmates should be able to trust that situations like that will not happen, and that our safety and dignity will be respected by those designated to supervise us. There is a clear protocol for officers already laid out in the inmate handbook, but it is seldom followed. Officers are allowed to make up the rules as they go and get away with it, which we find unacceptable.

Our final demand is that we be provided with rehabilitative and educational services that will help us to heal our addictions and gain new skills, and that will make it much easier for us to adjust to the outside world and achieve employment when we are released. Specifically, for our education we would like access to classes beyond GED completion, maintenance, and basic computer skills, access to a library, and English classes for those attempting to learn the language. We feel that the addition of these programs would significantly help us prepare for release and reentry into the world, which would lower reincarceration rates.

We also feel strongly that Rikers Island needs to have much better drug rehabilitation programs. Many women who come through here are addicts, and many women are imprisoned here because they are addicts. That's the area in which reentry rates seems to be the highest. This is likely a direct result of the failure of the meager programs that we are provided with. Thus, it seems only logical that serious and effective drug rehabilitation programs be provided to those who need them, assuming that the Department of Corrections would like to help work to achieve a better, healthier society and keep as many people as possible out of jail.

Working with my sisters to organize for change in the confines of jail has strengthened my belief in participatory democracy and collective action. I am inspired by the incredible resilience of the incarcerated women I have encountered, and I find faith in their ability to find commonality in a system that is utterly stacked against them. My time at Rikers has changed me permanently, an even more formative experience than Zuccotti Park itself. Most importantly I have learned that the only difference between the people we call citizens and those we call criminals is vastly unequal access to resources. As long as we deny the humanity of people in prison, we cannot imagine a truly free society.

Working with my sisters inside Rikers has been the most transcendent experience of my life. On the outside, I will continue to fight until they gain all the rights they deserve as citizens of this city, of this state, and of these United *States* of America.

"Thank you," I said and lingered there, for just a moment, in the world I felt so ready that morning to leave behind—that moment, just before I stepped back into the world I'd come from to begin with (no longer truly a part of either). I realized, then, that the words I'd just read would likely be my only bridge between those two worlds. Words that I vowed to repeat as often and as loudly as need be until all worlds shook with the power of their humanity, the same power that had shaken me of a prison of my own. In such a short time, they had released me from the constraints of who I should be, what I should think, what I should do . . . and instead, forced me to face, live, and breathe, *test* the person I already was. And through them I had explored freely the boundless possibility of the woman I could be. And when they allowed me to be the vessel for their message, they afforded me the voice I'd been searching for—one that understood both the language of power and the ability to share it equally. It was only when I put my faith in them fully and turned myself over completely to be willed by their voices that I found my own. The guards didn't free me that day, *the women did.* Their demands were my emancipation proclamation.

RICHARD FOULSER

Cecily McMillan is an activist, union organizer, and advocate for prison reform whose participation in and arrest during the Occupy Wall Street movement, along with her trial and conviction, have been widely covered by the national media, including *Vanity Fair,* the *New York Times, Cosmopolitan,* and *Rolling Stone,* among others. Her own writing has appeared in the *New York Times* and *AlterNet.*

NATION BOOKS

The Nation Institute

Founded in 2000, **Nation Books** has become a leading voice in American independent publishing. The inspiration for the imprint came from the *Nation* magazine, the oldest independent and continuously published weekly magazine of politics and culture in the United States.

The imprint's mission is to produce authoritative books that break new ground and shed light on current social and political issues. We publish established authors who are leaders in their area of expertise, and endeavor to cultivate a new generation of emerging and talented writers. With each of our books we aim to positively affect cultural and political discourse.

Nation Books is a project of The Nation Institute, a nonprofit media center dedicated to strengthening the independent press and advancing social justice and civil rights. The Nation Institute is home to a dynamic range of programs: the award-winning Investigative Fund, which supports ground-breaking investigative journalism; the widely read and syndicated website TomDispatch; the Victor S. Navasky Internship Program in conjunction with the *Nation* magazine; and Journalism Fellowships that support up to 25 high-profile reporters every year.

For more information on Nation Books, The Nation Institute, and the *Nation* magazine, please visit:

www.nationbooks.org

www.nationinstitute.org

www.thenation.com

www.facebook.com/nationbooks.ny

Twitter: @nationbooks